ISLAM

THE BASICS

Colin Turner

Routledge
Taylor & Francis Group

LONDON AND NEW YORK

First published 2006
by Routledge
2 Park Square, Milton Park, Abingdon, Oxon, OX14 4RN

Simultaneously published in the USA and Canada
by Routledge
270 Madison Avenue, New York, NY 10016

Reprinted 2006

Routledge is an imprint of the Taylor & Francis Group, an informa business

© 2006 Colin Turner

Typeset in Aldus Roman and Scala Sans by Taylor and Francis Books
Printed and bound in Great Britain by MPG Books Ltd, Bodmin

British Library Cataloguing in Publication Data
A catalogue record for this book is available from the British Library

Library of Congress Cataloging in Publication Data
Turner, C. (Colin)
   Islam: the basics/Colin Turner.
      p. cm.
   Includes bibliographical references and index.
   1. Islam. 2. Islam – Doctrines. I. Title.
   BP161.3.T89 2005
   297 – dc22

                                    2005013752

ISBN10: 0–415–34105–1   ISBN13: 9-78-0-415-34105-9 (hbk)
ISBN10: 0–415–34106–X   ISBN13: 9-78-0-415-34106-6 (pbk)

Taylor & Francis Group is the Academic Division of T&F Informa plc.

THE BASICS

With nearly 1,500 rich years of history and culture to its name, Islam is one of the world's great faiths and, in modern times, the subject of increasingly passionate debate by believers and non-believers alike. *Islam: The Basics* is a concise and timely introduction to all aspects of Muslim belief and practice. Topics covered include:

- The life of the Prophet Muhammad
- The Koran and its teachings
- Gender in Islam
- Sufism and Shi'ism
- Islam and the modern world
- Non-Muslim approaches to Islam
- Spirituality in Islam

Complete with a glossary of terms, pointers to further reading and a chronology of key dates, *Islam: The Basics* provides an invaluable overview of the history and the contemporary relevance of this always fascinating and important subject.

Colin Turner ~~~~~~~~~~~~~ Eastern and
Islamic Stud

ALSO AVAILABLE FROM ROUTLEDGE

For Mahshid, without whose love and inspiration,
nothing is possible ...

CONTENTS

A NOTE TO READERS

The layout of this book is straightforward and generally self-explanatory. The sequencing of the chapters has been designed with a view to gentle progression from the story of the Messenger of Islam, Muhammad, through the Message itself – the Koran – and on to the ideals, beliefs and practices connected with that message. These are, after all, the very basics of Islam, as the title of this book suggests.

The current interest in various politicised manifestations of Islam has occasioned the inclusion of Chapter 6, which looks at the role of radical Muslim groups and ideologies in the modern and post-modern eras. However tenuous the connections of 'political Islam' to the basics of Islam in the Koranic sense of the term, this modern phenomena cannot be ignored, which is why a discussion on the contemporary Muslim world concludes this book.

Similarly, the issues of Muslim law and theology, which strictly speaking do not fall under the category of 'basics', have also been covered, appearing in a number of detailed appendices.

Finally, a word concerning the Koran references. The translation I have used is that of Abdullah Yusuf Ali, arguably the most widely read translator of the Koran into English; different editions of his work – *The Meaning of the Holy Qur'an* – abound in the West, and readers should have no difficulty in acquiring a copy. References to the Koran in *Islam: The Basics* are always to Yusuf Ali's translation unless otherwise specified. The referencing system itself is easy to use. Chapter 3, verse 12, for example, would appear as 3:12; verses 9 to 11 of Chapter 101 would appear as 101:9–11, and so on.

Finally, just as this book assumes no prior knowledge of Islam, it also assumes no prior knowledge of Arabic, the language of the Koran. However, for the sake of those who may be acquainted with that language to some degree, Arabic terms have been used where relevant, but always together with their English equivalents.

INTRODUCTION

I am not a Muslim in the usual sense, though I hope I am a 'Muslim' as 'one surrendered to God', but I believe that embedded in the Koran and other expressions of the Islamic vision are vast stores of divine truth from which I and other occidentals have still much to learn, and that Islam is certainly a strong contender for the supplying of the basic framework of the one religion of the future.

(W. Montgomery Watt in *Islam and Christianity Today*, London, 1983)

A gentle word of warning: this is not a book written in order to 'explain' the events of 11 September 2001: plans to write this book were in place long before that grim Tuesday in Manhattan, when the world seemed suddenly to take leave of its senses.

There can be little doubt that the terrorist attack on the Twin Towers changed international politics forever, leading directly to the crippling of Afghanistan and the ongoing tragedy that is the destruction of Iraq. Yet it was not only the political world that was transformed by the attack on Manhattan; the world of publishing appeared to undergo convulsions too, but with a decidedly different, although at times equally disturbing, outcome. Almost overnight, it seemed, what had hitherto been a gentle stream of books on Islam and the Muslim world turned into a veritable flood. Listen carefully enough, a colleague quipped at the time, and beyond the crackle of gunfire you will hear a singularly more disturbing sound: the sound of a vast, ramshackle bandwagon, being jumped on by countless pairs of frenzied feet. Islam, it seemed, had resurfaced, Kraken-like, from its slumber, and everyone wanted to explain how and why it had lashed out with such violence.

Not every book which emerged in response to 9/11 was written with 'an eye for the main chance'. A number of valuable works reappeared, some of which had been out of print for years, and as a researcher and teacher in Islamic Studies I can hardly complain about the suddenly raised profile of my area of expertise and academic interest. The sad truth remains, however, that most of the books which emerged in the weeks and months after the destruction of the WTC saw Islam as the cause of a disease with multiple symptoms: 'fundamentalism' and terrorism, suicide bombing and the quest for 'weapons of mass destruction' being among the most salient.

It is to the eternal credit of my editors at Routledge that they commissioned the present book when they did, several years after 9/11, thus allowing it to stand apart as an academic work which aims to investigate one of the world's most important faiths, and which does not conflate the religion of Islam with the beliefs, ideals and actions of an infinitesimally small minority of individuals who claim to be acting in its name. They would not have been happy with a book on Catholicism which attempted to deconstruct the activities of the IRA, or with a work on Judaism which endeavoured to rationalise the modus operandi of Israel *vis-à-vis* the Palestinians; why, then, should they make an exception in the case of Islam?

Instead *Islam: The Basics* introduces Western readers to the very basics of Islam the *religion*: the faith as envisaged by the Koran, articulated by its Prophet, and practised peaceably by millions of adherents for centuries – long before the over-politicisation of certain motifs in the Islamic tradition led to the emergence of Islamism, which has everything to do with the discourse of power, and little or nothing to do with faith in God and conscious, personal submission to the Divine will, both of which constitute the beating heart of the Islamic revelation. At a time when the actions of a small minority of Muslims have, in the minds of many, become conflated with the teachings of the Koran and the ideals, beliefs and practices of Islam, the need for a sober and objective introduction to the world's fastest growing, yet arguably most misunderstood, religion is felt more acutely than ever. *Islam: The Basics* is an attempt to meet this need.

As attempts go, it has not been easy. Unlike most of the authors to whose works I have alluded, I do not claim to provide the definitive 'take' on what Islam is, has been or should be. Someone once said, 'I know what time is – until someone asks me to define it.' I can say the same about religion in general, for there is as yet no consensus as to what religion actually is. And I can certainly say the same about Islam, which, for me, will always be a highly contested, and contestable, phenomenon.

Part of the problem lies in the sheer diversity of intellectual, emotional and socio-political approaches to the Islamic revelation – the Koran – which are lumped together under one convenient umbrella. Yet one only has to scratch the surface to reveal that Islam is no monolith: it is a vast, multi-faceted entity with as many different forms of expression as there are people to express them. It is therefore impossible to talk about Islam without qualifying it.

For example, there is so-called Sunni Islam and there is Shi'ite Islam, and within both of these denominations – which some say are political, others religious – there are further divisions. (The word 'division' does not necessarily have negative connotations, and should be understood, unless indicated to the contrary, in the sense of partitions rather than as mutually exclusive or antithetical sub-groupings.) In Sunni Islam there are four main 'schools of law', which in practical terms means that a follower of one particular school will carry out the practical injunctions of the faith in a slightly different way to followers in the other three schools. In Shi'ite Islam, which has its own school of law, believers 'emulate' learned jurists in matters of practice, and the number of possible learned jurists is considerable. Shi'ite Islam breaks down further into a number of 'sub-sects' – the Ismailis are one example – with considerable theological and political differences.

Then, as we shall see, there is Sufism. Within Sufism there are tens if not hundreds of different 'brotherhoods', all of which hold certain key beliefs in common, but which differ on detail, or on broader conceptual issues connected with belief and personal spiritual progress. There are Sufis who adhere to Sunni Islam and Sufis who adhere to Shi'ite Islam, and Sufis who claim not to adhere to either. And just as there is overlap between all of these different approaches to Islam, there are within each 'type' or 'sub-type' of Islam internal theological and jurisprudential differences so diverse that one can only conclude, as many have, that there are as many kinds of Islam as there are individual Muslims. Given that humankind is made up of individuals, each understanding the world in his or her own unique way, is the astonishing diversity of approaches to Islam really that astonishing? Quite the contrary: not only is it to be expected, it is also to be applauded. After all, was it not the Prophet Muhammad himself who said, 'Difference of opinion among the people in my community is a Divine mercy'? The first premise, then, upon which this book has been written is the diversity at the heart of the Islamic experience.

The second premise is the need to separate the religion from the revelation around which it has accreted. The Koran and its ideals are one thing; the communal response to it – in the form of an 'organised religion' – is another. What Islam is – at least, what the Koran says Islam is – may often be at odds with what Muslims do, and this needs to be recognised. That Islam should be held responsible for the faults of Muslims makes absolutely no sense. There are numerous reasons for this, not least the slightly less obvious one that, in the eyes of the Koran itself, most of those who actually claim to be Muslims are in reality quite divorced from the Koranic ideal. To conclude, based on the actions of nominal Muslims, that Islam is this, or Islam is that, is to fall into the very trap which, at the outset of this Introduction, we were anxious to circumvent.

The third premise is that the overall interpretation of the facts in this book is mine. It is, for what it is worth, based on years of academic study of the Koran and Muslim theology, and half a lifetime of practical experience gained from living among people who self-identify as Muslims, both in Britain and abroad. This does not, of course, make it the definitive interpretation, for I do not believe that there is one. Hopefully, however, it will be a closer approximation to the Koranic vision of Islam than those whose approach is mediated by financial considerations alone, and who are ready to ride roughshod over intellectual honesty and academic integrity so long as the sales figures are rosy.

Welcome, then, to *Islam: The Basics*, a phenomenological study of the Islamic revelation as enshrined in the Koran, and as expressed in the beliefs and practices of Islam to which millions of human beings aspire.

Colin Turner
Durham, summer 2005

FURTHER READING

For the interested layperson, general introductory works which cover both the religion of Islam and the politics and history of the Muslim world abound, although they differ greatly in quality. One of the most readable, and least sensational, introductions to the emergence of the Muslim community, the doctrines of Islam, the question of tradition versus modernity, and the 'resurgence' of Islam in the twentieth century is J. L. Esposito, *Islam: The Straight Path* (Oxford University Press, 1994). For a concise introduction to the history of the Muslim world, my own *The Muslim World* (Sutton Publishing, 2000) is said to be one of the most accessible short overviews, taking the reader from the birth of Muhammad in AD570 up to the year 2000. And at just over 100 pages, it can be completed in two or three sittings. Finally, Neal Robinson's *Islam: A Concise Introduction* (Curzon Press, 1999) combines an overview of Muslim history with excellent insights into issues of religious faith and practice.

THE MESSENGER

The founder of twenty terrestrial empires and of one spiritual empire, that is Muhammad. As regards all standards by which human greatness may be measured, we may well ask, is there any man greater than he?

(Lamartine in *Histoire de la Turquie*)

If a man like Muhammad were to assume the dictatorship of the modern world, he would succeed in solving its problems that would bring it the much needed peace and happiness.

(George Bernard Shaw)

My choice of Muhammad to lead the list of the world's most influential persons may surprise some readers and may be questioned by others, but he was the only man in history who was supremely successful on both the religious and secular level.

(Michael J. Hart in *The 100: A Ranking of the Most Influential Persons in History*)

There can be very few people in the world who have not heard of Muhammad, Prophet of Islam. For Muslims, of course, he is the orphan who became apostle of God, communicating to all humankind the message of Divine Oneness and the key to man's existential dilemma: *islām* or conscious submission to the will of the One true Lord of all worlds. For those who choose not to follow his teachings, he is a man whose career formed the cornerstone upon which a vast empire, spanning from Spain to India, was founded, and the enigmatic, often controversial, founder of a world religion that today claims the allegiance of over a billion souls. As such, he is often lauded – even by his detractors – as both prophet and statesman, a figure whose significance is such that he was once voted the most influential man in world history by a panel of Western writers and academics. Few who have read anything about him come away without having formed an opinion concerning him, and many who know nothing at all about him will often venture an opinion anyway, swayed possibly by the latest news item on 'Islamic fundamentalism', or simply because it is human nature to pontificate on matters totally beyond our ken. But who is Muhammad, and what is his role in the genesis of that enigma known as Islam?

WHAT DO WE KNOW ABOUT MUHAMMAD AND HOW DO WE KNOW IT?

It has been argued, and not without justification, that we know more about Muhammad than we do about any other classical prophet or founder of religion. The wealth of information available on almost every aspect of the man's life is astounding, from detailed accounts of his role as prophet to the most intimate minutiae of his private life. Not only can we read about the trials and tribulations he faced in establishing his mission, or the wars he fought in defence of his community-state in Medina, but we can also peer directly into his private space, gleaning fascinating snippets of information on every facet of his conduct as an ordinary human being: how he ate and drank, how he behaved towards strangers, how he treated his family – and even how he urinated, took ablutions or made love to his wives. There is nothing, it would appear, that is taboo, and no place in the public or private life of this exceptional individual that we cannot enter.

Yet little if any of this information is available in the Koran, which is extremely sparing in its references to Muhammad: the Koran may be all things to all people, but a biography of the Prophet it most certainly is not. In fact, the amount of concrete biographical information on Muhammad in the Koran amounts to probably no more than a handful of verses, and he is mentioned by name a total of four times in all. If the wealth of detail that we have on Muhammad does not come from the Koran, then, what is its source? In short, how do we know what we know about the Prophet of Islam?

THE *HADITH*

The Meccan Arabs at the time of Muhammad were not known for their written literature: while poetry was their forte, for the most part this was communicated orally, with very little of it actually committed to paper. The art of memorisation was highly prized: legends from the past, and the history of each clan, were captured in verse and handed down by word of mouth from generation to generation.

By the time of Muhammad in the late sixth century, this pre-dominantly oral literary culture was still very much in evidence. However, with the growth of centres of commerce such as Mecca and the gradual settlement and urbanisation of the nomads, there was a commensurate rise in literacy, and in the popular perception of its importance and prestige. It is inconceivable, then, that the rise of a self-styled 'messenger of God' would not have been written about or at least commented on by writers and historians of the time. Equally, it is inconceivable that his close followers and companions would not have wished to record for posterity the sayings of a man whom the Koran described as a universal messenger to all humankind.

Muslims today do indeed believe that much of what Muhammad said and did was recorded for future generations. These written accounts are referred to individually as *hadiths*, and collectively as 'the *hadith*'. (The usual English translation is 'Prophetic Tradition' or simply 'Tradition'.)

The overriding problem with the Prophetic Traditions is that a written record of their existence did not emerge until 200 years after the Prophet's death, when six authoritative volumes of Traditions, each containing thousands of *hadiths*, were produced. Why, if accounts of the Prophet's life were recorded while he was alive, is there no record of their existence until the middle of the ninth century? There are several possible explanations for this:

(i) Although the accounts were written down while the Prophet was still alive, they were not actually collated until the middle of the ninth century. When the six definitive volumes appeared, the sources from which they were compiled were gradually lost. Today we have the six volumes, but no record of the written sources upon which they were based.

(ii) The accounts were not written down while the Prophet was alive, but were instead handed down orally from generation to generation. Eventually it was felt that to avoid the problem of possible errors in transmission, the accounts should actually be committed to paper.

(iii) The absence of written sources prior to the middle of the ninth century makes it unlikely that anything substantial was written down in the lifetime of the Prophet, although this cannot be proved beyond all doubt. Some of the Traditions which were produced two centuries after the death of the Prophet were based on hearsay and probably do date back to the time of Muhammad; most, however, are fabrications from a later age, constructed for political or ideological purposes.

The 'orthodox' Muslim position is that the Traditions which emerged from AD850 onwards are for the most part genuine, regardless of whether they were compiled from written or oral sources. Some Muslims concede that the possibility of later fabrication exists, and for this reason treat the Traditions with a certain amount of respectful caution. Non-Muslim critics of the Traditions tend either to accept the Muslim account, albeit with the obvious caveats, or to reject the whole corpus of Traditions as a later construction. The situation is not helped by the fact that the Traditions accepted as valid by the Sunni Muslims differ from the Traditions considered authoritative by the Shi'ites.

A closer look at the history and structure of the Traditions may help to show why the issue is such a controversial one.

The two main (Sunni) collections of Traditions are those made by Muhammad ibn Isma'il al-Bukhari (d. 870) and Muslim b. Hajjaj (d. 874), each of which, confusingly enough, is known as the *Sahih* or 'authoritative collection'. The *Sahih* of al-Bukhari contains around 9,000 *hadiths*, while the *Sahih* of Muslim has around 4,000; both collections contain numerous repetitions. The fact that both authors entitled their works *Sahih* indicates the conviction on their part that the Traditions they had included were genuine. Other compilers – the Shi'ite collectors of Traditions in particular – concede the possibility that spurious *hadiths* may have fallen through the net.

The *Sahih* of al-Bukhari is arguably for the vast majority of Muslims the most important 'religious text' after the Koran, and with the *Sahih* of Muslim it is considered the most authoritative collection of Traditions by all Sunni Muslims. Containing approximately 9,000 Traditions in nine volumes, it is arranged thematically and deals with the sayings and behaviours of Muhammad with regard to a wide range of issues such as belief, prayer, ablution, alms, fasting, pilgrimage, commerce, inheritance, crime, punishment, wills, oaths, war, food and drink, marriage and hunting. The *Sahih* of al-Muslim, with approximately 4,000 Traditions, is divided into forty-two 'books', each dealing with a different theme.

The topics covered by al-Muslim are similar to those one finds in the *Sahih* of al-Bukhari. The differences in methodology employed by the two compilers is minimal. Bukhari was renowned for his precision in testing the authenticity of Traditions and tracing their 'chains of transmission', and he was the founder of the discipline known as *'ilm al-rijāl* (lit. 'science of men') or the detailed study of those individuals who transmitted *hadith* orally. Muslim b. Hajjaj for his part divided the Traditions into three main categories according to the level of knowledge, expertise and excellence of character of the transmitter, and also the degree to which the Tradition was devoid of contradictions, falsities or misrepresentations.

Each Tradition has two parts: a main body of text, known in Arabic as a *matn*, which includes the actual account of what the Prophet either said or did; and an *isnād* or 'chain of transmitters' – the list of people, reaching back to one of Muhammad's companions, who have handed the account down orally through history. For example, a typical *hadith* would read as follows:

X said that Y said that W said that V heard the Prophet say: ' … '

The text of the above *hadith* indicates a saying of Muhammad, uttered by him either as a general comment or word of advice, or in response to some question or other. These recorded sayings were not said by him in his capacity as Prophet, and clearly do not hold the same status as the utterances which constitute the Koran.

The *hadiths* do not record only the sayings of the Prophet, however: they also record his behaviour, as witnessed by others. A typical *hadith* of this kind would read as follows:

> X said that Y said that W said that V saw the Prophet do ...

The form of the *hadith* clearly keeps itself open to possible adulteration, by the simple process of 'Chinese whispers' if not by blatant manipulation or fabrication by those who wish, for whatever reason, to put words in the mouth of the Prophet. Controversy concerning the authenticity of the *hadith* material still continues today, with groups polarised sharply in their assessment of the validity of the Traditions not only as a reliable source for a biography of the Prophet but also as the theoretical cornerstone of Islamic jurisprudence.

THE BIOGRAPHY OF THE PROPHET

Another important source of information on the Prophet is his biography or *sira*. However, this is surrounded by the same problems and controversies as the Traditions.

The biography of Muhammad is problematic in that it was not written until over a century after his death. Its author, Ibn Ishaq, was a native of Medina, where he devoted much of his time to the collection of *hadith*, anecdotes and reminiscences concerning the early years of the Muslim community and the life of Muhammad in particular. The work itself, produced at the beginning of the eighth century, has not survived. However, many early Muslim historians quoted from it extensively, and so it has been possible to reconstruct most of Ibn Ishaq's book by excavating it from the writings of others.

While the *sira* is of immense historical importance as the earliest known source of information on the Prophet's life, it has come under fire from many historians – quite a few of them Muslim – as unreliable, presumably on the same grounds that the *hadith* may be unreliable. One must, therefore, treat it with caution when trying to piece together parts of the enigmatic jigsaw that goes to make up the life of one of the world's most illustrious figures.

There is actually much debate within the community of historians who research the birth of Islam and the rise of the Muslim world as to which, if any, of the early Muslim historical sources are of any real use at all, with some critics going so far as to say that the life of Muhammad is impossible to reconstruct, while others claim that much of what has passed traditionally as early Muslim history is, in fact, a product of later fabrication.

In the absence of viable alternatives, however, they are as reliable or unreliable as any historical source of similar antiquity is likely to be, and thus we must give the benefit of the doubt to the traditional Muslim account, which is certainly as credible as, and for the most part considerably more credible than, any of those accounts proffered centuries later by certain revisionist historians with particular axes to grind. To begin that account, we need to go back over 1,400 years to Mecca, in the Arabian peninsula, birthplace of Muhammad and cradle of the religion of Islam.

PRE-ISLAMIC ARABIA

The old idea that Islam is a religion of the desert, designed for a desert mindset, is one of those myths that seem to persist even when they have been proven false; the notion that Islam was spread by the sword is another. Almost as deep-rooted is the assumption that the history of Islam is the same as that of the Arabs, and that prior to the arrival of Muhammad they had little if any history to speak of. Yet Islam did not emerge into a vacuum; nor was its founder, or the society of which he was a part, without a past. It is to this past – the history of pre-Islamic Arabia – that we must look in order to better contextualise, and thus understand, the mindset of Muhammad, the advent of Islam, and the genesis of Muslim civilisation.

Although Arabia and the Arabs were known to the chroniclers of ancient history, for the purposes of this book we shall begin our story in the middle of the sixth century AD, some 500 years after the death of Jesus Christ. Our scene is set in the vast Arabian peninsula, an area of mainly rock and desert approximately 700 miles wide and 1,000 miles long. Those who lived there eked out their existence under the harshest of physical conditions, scorched for most of the year by a relentless sun, which made survival something of an achievement. Yet on its coasts were dotted numerous small ports, home to enterprising seafarers, forming an important part of the trade network which linked India and Mesopotamia to East Africa, Egypt and the Mediterranean. Also, for several hundred years before, and for a century after, the birth of Christ, the southern part of Arabia had been the locus of several prosperous kingdoms, with civil institutions as advanced as any in the world at that time. However, a variety of socio-economic factors led to gradual changes in the demographic structure of the peninsula. Among them, according to historians of the time, was the bursting and subsequent collapse of the great dam of Ma'rib in the Yemen. Consequently, the inhabitants were forced to migrate northwards where, untouched by the civilising influence of the two great empires of the region, namely Byzantium and Persia, the migrants formed a tribal society based on pastoral nomadism. This was the Arabia of Muhammad's day – an Arabia which, in many respects, has changed little since.

ARAB SOCIETY AND CULTURE

Some Arab tribes in the peninsula were involved in trade between the Mediterranean and the southern seas. A larger number, however, made a precarious living in the desert by raiding other tribes or plundering trade caravans, or by herding camels, sheep and goats in a life that was lived constantly on the move. Yet the old image of the 'uncivilised Bedouin' is most misleading, for in fact desert life was lived to the highest of values. Qualities such as manliness, valour, generosity and hospitality were valued highly; even the intertribal raids and vendettas occurred to precise, unwritten rules. The Arabs were also lovers of poetry, producing a sophisticated literature that was communicated orally from father to son, and from tribe to tribe. Indeed, it was the unquestioning loyalty to one's tribe, and the values it represented, that lay at the heart of Bedouin life, and the idea of individual identity outside the tribal set-up was unknown.

By the end of the sixth century, certain changes had begun to occur. The population was growing, and with it the development of sedentary life. The town of Mecca was one such oasis. Situated at the junction of two major trade routes, it had enjoyed a certain amount of prestige since ancient times. More important, however, was its prominence as the most sacred city of the desert Arabs – a status it still enjoys, albeit under very different circumstances.

The pre-Islamic Arabs have often been misleadingly described as 'pagans'. The Arabs believed in a whole host of nature gods and goddesses, demons and spirits. The focus of their worship was a cuboid structure, the *ka'ba*, situated in the middle of Mecca and originally built, so later Muslims claimed, by the prophet Abraham. Around the *ka'ba* stood a whole panoply of effigies – originally 360 in number – to which the Arabs would pray and offer sacrifices. Overlooking all of these was *al-ilāh* or 'the god' – the Arabic of which was later shortened to give the word 'Allah'.

The 'Allah' of the pre-Islamic Arabs was very different, conceptually, from the Allah which would appear later. He was indeed seen as the 'supreme god', but a god that was rather remote from everyday life. He was posited as the creator of the heavens and the earth but he was not the only god or object of worship. However, Bedouins were not actually polytheists, as they have usually been portrayed, but henotheists: those who accept many gods in addition to one central deity. The difference between polytheism and henotheism is slight, but the latter term defines more precisely the religious outlook of the Meccans prior to the advent of Islam.

During the four 'sacred months' of the year when inter-tribal warfare was forbidden, the Meccan pantheon of gods would play host to pilgrims from all over the peninsula, who would journey there in order to pay homage to their objects of worship. Apart from offering the Arabs a focal point for identification with their gods and goddesses, the pilgrimage was also an important source of income for the Meccans, who saw their city emerge as the most prosperous in the region.

However, as Mecca and its elites grew wealthier, the divide between rich and poor increased, and hitherto unquestioned tribal loyalties were called into question by the demands of commerce and consumerism. On the eve of the advent of Islam, historians tell of a city in which the old tribal values had been abandoned, and in which a dog-eat-dog culture had begun to emerge, fuelled by greed and envy. It was from this milieu that Muhammad, messenger of God and admonisher of humankind, was to emerge.

MUHAMMAD'S BIRTH AND CHILDHOOD

Muslim tradition holds that Muhammad was born in Mecca in the year 570. His father, Abdullah, died shortly before Muhammad was born; his mother, Amina, passed away shortly afterwards. Muhammad's status as an orphan is referred to openly in the Koran:

> Did He not find thee an orphan and give thee shelter (and care); and He found thee wandering, and He gave thee guidance. And He found thee in need, and made thee independent.
>
> (93:6–8)

The Koran is silent on almost all other aspects of Muhammad's early years, and for insight into the evolution of his character we have to rely – albeit with due caution – on the *hadith* reports mentioned earlier. According to these, Amina's pregnancy and Muhammad's birth were attended by various miraculous signs. For example, people reported seeing a light shining out from Amina by which the castles in far-off Syria could be seen.

Apparent miracles continued to follow Muhammad through his early years. According to Meccan custom, the orphaned child was fostered out to a Bedouin wet-nurse. The *hadith* reports recount how this nurse's breasts were always full of milk, of how her sick donkey suddenly got well again, and of how her clan in general prospered thanks to the auspicious presence of the young Muhammad.

YOUTH AND EARLY ADULTHOOD

On Muhammad's youth and early adulthood the Koran is largely silent, and even the *hadith* reports offer little of substance. By his early twenties it appears that he had become a seasoned participant in the commercial life of Mecca. His experience and sense of fairness were seemingly such that he acquired the nickname *al-amin* or 'the trustworthy', and it was probably traits such as these that brought him to the attention of a prominent Meccan business-woman and widow named Khadija. She hired him to manage her business affairs and, impressed by his impeccable conduct and savoir-faire, later proposed marriage to him. This union with Khadija, who was apparently fifteen years older than Muhammad, was by his own admission the happiest of all his marriages.

From the age of twenty-five to forty, Muhammad virtually disappears from the history books, and at this point in time there is no outward sign either in his character or in his particular circumstances to suggest that his life would be anything but run-of-the-mill, at least in the context of seventh-century Mecca. Yet all of this was to change, and in a way that would transform Muhammad – and all of human history – beyond recognition.

THE CALL

According to Ibn Ishaq's biography and the later *hadith* literature, Muhammad had always been a serious, introspective youth who had never been entirely at ease with the pagan values of Meccan society. Muslim hagiographers claim that Muhammad had denounced idol-worship at an early age, adopting the outlook of the fabled monotheistic hermits – the *hanifs* – who believed in one God yet adhered neither to Judaism nor Christianity. For Muhammad 'the trustworthy', the social unrest and erosion of justice and economic equality was as detrimental to society as the idolatrous norms which underpinned it.

What is more or less certain is that, in keeping with nomadic tradition, Muhammad was given to long periods of isolated meditation, during which he would ponder the mysteries of human existence and pray for guidance. During one of these retreats, in a cave on nearby Mount Hira, Muhammad received his first 'divine visitation'. A vision – later identified by Muhammad himself as the Archangel Gabriel – appeared bathed in light, saying:

> Read! In the name of your Lord and Cherisher, who created – created man, out of a clot of congealed blood; Recite! And your Lord is Most Bountiful – He Who taught (the use of) the Pen – taught man that which he knew not.

> (96:1–5)

Muhammad may have been a grown man – he is said to have been forty when he was first 'called' – but the experience left him shaking like a bewildered child. Terrified by this fantastic vision, he was convinced initially that he had been visited by demons. His mind abuzz with doubts and uncertainties, and his heart aflame with fear and awe, Muhammad ran down the mountain track and back into the apparent safety of pagan Mecca, convinced that he had fallen foul of the wily demons who inhabit the desert wilderness.

However, Khadija reassured him that this was not the case, and as the visions continued, Muhammad's belief that he had indeed been singled out for some kind of prophetic mission increased. The source of the messages, he concluded, was not the devil but Allah – God Himself – the same God Who had revealed Himself to Abraham, to Moses and to Jesus before him.

THE MISSION BEGINS

Muslim tradition is unclear exactly for how long Muhammad was left to wrestle with his thoughts before God spoke to him again: some say six months, others as much as two years. However protracted this apparent break in communication was, to Muhammad it must have seemed like an eternity, and one can hardly imagine how frustrated and alienated it must have left him. When the second 'visitation' finally occurred, and God 'spoke' to him again, his relief must have been palpable as Muhammad could no longer doubt either the provenance of the message or the nature of the mission:

> O thou folded in garments!
> Stand (to prayer) by night, but not all night, –
> Half of it, – or a little less,
> Or a little more; and recite the Qur'an in slow, measured
>   rhythmic tones.
> Soon shall We send down to thee a weighty Message.
>
> (73:1–5)

It appeared that Muhammad was being instructed to modify his spiritual exercises by standing for only part of the night in prayer. He was also told to repeat the revelation he was receiving more carefully, for this was clearly only the beginning of a long series of revelations yet to come. And for the first time he was able to put a name to the words he was hearing: the *qur'an* or 'recitations'.

What he was receiving by way of revelation was something that he must recite, first to himself and then, it seemed, to those around him. For what good was a recitation – and the recitation of a 'weighty Message' at that – if it was not to be heard by others? When another revelation occurred shortly afterwards, Muhammad was convinced that the mission was not something that he could keep to himself for much longer:

> O thou wrapped up (in the mantle)!
> Arise and deliver thy warning!
> And thy Lord do thou magnify!
> And thy garments keep free from stain!
> And all abomination shun!
> Nor expect, in giving, any increase (for thyself)!
> But, for thy Lord's (Cause), be patient and constant!
>
> (74:1–7)

THE FIRST 'CONVERTS'

In the days and weeks that followed, and as further revelations appeared, Muhammad worked in earnest on those closest to him. Khadija, his wife; his young cousin Ali; Abu Bakr, a wealthy merchant and close friend who was also given to introspection and meditation; and his manservant Zayd, are all said to be the first to accept the messages revealed to Muhammad.

Muhammad's immediate family, together with the small, slowly expanding group of intimate companions whom Muhammad could trust to keep his mission a secret, formed the first faith community in Muslim history. The early Meccan verses deal almost exclusively with the fundamental principles underlying the Koranic worldview: the unity of God; the concept of prophethood; man's accountability for his deeds; and the inevitability of the 'final judgement' and the afterlife which follows. One of the distinguishing features of the Meccan phase of Muhammad's career was its emphasis on the primacy of belief, without which the performance of rite and ritual is meaningless. For the early Muslim community, it was the spirit rather than the letter of the law that was important. That is not to say, however, that they did not give external expression to their faith in the form of prayer, be it personal or communal, but rite and ritual are largely absent from the Meccan verses of the Koran.

PRAYER RE-ESTABLISHED

By Muhammad's time, the original form of the Abrahamaic prayer had long since been forgotten, and the prayer offered by the Meccans as they circled their gods was 'nothing but whistling and clapping of hands' (8:35). Muhammad now worked to revive the great prophet's institution of formal prayer by teaching his household how to stand, bow and prostrate before God, and how to interpose certain recitations from the Koran between the various movements. While the practice of formal prayer would undergo further modifications in years to come, the embryonic form of *salāt*, canonical prayer, offered clandestinely by Muhammad and his household would not have been dissimilar to that which is offered by millions of Muslims today.

That prayers were offered in secret indicates how sensitive the situation had become. Muhammad was a man held in high esteem by his kinsmen and by Meccan society at large, renowned for his trustworthiness and with no history of madness or mental instability. By rights, the high regard of his peers should have worked in his favour, serving to convince even the most sceptical among them of his sincerity. But given the nature of his claim, and the tumultuous consequences and implications it would surely have for Meccan society as a whole, would an untarnished reputation be enough to protect him?

THE MISSION GOES PUBLIC

> Therefore expound openly what thou art commanded, and turn away from those who join false gods with God. For sufficient are We unto thee against those who scoff, – Those who adopt, with God, another god: but soon will they come to know.
>
> (15:94–96)

Only when Muhammad was sufficiently convinced of the veracity of his mission was he commanded to 'go public', despite his doubts and insecurities. However, the Koran makes it quite clear that the mission has to be universalised and offers Muhammad reassurance:

> And admonish thy nearest kinsmen,
>
> And lower thy wing to the Believers who follow thee.
>
> Then if they disobey thee, say: 'I am free (of responsibility) for what ye do!'
>
> And put thy trust on the Exalted in Might, the Merciful.
>
> (26:214–217)

Tradition has it that his first attempt at a public declaration of faith was made from the top of a hill near Mecca, where a small crowd soon gathered to hear him speak. 'What would you do, fellow clansmen, if I were to tell you that on the other side of this hill, enemy horsemen lie in ambush? Would you give me credence or not?' The audience affirmed in one voice that they would, aware as they all were of Muhammad's reputation as an honest and trustworthy man. 'Know then, my people, that I come to you as an admonisher, warning you of a severe punishment if you do not refrain from worshipping idols and affirm that there is no god but Allah!'

His second attempt at preaching came a few days later, at a dinner given for members of his family and tribe in his own home. Again, his sudden and wholly unexpected sermon was greeted with stony silence, shattered only by the derision heaped upon Muhammad's young cousin, Ali, who had stood up to second Muhammad's declaration and offer his support.

In the days that followed, news of Muhammad's attempts to steer his kinsfolk away from idolatry percolated through Meccan society, with an initial trickle of converts to the new faith growing steadily into a constant stream. As more and more Meccans joined Muhammad's mission, the consternation of the Qurayshi elders increased. If Muhammad was serious about his mission, and intent on trying to draw people to his side, the Quraysh's whole way of life lay in very real danger.

THE THREAT TO THE QURAYSH

The Quraysh were the most important tribe in Mecca and enjoyed the kind of political hegemony over society that they were not about to give up lightly. The Quraysh were, insofar as they held the unofficial position of 'guardians of the ka'ba', the de facto religious leaders of Mecca. The administration of the sacred precinct and the overseeing of the rites and rituals conducted there were carried out by members of the Quraysh, which in time had earned the soubriquet 'family of Allah'. And since pilgrimage to the pantheon was linked inextricably to the economy of Mecca, the financial considerations of the Quraysh also had to be taken into account.

For Muhammad to stand up and denounce the way of life of the Quraysh was, then, to threaten the tribe on several fronts. However, it was the psychological effect that Muhammad's missionary zeal must have had on the Quraysh that was the most galling. For Muhammad was calling into question not so much how they exercised political control or made their money, but their complete worldview and value system. By denouncing their idols, he was in effect denouncing everything they held sacred, from their tribal affiliation to their veneration of desert custom, from the quasi-animistic worship of the natural world through the medium of idols to their idealisation of Bedouin qualities such as generosity, manliness and family honour. All of these were now called into question by this relatively unknown, unlettered orphan-turned-trader named Muhammad, who seemed intent on turning the world of the Quraysh on its head.

THE FLIGHT TO ABYSSINIA

The persecution of Muhammad and his followers, which had begun with sporadic incidents of name-calling and stone-throwing, took a sinister turn when the Quraysh, unable to punish Muhammad directly, targeted the weakest and most vulnerable among his community, in particular those slaves who had warmed to Muhammad's message and joined his mission early on. Among these was a young convert, Ammar, who was left out in the hot sun to recant, alongside his mother, Sumayya, and his father, Yasir. Tragically, the blows of the oppressor proved too much for Sumayya, whom history records as the first martyr of Islam.

Sumayya's death was a psychological watershed in the evolution of the Muslim community, forcing Muhammad and his companions to consider their future carefully. One option might have been to flee Mecca en masse, but there was no divine sanction for this, and in any case, where would they go? To stay, however, would be to tempt fate and invite even more drastic forms of repression. The more violent the opposition, the greater the possibility that new converts would abandon the faith, or that the community would be driven underground.

For a while the Muslims were in turmoil. Then, with Muhammad's blessing, a compromise solution was reached. A group of Muslims – eleven men and four women – were despatched on a merchant ship to Abyssinia. Its ruler, the Negus, was renowned for his tolerance and generosity, and it was in the hope of finding refuge at his court that the first Muslim migrants set sail for the African coast.

In retrospect, this first migration to Africa looks more like an early attempt to spread the message of Islam than a measure adopted in order to escape persecution, for many of those who had been tortured on account of their faith elected to stay behind. Sensing that this might be the case, the Quraysh appealed to the Negus to send the Muslims back to Mecca, claiming the Muslim faith opposed Christianity and was disrespectful to Christ. The Negus decided to find out for himself and invited the Muslim migrants to defend themselves against the Quraysh's accusations. Satisfied with their account of themselves and their faith, the Negus dismissed the entreaties of the Quraysh and invited the Muslims to stay in Abyssinia for as long as they wished. Such was his hospitality that further small waves of Muslim migrants – several dozen – were to make the journey to Africa over the next few years.

THE EMBARGO

In the seventh year of Muhammad's mission, the leaders of the Quraysh took steps to isolate him, his followers, and the clansmen of his uncle and protector, Abu Talib, by cutting them off from the outside world: their food supplies were disrupted indefinitely and other clans were warned not to have social or commercial dealings with them. The embargo would continue, its instigators insisted, until Abu Talib agreed to withdraw protection from his nephew, thus effectively surrendering Muhammad and his followers to the Quraysh. Abu Talib's support for Muhammad was unwavering throughout the three-year boycott, which almost brought Muhammad and his clan to their knees. Eventually, affected deeply by the impoverishment of the embargoed clans, some of the Meccan elders relented and declared the boycott agreement null and void.

The former stream of converts to the Muslim cause had by now been reduced to a mere trickle, and these were for the Prophet of Islam among his darkest days, later referred to as his 'year of grief'. This was compounded by the loss of his uncle and wife within a very short space of time. In losing his uncle, he also lost the main source of political support against the Quraysh; in losing Khadija, he lost an invaluable source of psychological and emotional support, the importance and centrality of which he would never underestimate.

THE 'NIGHT JOURNEY'

It was possibly at his lowest ebb that Muhammad experienced what was arguably the most intense spiritual experience of his life, in which it is said he left his physical body and ascended 'into the heavens', where he underwent a series of visionary, psycho-spiritual experiences described in the Koran as an 'ascension' (*mi'rāj*) or 'night journey' (*isrā*) – the latter denoting the fact that it happened while he was asleep. The scriptural account is brief:

> Glory to (God) Who did take His servant for a Journey by night from the Sacred Mosque to the farthest Mosque, whose precincts We did bless, – in order that We might show him some of Our Signs: for He is the One Who heareth and seeth (all things).
>
> (17:1)

For a full account one has to look, with customary caution, to the *sira* and the *hadith*. According to the Traditions, Muhammad underwent what may be described in today's terms as an 'out of body experience'. It is said that his celestial journey brought him into contact with all of the monotheistic prophets who had preceded him, from Adam down through Noah, Moses, David, Jesus and himself. This gave him confirmation of the validity of his own prophethood and the continuity of the message of 'submission' (*islām*).

Whether Muhammad experienced this nocturnal epiphany in body or in spirit is of little importance; nor does it matter whether the 'farthest Mosque' he visited is the mosque in Jerusalem, as most Muslims claim, or a metaphor for the 'highest degree of submission', which is how it has been described by others. For Muhammad himself the experience was all too real: a validation of his prophethood and his mission that came at a time when it was most needed, giving him the psychological and spiritual strength to weather the turbulence of storms yet to come.

THE SEARCH FOR SUPPORT AND THE OASIS OF YATHRIB

Deprived of the political backing of Abu Talib, wherever he went it was clear that Muhammad's reputation had preceded him, but unfortunately it was his reputation not as prophet of God but as a madman, spouting lies against the tribal deities and the Bedouin way of life. When help did come – as God had promised it would – it came from the unlikeliest of sources: an oasis town to the north of Mecca with a large Jewish population and a history of internecine strife. That town was Yathrib.

The people of Yathrib mostly belonged to two main Arab tribes, the 'Aws and the Khazraj, and the town's large Jewish community. For the Jews, of course, monotheism was nothing new, and the fact they themselves were awaiting the advent of a messiah meant that they approached the news of a new Meccan prophet, claiming allegiance to the one true God, with cautious optimism. Some ten years into his mission, Muhammad was able to make an impact on several members of the Khazraj tribe during one of their annual pilgrimages. They took the message of Islam back with them to Yathrib, and the following year, a dozen members of the Khazraj returned to Mecca to declare their acceptance of Islam and the prophethood of Muhammad. Twelve months later, a contingent of some seventy-two citizens of Yathrib professed their acceptance of Islam under what later became known as the 'Oath of Aqaba'. His search for support was over.

THE MIGRATION

Known in Arabic as the *hijra*, the ensuing migration of the Muslims from Mecca to Yathrib was a psychological turning point of inestimable importance, marking the transformation of an oppressed faith minority into a small community-state, and eventually into the nucleus of a whole empire. The migration plays such an important part in the group consciousness of the early Muslims that its date was used to mark the inception of the lunar calendar that is still used today throughout much of the Muslim world.

Slowly, and almost imperceptibly at first, the Muslims of Mecca began to leave. Eventually, when only Muhammad and a small handful of his closest companions were left, the Quraysh realised what was happening. Mindful that the migration would signal in effect the export of the new faith to other corners of the peninsula, the elders convened an emergency meeting. Their conclusion, inevitably, was that to stop Islam, one had to stop Muhammad and to do that they had to kill him.

According to the *hadith* literature, Muhammad soon learned of the plot to assassinate him and drew up plans for his own personal flight from Mecca accordingly. On the night of the planned assassination, Ali acted as decoy by sleeping in Muhammad's bed. As his would-be assassins approached the bedchamber, only to discover his young cousin sleeping soundly, Muhammad and his companion Abu Bakr were able to escape on camelback. Stories later described how Muhammad and Abu Bakr took shelter in a cave, and how their pursuers would have found them had they not been fooled by a spider's web, woven miraculously across the mouth of the cave, giving the impression that no-one could have entered. The following day, Muhammad and his companion carried on to Yathrib, where a tumultuous welcome awaited them from both the *muhājirūn*, or the migrants from Mecca, and the *ansār* or 'helpers' – the people of Yathrib who had given them refuge.

THE 'CONSTITUTION OF MEDINA': BLUEPRINT FOR A PLURALISTIC SOCIETY?

The *hijra* over, Yathrib was renamed Medina – an abbreviation of the honorific *Madinat al-Rasul* or 'City of God's Messenger'. This nominal change of identity was followed by a more fundamental reorientation of socio-political and religious values as Muhammad began to transform what had hitherto been a Muslim community (*umma*) into a community-state. Medina was, after all, a melting-pot in which Jewish and pagan tribes lived cheek by jowl, and to which the Muslim immigrants were coming very much as a minority. The task facing Muhammad was to unite these disparate elements as justly and judiciously as possible.

As God's messenger, Muhammad's religious leadership of the Muslims was sanctioned by divine decree. However, as political leader of Medina, Muhammad's jurisdiction over the numerically larger group of non-Muslims in the city could not be justified by his position as God's Prophet. The legitimacy of Muhammad's rule over both the Muslims and non-Muslims of Medina was based on a series of agreements known collectively as the 'Pact of Medina' (*Mithāq al-Madina*) and preserved in a document that has reached us via Muhammad's biographer, Ibn Ishaq.

This document, sometimes referred to as the 'Constitution of Medina', outlines the reciprocal rights and duties agreed between the *muhājirūn*, the *ansār* and the Jewish clans of Medina. According to the Pact, these disparate groups were to form one community or *umma*, 'distinct from all others'. Those 'others' were mainly the pagan Quraysh of Mecca, the community's first and most tenacious enemy. Any pagans still residing in Medina were free to join the new community so long as they accepted the provisions of the Pact: failing this, they were free to live peaceably in the midst of the new community so long as they refrained from taking up arms to oppose it.

The Pact is important because it is one of the very earliest examples we have of what is basically the blueprint for a truly pluralistic community – one in which all groups are accorded equal protection, rights and dignity, regardless of their ethnic background or religious orientation. As such it was without precedent in Arab history, not least because the underlying principles upon which society was now structured were based on faith – in the widest sense of the word – rather than ties of blood and tribal allegiance.

FROM JERUSALEM TO MECCA: A CHANGE IN THE DIRECTION OF PRAYER

During the second year of the migration to Medina, several Koranic verses were revealed which directed Muhammad to change the *qibla*, or the direction in which Muslims faced when performing the five daily prayers. The Koran commanded Muhammad and his followers to turn away from Jerusalem and face the sacred precinct of the *ka'ba* – the *masjid al-harām* – in Muhammad's native

Mecca, the birthplace of the Koranic message and the prophetic mission.

The change of *qibla* heralded by the revelation of these new verses was an important milestone in the evolution of the young Muslim community, a conscious rite of passage which served to separate the Muslim *umma* conceptually from that of its Jewish co-monotheists and which contributed to the formation of a religious identity distinct from all others. It also reflected an undeniable cooling of the relationship between Muhammad and the Jews, some of whom had begun to criticise him openly.

However, Jewish antipathy towards Muhammad was in no way as vehement as the opposition of the Quraysh. It was the actions of one armed group that precipitated the first major military encounter between the Muslims of Medina and the pagan Quraysh of Mecca. The Battle of Badr, as it later came to be known, was the first of several famous victories for the Muslims and, as such, marked a psychological turning point in the fortunes of the growing community that cannot be overestimated.

WAR: THE BATTLE OF BADR, THE BATTLE OF UHUD AND THE BATTLE OF THE DITCH

The Battle of Badr was the first of several full-scale military encounters between the Muslims and the Quraysh. It was precipitated by a small group of armed Muslims ambushing a Qurayshi caravan in January 624, during one of the 'sacred months' when all bloodshed is in theory forbidden. The raid was seen as a provocation that could not go unanswered. The opportunity for revenge came on 15 March 624, on the coast road from Syria to Mecca at a place called Badr.

Muhammad's main objective at Badr was to intercept another Qurayshi caravan on its way back to Mecca. The Meccans had presumably through their own spies received news of Muhammad's intentions and responded by despatching a force of approximately 1,000 Meccans to Badr, the intention being to overwhelm the smaller Muslim force and to prevent them from disrupting the Meccan caravan trade in the future.

The Muslims' victory over the Meccans at the Battle of Badr must have felt it was almost as though the divine seal of approval had been stamped on Muhammad's mission. Their elation was not to last long, however, for within a year the Meccans had regrouped and were bent on revenge for the ignominy and humiliation of their defeat. When reports reached Muhammad that Qurayshi forces were amassing with the intention of attacking Medina, he consulted with his companions and followers concerning possible battle strategies. Consultation or *shurā* had been an integral feature of Muhammad's socio-political leadership from the outset, for while he was above question as far as his prophetic status was concerned, in mundane matters such as economic policy or battle strategy, he was as fallible as his peers. However, Muslims ignored the Prophet's advice on battle strategy by leaving their fortifications and rushing into the fray, eager for Meccan blood and the spoils of victory.

The battle which ensued, fought near the hill of Uhud outside Medina, was not the total military disaster for the Muslims that some historians have painted it. The Meccan objective, which was to destroy the embryonic Muslim community and remove Muhammad from its helm, was never realised: content with having rubbed the Muslim community's collective nose in the dust, the Meccan commander Abu Sufyan ordered his troops back to Mecca. Militarily, the outcome of Uhud remains inconclusive. For Muslims, however, Uhud betokened a massive spiritual and moral defeat, occasioned, or so many believed, by the zeal and greed of the Muslim army.

It was another two years before the Meccan leaders felt confident enough to deal what they hoped would be a death blow to the Muslim community-state. In March 627, with an army of some 10,000 men, the Meccans subjected Medina to a siege, but were ultimately unable to take the city. The 'Battle of the Ditch' – so called because one of Muhammad's Persian followers had suggested that they dig a trench around the city to foil the Meccan cavalry – culminated in a resounding victory for the Muslims.

MUHAMMAD AND THE JEWS OF MEDINA

Muhammad's attitude to the Christians and Jews was informed by the Koranic assertion that, as 'people of the Book' and fellow monotheists, their creed was also *islām*, and that they too were *muslim*, just as he was. The 'Constitution of Medina' asserted that as co-believers in the same Creator, Jews and Christians would exist in peace and harmony with the Muslim community.

In practice, however, Muhammad's relationship with the 'people of the Book' was rather different. The Jews of Medina had watched developments in Mecca with guarded optimism, mindful perhaps that Muhammad might have been the messiah whose appearance they awaited. As time passed, however, their attitude changed. Gradually, antipathy turned to acrimony, and the sources reveal how, on numerous occasions, rogue members of the Jewish community of Medina collaborated with the Quraysh in their endeavours to extirpate the nascent Muslim community.

The most significant clash came during the Battle of the Ditch, when the Jewish clan of Banu Qurayza collaborated with the Quraysh in an attempt to break the siege. Had they succeeded, Medina would have fallen and the Muslim *umma* would have been destroyed. This open act of treachery was a clear violation not only of the Pact of Medina but also of Jewish law, in accordance with which the Jews had been allowed to live, and by which, it was decided eventually, the Banu Qurayza should be judged. The punishment meted out to the treacherous clansmen was uncompromising: their property was confiscated, the women and children were taken into captivity, and several hundred adult males were executed.

WAR AND PEACE

It may be argued that the natural state of man – the state adumbrated by the Koran as the ultimate human ideal – is peace, or *salām*. And the safest, surest way of securing that peace is through submission – *islām* – to God's will. However, the fact that much of Muhammad's Medinese career was taken up with military matters has done very little to bolster the claim that Islam is a 'religion of peace'. This mantra is repeated every time Muslim apologists or their liberal defenders rush to dissociate themselves from the latest atrocity perpetrated by so-called 'Islamic terrorists'.

One cannot deny that the Koran does accommodate the possibility of armed conflict between individuals and between nations. However, the Koran lays down strict regulation for warfare, and endeavours at all costs to prevent the outbreak of hostilities, particularly between fellow believers but also between believers and unbelievers. Notwithstanding attempts to prove the contrary, there is nothing in the Koran to support the old assertion that Islam has to be spread 'by the sword'. When one considers that, on several occasions, the Koran confirms that belief in God must be the result of a choice rather than coercion, one realises how baseless that assertion is.

One may say therefore that historically, Islam has been peace-loving but not pacifist: the example of Muhammad himself shows that if war is unavoidable, then it is undertaken – but only on the proviso that all legal, moral and ethical provisions and precepts governing armed conflict are adhered to meticulously.

PEACE BREAKS OUT – THE TREATY OF HUDAYBIYA

> But if the enemy incline towards peace, do thou [also] incline towards peace, and trust in God: for He is One that heareth and knoweth [all things]
>
> (8:61)

Around the sixth year of the *hijra*, to signal their peaceful intention, Muhammad and those ready to accompany him went forth from Medina unarmed, clad in ritual pilgrimage garb. The Meccans, unsure of Muhammad's motive, sent a contingent of cavalry out to intercept the pilgrims. When Muhammad gained wind of this, he changed course, finally camping at a place called Hudaybiya so that he might reconsider his plans. After several difficult days of negotiation, the Meccans finally conceded that the Muslims had come in peace, and a treaty was finally concluded between the two sides, which came to be known as the Treaty of Hudaybiya.

The Treaty – described in the Koran as a 'clear victory' – actually worked in favour of the Muslim community-state, for the outbreak of peace allowed tribes hitherto forbidden from entering Medina to travel to Muhammad's community-state in order to hear and experience the prophetic message for themselves. The several years of peace that ensued gave the growing community of Muslims in Medina the opportunity to grow and expand without the constant threat of external aggression. They made the most of this period of respite by strengthening their own community at

home and taking the message of Islam beyond the confines of
Medina to tribes and communities across the length and breadth of
Arabia. Delegations were also sent to various leaders outside the
peninsula, such as the rulers of Rome, Egypt and Sassanid Persia,
who were invited to ponder Muhammad's message and, should
they wish, accept Islam. While reception to these missions was not
entirely negative, none of the leaders approached actually accepted
Muhammad's invitation to submit to the faith. Yet he felt that he
had done his duty by inviting non-believers to believe. So long as
they did not take up arms against him, they were to be left as they
were; the fact that he did not take up arms against any of them is
further evidence of the non-coercive nature of his mission

SOCIAL CHANGES IN THE NEW COMMUNITY-STATE

The battles fought by the Prophet against his Meccan enemies
account for a relatively insignificant portion of the Medinese phase
of his prophethood. There was a far more important agenda to be
followed, namely the cultivation of a society in which believing
men and women would have the amplitude and opportunity to
express their belief outwardly. Furthermore, society needed to be
cleansed of those practices that were a legacy of henotheism: some
rules, conventions and social habits had to disappear altogether, while
others would be adapted to suit a monotheistic faith community.

Muhammad was thus obliged to pay a great deal of attention to
the reworking of society along Islamic precepts, be they moral,
ethical or socio-political. And this new social experiment would
have at its heart not loyalty to the tribe, as had been the case in
pre-Islamic Mecca, but a common belief in one God. In this community of believers, everyone was equal in the sight of God. Even
those who believed not in the Koran but in the Torah and the
Gospel which preceded it were accorded a place in the new scheme
of things, as laid down in the Constitution of Medina.

Many of the verses revealed in Medina are legislative in nature,
containing guidance on practical matters such as prayer and fasting,
marriage and divorce, buying and selling, and taxation and inheritance. Islam the religion of personal submission to the will of God
was now externalised as Islam the collective submission of the
community. To this end, the Koran prescribed far-reaching changes

in the social fabric, with prescriptions designed to do away with the old injustices. Among other changes, the rights of women, as individuals equal to men before God, were guaranteed. By way of a short excursus, and conscious of the topicality of the issue, it is to the question of women and the feminine that we now turn.

WOMEN: THE KORANIC VIEW

While it is true that Muslim women have not always been treated as equals of Muslim men, this inequity is largely a symptom of the uncompromisingly patriarchal cultures of the Muslim world, most of which claim to have been shaped by Islam, but which actually reflect little, if anything, of the egalitarian ethos of the Koran, in which male and female are seen as absolute equals before God, be it spiritually, physically and socially. Unfortunately, the fact that Islam is almost always refracted through the prism of local culture means that outsiders are wont to attribute sexual inequality to the dictates of religion. It is not only in the context of the gender divide that the misidentification of a cultural tradition with a religious norm leads to confusion: in areas as trivial as food and dress, actions and practices to which people are habituated culturally are often misconstrued as being a result of religious diktat. Thus the all-encompassing veil, for example, which women in Muslim countries use to cover themselves, is described as 'Islamic dress', when in actual fact it was used as a status symbol long before the advent of Islam.

There are many other facets of life in Muslim countries which are seen as 'Islamic', but which are in fact merely products of the regional or national culture. What Muslims do, or wear, or eat, does not necessarily reflect the teachings of Islam, just as the habits and practices of people in the West are not by default a product of Christianity. In short, if Muslim women have not always been treated as the equals of Muslim men, one should not look automatically to the teachings of the Koran for a reason.

THE JOY OF SEX IN THE MUSLIM TRADITION

One of the charges levelled at Muhammad, particularly by his medieval Christian detractors, is that he was a lecher, and that the polygamy allowed by Islam was symptomatic of the Prophet's obsession with sex. The fact that Muhammad himself married no fewer than eleven times was seen as confirmation of his libertinism. Add to this the Koranic promise of 'intimate companions' for the believers in the hereafter, and it is not difficult to see how the criticisms of Islam as a religion that promotes sexual licentiousness might have come about.

That is not to say, of course, that they were in any sense warranted. The Islamic policy is always one of gradual change. The issue of alcohol is a case in point: so used to inebriation were the desert Arabs that prohibition could not have been brought in overnight; instead, it was abolished gradually, over a period of several months or years. Polygamy was never abolished outright; rather, the conditions governing marriage to more than one woman were made so stringent as to be practically unfeasible.

On sex itself, Islam would appear to be refreshingly realistic. While sex must always be a matter for couples who have accepted a contract of marriage, there is very little – sexually – that a man and woman may not do in bed once they are man and wife. The only act which appears to have been outlawed is anal sex; apart from that, so long as the sex is consensual, a couple may enjoy each other in any way they desire. The Prophet, for example, reminded men that they were not the only factors in the sexual equation, and that women deserved to derive as much pleasure from the sexual act as men; to this end, he advised couples to indulge in much loving foreplay before sex, in order to ensure that the woman gains as much satisfaction from the experience as possible. As always, however, the Koran advises restraint, for anything which is taken beyond the bounds of moderation may become problematic if not brought under control.

Sex outside of marriage is, of course, prohibited by the Koran, with rather stringent punishments reserved for those who commit fornication or adultery. Punishment by stoning, however, is not Koranic, and thus should be seen as an aberration.

Sex between members of the same gender is also outlawed by the Koran, although no specific punishments are prescribed. Masturbation is not discussed by the Koran, and is thus presumably allowed, although there are *hadiths* which appear to prohibit it.

MUHAMMAD'S MARRIAGES

Muhammad's first marriage, to the wealthy businesswoman Khadija, lasted almost a quarter of a century and was monogamous throughout. The sources imply that theirs was a true love match in a society where marriage was an issue more of socio-political expediency than of romance and the emotions.

His second wife, Sawda, was an early convert to Islam and the widow of one of his close followers. Subsequent to the *hijra*, Muhammad married a further nine times in all, mostly to widows of companions who had lost their lives fighting the Quraysh. Muhammad made at least two political marriages: the first was to Maria, a Coptic slave girl; and the second to a Jewess who had been captured in battle.

By far the most controversial of Muhammad's relationships were his marriages to Aisha, the daughter of his close companion Abu Bakr, and to Zaynab, the divorced wife of his adopted son Zayd. The marriage between Muhammad and Aisha was contracted when she was probably no more than ten years old: the sources do not mention her age directly, but say that when she went to live in the Prophet's house, she passed much of the time playing with her toys, and was often joined in her games by Muhammad himself.

A relationship between a man in his early fifties and a child of ten is bound to raise more than a few eyebrows today, particularly in Western cultural milieus where sensitivity regarding issues such as paedophilia is heightened. Unsurprisingly, one of the charges levelled against the Prophet by his detractors is that his relationship with Aisha was tantamount to child abuse. A marriage between an older man and a young girl was customary among the Bedouins, as it still is in many societies across the world today. It was not unheard of in Muhammad's time for boys and girls to be promised to each other in marriage almost as soon as they were born, particularly if the union was of direct political significance to the families concerned. However, such marriages were almost certainly not consummated until both parties had entered adulthood, which Arabs in the seventh century tended to reach at an earlier age than Westerners today. It is highly unlikely that Muhammad would not have taken Aisha into his bed until she was at least in her early teens, which was wholly in keeping with the customs of the day, and in context not in the least improper.

MUHAMMAD'S LATER LIFE: THE CONQUEST OF MECCA

The eighth year of the *hijra* saw a breach of the Pact of Medina when a clan allied to the Quraysh attacked one of the first clans to have allied itself to the Muslim *umma*. This brought Muhammad and his Muslim army to the gates of Mecca in search of justice. Outnumbered by Muslim fighters, the Quraysh had little option but to surrender immediately, thus allowing Muhammad to reclaim his birthplace in a bloodless victory, putting Mecca once more at the very heart of Islam.

Muhammad's first act upon conquering Mecca was to announce a general amnesty for all those who had hitherto opposed him. Upon witnessing this, a number of the Quraysh converted to Islam, although it was clear that no-one was under duress to do so. Then, to demonstrate Islam's abhorrence of idolatry, Muhammad smashed the statues and images that littered the *ka'ba*. Whilst he had destroyed the physical signs of idolatry, the removal of self-worship from the hearts of the unbelievers was a matter for the unbelievers themselves: belief or unbelief must be the result of a choice, the Koran asserted, and not the result of coercion. In a sermon delivered within the Sacred Precinct, the Prophet reiterated the belief that there can be no compulsion in religion, and that those who did not wish to bow down to Islam were free to go about their business without let or hindrance, provided they extended the same courtesy to others.

THE FAREWELL PILGRIMAGE

In the tenth year of his mission, Muhammad's performance of the *hajj* attracted vast crowds to Mecca. Thousands of Arabs had become Muslim, and peace had brought easy access to Mecca for all.

In what would later be termed the 'farewell pilgrimage', Muhammad stood atop a hill – the 'Mount of Mercy' – on the plains of Arafat, and delivered a sermon which, even to the unsuspecting, must have had an air of finality about it.

The sermon had a premonitory tone, as though he was aware that he would not be with his followers for much longer. When the end came, it was mercifully brief: Muhammad died in the spring of 632, the eleventh year of the *hijra*, after a high fever. One can imagine the consternation with which his passing must have been met by the Muslim community at large, particularly since the *umma* was scarcely a decade old. Some refused to believe that the Prophet had gone forever, and that he would one day return, messiah-like, to lead them. Muhammad's companion Abu Bakr moved quickly to disabuse the people of these notions. 'O people,' he declared, 'if anyone worships Muhammad, let them know that Muhammad is dead. If anyone worships God, God is the One that lives, the Everlasting.'

MUHAMMAD THE MAN: APPEARANCE, CHARACTER AND PERSONALITY

While the Koran builds up a picture of Muhammad the prophet, with all of the virtues pertaining to his prophetic status, such as trustworthiness, honesty, integrity, steadfastness and a whole host of attributes too numerous and formulaic to mention, Muhammad the man is still something of a mystery.

However, the *hadith* books contain vivid descriptions of him, covering as they do even the minutiae of his life in rich detail. From the Traditions we learn what he looked like and how he walked; we learn what he wore, ate, liked and disliked. They tell us how he bathed and cooked and sewed, and how he put on his clothes or performed his ablutions. There are anecdotes in these collections which inform us whether he entered the lavatory with his left foot first or his right foot, or whether he prayed with his hands folded across his chest or hanging by his side; there are even anecdotes which reveal how he never made love to his wives without engaging in foreplay first, mindful as he was of the woman's equal right to sexual satisfaction.

We know that he was slow to anger or pass judgement, and that he had a sense of humour. We know that he adored children, and that one of the greatest tragedies of his life was the loss in infancy of at least one son, his beloved Ibrahim. We know that he doted on his daughter, Fatima, and the children – Hasan and Husayn – that she bore from her union to the Prophet's cousin, Ali. We know that when he walked, he did so heavily, as though he were strolling downhill, and that when he turned to speak to someone, he turned his whole body, giving the other person his complete attention. We know all of this and more. To say that Muhammad's is a life well chronicled is an understatement: there is virtually no area of the man's life which did not come under the scrutiny of his close companions, who preserved for posterity everything they ever saw him do or heard him say.

No portrait of Muhammad exists, and there is an unspoken rule among Muslim artists and painters that no likeness of the Prophet should be attempted, given the fact that any portrait would be conjecture, and would more likely than not become an icon – Islam's warnings against personality worship notwithstanding. That people do tend to place Muhammad on the kind of pedestal that sits on a fine line between reverence and idolatry may be true, and it is partly for this reason that Muslims have baulked against the old Western use of the word 'Muhammadanism' to describe the religion of Islam.

Yet there is something 'Muhammadan' about a religion in which believers are encouraged to base their lives on the example bequeathed to them in the form of Muhammad's *sunna* or practice. Interest in the incidental detail of Muhammad's life has always been enormous for this very reason: to know what Muhammad did is to know what everyone must do. There are some who endeavour to emulate Muhammad in everything they do, down to the most trivial of things such as putting on shoes, or taking off clothes.

The Koran describes Muhammad as a 'wonderful exemplar', and surely it is those moral and ethical traits of the man that are to be emulated rather than the way he brushed his teeth or wound his turban. Muhammad's example left for his followers to emulate was, apart from the Koran, the very notion of *islām* itself – the significance of which we shall discover in the chapters to come.

MUHAMMAD: REVOLUTIONARY OR REFORMER?

A popular question on undergraduate examination papers is 'Was Muhammad a revolutionary or a reformer?' As with all issues in history, there are no right or wrong answers in the absolute sense of those words; after all, it is almost always a matter of personal perspective, particularly in the appraisal of events so far removed from our own experience, with different frames of reference and often wildly diverging definitions of the same term: what constituted 'freedom' for the seventh-century Arab, for example, would no doubt stand at variance with our understanding of the concept. Another exam favourite is 'Was the first Islamic state at Medina a democracy?', a question that is virtually meaningless given the fact that democracy was a totally unknown concept in seventh-century Arabia, and quite alien to the Bedouin mind.

On one level, the concepts of 'revolution' and 'reform' are just as inapplicable, yet this has never prevented modern historians from discussing Muhammad's career in such terms. Opinion seems to be cyclical: for years it was fashionable to see Muhammad as a revolutionary, sweeping away the heathenism and corruption of the Meccan oligarchs and introducing a radically new socio-political programme based not on the old values of the desert but on the new theocracy of the Medina community-state; such views were particularly popular among the Islamist ideologues of the 1960s and 1970s. Later opinion favours a more conservative interpretation, citing Muhammad's retention of certain pre-Islamic rites as evidence of a reformist agenda. Prior to the advent of Islam, Arabs had made pilgrimages to Mecca; Muhammad retained the annual *hajj*, but gave it an Islamic orientation, banishing the idols from the Sacred Precinct and purifying the old rituals to bring them in line with the requirements of *tawhīd* or Divine unity. Other rites and rituals were similarly 'Islamicised', while a whole raft of social reforms concerning women, orphans and the poor were advocated.

Historical appraisal has focused largely on the Prophet's actions: if Muhammad abolished a particular institution, such as infanticide, then clearly he was a revolutionary; if he modified it somewhat, as he did with the laws of marriage, then he was a reformer, and so on. Where it is more difficult to judge is in the domain of personal and psychological change. It is true that the retention of the *hajj*, say, represents in one sense a reform of previous tradition, the ejection of the idols from the *ka'ba* was a psychological watershed in Arab religious life. We may be correct in describing the Islamicisation of pagan rite as a kind of reform, but when we deconstruct such phenomena and the impact that they must have had on Meccan society, the radical nature of the change becomes only too apparent. Muhammad was, therefore, a reformer in some matters and a radical in others, just as one might expect of a monotheistic prophet whose first and most important aim is to facilitate the regeneration of the human soul – a complex entity which is receptive now to reform, now to revolution, but rarely to one at the expense of the other.

MUHAMMAD AS PROPHET

It has often been said that the greatness of prophets lies in their ability to help man interpret the world in accordance with their God-given natures – an ability that is dissipated when man 'gives himself to the world' rather than to God, his point of origin and his final destination. There is in all prophets a faculty which enables them to help others to cultivate new perspectives on old problems, and to achieve fresh insights into the nature of the cosmos of which they are part, and the short life they have been given on earth. In short, the prophet comes to teach each man how to read the book of his own existence, and how to benefit from what he reads. As such, the prophet is an interpreter, sent to make sense of man's most intractable existential dilemma: his coming into existence, his short stay on earth, and his inevitable demise.

In this sense, then, Muhammad's greatness – whether one believes he was a divinely ordained prophet or not – seems beyond question. For along with many other visionaries in history – be they 'religious' prophets such as Buddha or Jesus, or 'secular' prophets such as Gandhi or Marx – Muhammad was brave enough to challenge the status quo on every count, risking much in the process, for the sake of the truth he believed in. By exposing the falsity of idol-worship and the inauthentic nature of a life which, while lived in denial of eternity, endeavours to create a bogus eternity here on earth, he opened the eyes of those around him to the reality of human existence, and by so doing helped them to address the major issues of their times.

Greatness is also predicated on those whose vision endures. Muhammad's vision has endured for 1,400 years, and seems to be as strong – in theory at least – as it ever was. Whether that vision will be carried forward into the future depends largely on those who perpetuate it. It is to the document which best enshrines that vision – namely the Koran – that we turn next.

FURTHER READING

An excellent introduction to the life and achievements of Muhammad comes in the form of W. Montgomery Watt's scholarly yet
eminently reader-friendly *Muhammad: Prophet and Statesman*
(Oxford University Press, 1961). Watt is one of Britain's greatest
scholars of Islam, and his approach is that of a sympathetic but
cautious non-Muslim admirer of the Prophet and the Islamic tradition. For a slightly more traditional approach to Muhammad, one
would have to go far to beat the magisterial *Muhammad: His Life
based on the Earliest Sources* (The Islamic Texts Society, 1983),
which draws on the *hadith* and the *sira* – to recreate the life and
career of the Prophet.

2

THE MESSAGE

The Koran describes God, the principles of belief and the fate of man in the world to come, but it is no work of theology; it contains accounts of past prophets and faith communities of old, but it is no history book; it contains invocations and words of inspiration, but it is no book of prayer.

Legal issues are discussed in it, but it is no book of law; it tells us how the Creator fashions the cosmos and makes the world turn, but it is no treatise on cosmology; it describes the alternation of day and night, and the development of the foetus in the womb, but it is no compendium of natural science.

It examines the heart and mind of man, and the existential dilemma of being human but longing for the divine, yet it is no work of popular psychology.

It is all of those things and it is none of those things: more than any other book can it truly be said of the enigmatic Koran that it is far more than simply the sum of its component parts.

THE KORAN AS CORNERSTONE OF ISLAM

In the recorded history of humankind, few events have had the kind of impact on human society created by what Christian theologian Kenneth Cragg once termed the 'event' of the Koran. Starting out as a loosely assembled collection of utterances believed to have emanated from God, and committed to writing over a period of years on a motley assortment of materials such as deerskin and camel bone, the Koran grew in stature and influence until, just a century after Muhammad's death, it had become the intellectual and emotional focal point for a faith community that stretched from Spain to India.

Some 1,400 years later, virtually nothing has changed – including, Muslims assert, the text of the Koran itself, which reads today exactly as it read at the time of Muhammad. The Koran is still the hub around which the global Muslim community claims to revolve, only today that community is a billion strong, and the profile of the 'Holy Book' extends far beyond the faith community of which it is an integral component: there can be few non-Muslims who are unable to identify the Koran as the 'sacred book of Islam'.

Despite the differences of outlook, approach and ideology that exist among the world's believing Muslims, one of the few things on which they enjoy unanimity is their acceptance of the Koran as the eternal word of God, vouchsafed to Muhammad 1,400 years ago and revealed to him in a series of angelic 'visitations' over a period of twenty-three years. As such, the Koran forms the cornerstone not only of the Muslim worldview and belief system, but also of Muslim law, theology, philosophy and, in recent years, much of Muslim social policy and political theory. None of these things is, of course, monolithic: given the diversity of the Muslim world, it is perhaps more accurate to talk of 'worldviews, systems, theologies and theories', for it would of course be a gross over-simplification to say that all Muslims believe in the same things in the same way, or, indeed, approach the same truths or embrace the same practices in the same manner. Nevertheless, however divergent their paths may be, Muslims the world over would claim that they all lead back to the Koran.

Whether some Muslims interpret it differently, or whether others misinterpret it, wittingly or unwittingly, for their own personal or political purposes, the ineluctable fact remains that the Koran is the theoretical centre of the Islamic universe, occupying a position in Islam analogous in its centrality to that occupied by Jesus in Christianity. For just as Jesus was the *logos*, or the 'word' of God 'made flesh', so too is the Koran the eternal 'word' of God, translated into the tongue of man.

THE KORAN AND POPULAR PIETY

The Koran sees itself as a vehicle through which, it is believed, the word of God is conveyed to man. While the Koran is held to enshrine the 'eternal word' of God, as a material object – a book, comprising leaves of paper upon which human words have been written in a human language, all held between two covers – it itself is not sacred.

Nevertheless, for many Muslims it is not 'just a book' but a 'Book', a holy scripture that is sacrosanct in every respect. The inability or unwillingness on the part of pious but ultimately unthinking Muslims to make a distinction between form and substance is no doubt one of the many manifestations of man's proclivity to venerate that which is tangible rather than that which cannot be seen or touched.

Whether or not popular Muslim perception holds the Koran to be sacred, it is treated as such by the vast majority of ordinary Muslims. In many Muslim households the 'Holy Book' occupies an elevated position in the literal as well as the metaphorical sense, for it is often to be found on the highest bookshelf, a Book above all other books. Although the Koran is a text that is designed to be read and pondered at all opportunities, for many Muslims the bookshelf is often where the Koran remains. It will be taken down or consulted only on special occasions, such as births, deaths, marriages, or, in one particular custom, as a quasi-magical object that is waved above the heads of those setting out on long journeys. For many Muslims, the existence of a Koran in the house is crucial to the good fortune of the family, like a charm or amulet that wards off the 'evil eye'. Others wrap the Koran in sumptuous material, mindful that the book cannot, in its own words, 'be touched by the impure'. Hence those who are in a state of ritual impurity on account of not having taken their ablutions, or women who are menstruating, are barred from actual physical contact with the pages of the Koran. Little thought do most Muslims give to the possibility that the 'impurity' implied by the Koran may be the 'impurity of heart', which renders one unable to 'touch' the Koran because one's heart is unwilling to embrace the truths it enshrines.

For another, rather different kind of Muslim believer, the Koran is seen as a kind of 'guidebook' that was sent to lift the veil on the

Creator and make Him known. For them, the Koran is the eternal word of God made manifest in human tongue, revealed to clarify man's position on earth and to help him understand why he is here. In this worldview, the Koran may be seen as an aid to decode the riddle of existence. For Muslim believers such as these, the Koran is both 'of this world' and of the 'realm of the Unseen'. It is of this world in the sense that it is made of ink and paper, and it is of the realm of the unseen in the sense that it emanates from One who is above time, space and the realm of materiality. As such, it is treated with the kind of respect that should be accorded to anything which enshrines the sacred, but it is not revered as though it itself were an object worthy of veneration.

It is important to allow for often quite marked differences of opinion with regard to the Koran among Muslims. Those who classify themselves as Muslim, or as believers in the Koran, are not one vast monolithic group of people who all look at revelation in the same way, and it is important to make distinctions between different conceptual and intellectual approaches. It is also particularly important that we distinguish the popular Muslim perception of the Koran from the way that the Koran perceives itself, namely as an 'inspired message' and 'book of wisdom' that was sent 'in Arabic' as a 'guide and mercy' to 'all the worlds'.

THE KORAN AND THE WESTERN READER

For Western, non-Muslim readers with no knowledge of Arabic, approaching the Koran with a view to gaining at least a rudimentary understanding of its message can be quite daunting, and first impressions of the book are often less than favourable, to say the least. Preconceptions as to the role of the Koran in Islam and its significance for Muslims today are probably unavoidable, given the high profile of Islam and the Muslim world in the modern media; paradoxically, this is no bad thing if it prompts people to study the book for themselves and not take anything purely on hearsay.

However, willingness to put one's prior assumptions aside and uncover the 'facts' for oneself do not make that initial encounter with the Koran any less problematic. The Koran is not an 'easy read', and if Western readers expect to sail through the book from cover to cover and emerge with a full grasp of the Koran and its underlying message, they will be disappointed. The obstacles to reaching the heart of the Koran are many, and while they are by no means insuperable, it does seem at first that they are part of some inner conspiracy designed to preserve the book's innermost truths from those unprepared to appreciate them.

Nothing could be further from the truth, of course: the Koran itself declares that it was sent down as a 'guide to humankind', and in this sense its message is open to everyone, in all places and at all times. However, readers approaching the Koran from different ideological or faith perspectives should naturally expect different things: one tends to take from the Koran in accordance with what one brings to it, and this includes any preconceived ideas concerning its validity and authenticity. What all newcomers to the Koran ought to bear in mind is that the book is an address to those who have already attained belief in God, and who have either affirmed the prophethood of Muhammad or at least considered the possibility that he is the Messenger of God. Of itself, the Koran says:

> This is the Book; in it is guidance sure, without doubt, to those who fear God; who believe in the Unseen, are steadfast in prayer, and spend out of what We have provided for them; and who believe in the Revelation sent to thee, and sent before thy time, and (in their hearts) have the assurance of the Hereafter
>
> (2:2–4)

Having attempted to put aside our preconceptions, and bearing in mind that the Koran is meaningful only in the context of belief in God and prophethood, the next obstacle to try to overcome is that of language. The illustrious Scottish essayist and historian Thomas Carlyle, who wrote about the charisma and heroism of Muhammad in the most glowing terms imaginable, clearly encountered problems in his attempts to understand Muhammad's written message, for he describes the Koran as:

> A wearisome confused jumble...endless iterations, long-windedness, entanglement; most crude, incondite – insupportable stupidity, in short.

Such criticisms become easier to understand when we bear in mind that he was hampered by the same obstacle that faces all of those who lack a grasp of Arabic: he read the Koran in translation, and possibly even a translation of a translation. I shall say more about the somewhat involved issue of Koran translation in a later section of this chapter.

A third obstacle to Western readers is the form or structure of the Koran. For while it is relatively easy to deflect criticisms regarding language, particularly when these come from people who have no idea how the original Arabic reads, it is considerably more difficult to explain away the apparent shapelessness of the Koran. Arguably the most common criticism of the Koran by its detractors concerns its form, and Arabic-speaking readers are perplexed by it. The chapters and verses which make up the Koran seem to have been put together almost arbitrarily. None of the 114 chapters which make up the Koran possesses any kind of discernible linearity, with scenes, pro- tagonists and themes changing often with such rapidity and apparent lack of motive that the reader is hard pressed to keep up with the narrative or to know what is coming next, and why. In short, for its most vociferous critics, the Koran appears to be little more than a formless collection of passages, some linked together in a semblance of interconnectedness, but mostly devoid of anything resembling a common thread. Before we can decide whether the Koran is really as shapeless and unapproachable as its harsher critics allege, there are many other things to ponder, and it is best to reserve judgement on the issue for the time being – at least until the end of the chapter.

THE STRUCTURE OF THE KORAN

We shall first look at the book as it appears now, before going back through history to the time of Muhammad to see how it appeared when it was first revealed, and how it was preserved and trans- mitted in its present form.

THE INTERNAL DIVISIONS OF THE KORAN

Slightly shorter in length than the New Testament, the Koran has two main internal divisions: the *āyā* and the *sūra*. These are usually translated as 'verse' and 'chapter' respectively, and repre- sent divisions which are similar in conception and structure to the chapters and verses of the Bible.

THE ÂYÂ OR 'VERSE'

As well as denoting a 'verse' of the Koran, the word *āyā* also means 'clear sign' or 'indication'. It can be a 'sign' in the sense of something that points to God, such as a miracle; a human indication of God's presence, such as a Prophet; or indeed any of the created beings in the cosmos, all of whom point through their very existence to the names and attributes of their Creator. In fact there are numerous occasions in the Koran where the word can be understood either as 'sign' or 'verse'.

Each of the numbered lines below constitutes a 'verse' of the Koran. Together, the 'verses' form arguably the most famous 'chapter' of the Koran, namely the opening chapter or *al-Fātiha*:

1   In the name of God, Most Compassionate, Most Merciful!
2   Praise be to God, the Cherisher and Sustainer of the Worlds;
3   Most Compassionate, Most Merciful;
4   Master of the Day of Judgement.
5   Thee do we worship, and Thine aid do we seek.
6   Guide us to the Straight Path –
7   The way of those on whom Thou Has bestowed Thy Grace, not those whose lot is wrath, or those who have gone astray.

The *Fātiha* is an invocation that is used as part of the five-times-a-day canonical prayer, or on any occasion when believers feel the need to praise God. Readers will see that the Koranic *āyā* is not necessarily self-contained, be it syntactically or thematically: a single sentence often straddles two or more 'verses', while others contain no more than two or three words. The verses of the Koran, then, come in different lengths and forms; some 'chapters' have comparatively few verses, while others have hundreds: the second 'chapter' of the Koran, *al-Baqara*, contains no fewer than 286.

THE SÛRA OR 'CHAPTER'

Etymologically, the word *sūra* denotes a 'row' or a 'fence' – something that is used to partition off one thing from another. There are 114 such 'chapters' in the Koran of unequal length; in modern printed editions, as in the manuscripts of Uthman's era, the sequence in which the 'chapters' appear is ordered roughly in accordance with 'chapter' length: the longest chapters – those revealed mostly in Medina – come at the beginning, and the shorter ones – those revealed mostly in Mecca, at the outset of the Prophet's career – towards the end. The exception, of course, is the *Fātiha*, which always appears as the opening chapter of the Koran. Appendix B shows the Arabic names of all 114 *sūras*, together with their English equivalents, in the sequence in which they appear in the Koran.

In most cases, the name by which each *sūra* is known either reflects the general tenor of the *sūra* or stands as a kind of thematic 'shorthand' for a particular subject included in the narrative. For example, the second *sūra* – *al-Baqara* or 'The Cow' – is a reference to the 'golden calf' idolised by the Children of Israel. Each *sūra*, with the sole exception of *sūra* 9, begins with the formula, 'In the name of God, Most Compassionate, Most Merciful', which is also the first line of the opening chapter, *al-Fātiha*.

While most of the chapters – particularly the shorter ones revealed in Mecca – were communicated to the Prophet as complete units, others were revealed over a period of days, weeks, months and even years. These chapters are said to be 'composite', which means simply that they are made up of verses which were revealed at different times, and often out of sequence, and which were inserted in particular chapters afterwards, according to their subject matter.

HOW THE KORAN WAS REVEALED

It is impossible to know for certain precisely when, where and how the Koran was communicated to Muhammad: any information we have comes mainly from the *hadith* and the *sira*, which is why any conclusions we draw regarding the dynamics of revelation – or, indeed, any aspect of early Muslim history – must remain provisional.

Evidence from the Traditions suggests that Muhammad experienced a steady stream of revelatory experiences over a period of twenty-three years, from his initial experience at the age of forty on Mount Hira to a final revelation just nine or ten days before his death. Apart from a short period at the beginning of his mission known as the *fatrat* or 'interval', where God appeared to fall silent and Muhammad began to doubt his sanity, the message was communicated at frequent intervals, enshrined in single verses, groups of verses and, at times, whole chapters.

Muslims believe that the 'veil' from behind which God talked to Muhammad was the archangel Gabriel, who appeared to Muhammad in different forms from one revelatory experience to the next. Muslim scholars have traditionally tried to identify the situations in the Prophet's career which precipitated the 'descent' of certain verses. Known as *asbāb al-nuzūl*, which may be translated loosely as 'reasons for revelation', these are various events in the early history of Islam – such as the Battle of Badr, for instance – which occasioned the emergence of a certain verse or chapter. Many books have been written about why certain verses were revealed when they were revealed. However, this is not an exact science; nor does it detract from the Muslim belief that while many verses are indeed contextual, they are at the same time relevant for all times, and must be interpreted accordingly.

Muslims believe the Koran was sent piecemeal over a number of years to reflect the gradual awakening of man to the truth the message contained. They also believe it was done through consideration for Muhammad who found his revelatory experiences extremely taxing, as well as practically making it easier for people to memorise the verses to pass down in their oral tradition.

THE KORAN AND THE MECCA–MEDINA DIVISION

There are substantial thematic and stylistic differences between those chapters revealed in Mecca and those revealed in Medina. The provenance of most chapters – whether they were revealed in Mecca or Medina – is known from the Traditions, and modern printed editions of the Koran usually indicate this at the beginning of each chapter. Some chapters, and particularly those which are known to be composite, are more difficult to classify in this way. Generally, however, there are a number of ways one can determine a chapter's origins.

THE MECCAN CHAPTERS

Meccan chapters deal more with those issues connected to the so-called 'fundamentals of religion' – Divine Unity, Prophethood and

The Last Day – than with the 'pillars of Islam' or rite and ritual. Thus if a chapter focuses on God's oneness, on the stories of the prophets of old, on the dangers of attributing partners to God or any other kind of moral corruption, or on the fate of man in the world to come, it is more likely to have been revealed in Mecca than in Medina.

Meccan chapters and verses are also likely to be shorter than their Medinese counterparts, and their language is often poetic, highly figurative and not without a certain sense of drama. To the pre-Islamic Arab, the oral–aural phenomenon of the Arabic Koran must have been quite literally stunning, regardless of whether or not the moral message it enshrined was taken on board. Tradition has it that idolaters in Mecca would fall down in prostration at the eloquence of the verses alone; some are even said to have accepted the Koran simply on account of the literary excellence on display in those early Meccan verses.

THE MEDINESE CHAPTERS

The chapters of the Koran revealed in Medina are for the most part longer and more complex than those revealed in Mecca. While the subjects covered by the Meccan verses are taken up again in Medina, they are discussed differently, in keeping with the general change in tenor that the Koran seems to undergo once Muhammad has migrated from Mecca and begun to establish the new community-state.

Although an oversimplification, there is some truth to the assertion that while the Meccan stage of the mission focused primarily on 'introducing God', the Medinese stage concerned itself mainly with 'introducing God's laws'. The 'legislative verses' – those verses which discuss rite, ritual and law – were revealed in Medina, where Muhammad was involved in the formation of a whole faith-based community in need of ethical norms and legal precepts. Although eloquent, the Medinese sections largely dispense with the literary tropes and conventions of the Meccan verses.

THE LANGUAGE OF THE KORAN

The Koran makes it quite clear that just as all prophets are instructed to take the divine message to their own people first, it is only natural that their message be couched in a language that their home communities understand. In the case of the Koran, of course, this language was Arabic. Why did God choose to communicate with man in Arabic, or through an Arab? Muslims tend to reply by pointing out that God has to reveal Himself somehow, and if He had revealed Himself in Norse, for example, or Mongolian, people would have asked the same question. Others adopt the Koranic approach and say that had the Koran been revealed in a language other than Arabic, the Arabs would have rejected it outright:

> Had We sent this as a Qur'an [in the language] other than Arabic, they would have said: 'Why are not its verses explained in detail? What! [a book] not in Arabic and [a Messenger] an Arab?'
>
> (41:44)

Muslim scholarly opinion is divided with regard to the 'purity' of the Arabic used in the Koran: some claim that the Koran contains no foreign words at all, while others concede that it does include a number of words derived from other languages. Some non-Muslim critics of Islam have tended to argue in favour of the existence of foreign words in the Koran, believing – erroneously – that to prove the 'impurity' of the Arabic in the Koran is to disprove the Koran's claim that its Arabic is 'pure and clear' (16:103).

Like any other language, the Arabic used in Mecca at the time of Muhammad would undoubtedly have assimilated words of foreign origin. What was important for its audience was that the words of the Koran be understandable, and not that they should possess the somewhat questionable quality known as linguistic 'purity'. The fact that the Koran includes words derived from Persian, Syriac or Abyssinian has little bearing on its claims to emanate from the sacred, which is why attempts by critics to prove the non-Arabic origin of some of the language in the Koran, and counter-attempts by Muslim apologists to prove that the Koran is free from the linguistic 'impurity' of foreign loanwords, are a waste of time.

THE LITERARY STYLE OF THE KORAN

Scholars, both Muslim and non-Muslim, have often debated whether it is legitimate to describe the Koran as 'literature'. While it clearly belongs to none of the traditional literary genres – epic, lyric, drama, novel, short story – it does have certain features which are definable as 'literary'.

Indeed, the Koran is written in a language wholly divergent in syntax and structure from any other, including the 'secular' Arabic literature of pre-Islamic times. As many experts in Arab literature will attest, it is distinguished by excellences of sound and eloquence, of rhetoric and metaphor, of assonance and alliteration, of onomatopoeia and rhyme, of ellipsis and parallelism. So sublime were these that certain Arab poets of the day would fall down in prostration at the inimitable eloquence of the Muhammadan message, while the first recipients of the Divine message were moved to deem it miraculous.

That it is literature in the classical sense of the word seems to me beyond doubt; that it is, in the context of its own time, excellent literature, is also taken as given. If the Koran is the word of God, it is the word of God as communicated through the medium of human language, and while it may not have the same function as a work of fiction or a collection of prose essays, it is no less a work of literature than others. To see the Koran as revelation but not literature is to deny the human aspect of Koranic language, without which the message would never have been communicated. To see the Koran as both is to understand how the word of God manifests itself not only in human speech, but in all creation – a view that lies at the heart of Koranic discourse.

Non-Muslims, of course, may accept the Koran as literature but not revelation. However, if Muslims and non-Muslims can find common ground in their acceptance of the literary nature of the Koran, many of the old stumbling blocks to dialogue may be lifted. For this, re-orientations of perspective are required from both sides, and thankfully there are indications, in the academic world at least, that such a rapprochement is not beyond the bounds of feasibility.

MESSAGE AS MIRACLE: THE 'INIMITABILITY' OF THE KORAN

According to the Koran, one way in which past prophets offered proof of their prophethood was through the working of 'miracles'. The word 'miracle' in Arabic is *mu'jiza*, derived from a verb which means, among other things, 'to render unable'. Many extra-ordinary feats have been attributed to Muhammad. However, the absence of any mention of the Prophet's wonder-working in the Koran has led some Muslim scholars to talk of the Koran itself as Muhammad's enduring miracle. After all, how could a man who was allegedly 'unlettered', and most certainly uneducated in the modern sense of the word, produce a book the supreme eloquence of which reduced even Muhammad's harshest critics to awestruck silence?

The miraculous aspect of the Koran is described by Muslim scholars as its *i'jāz* or 'inimitability'. The Koran, it is believed, has no equal: however hard he may try, man will never be able to match the holy Book in terms of eloquence, beauty or wisdom.

Few appear to have risen to the challenge, aware no doubt that the Koranic claim is almost certainly rhetorical in intent.

THEMES OF THE KORAN

The Koran defies definition most resolutely, as though it is deter-mined not to yield to the will of those who would deconstruct it chapter by chapter, verse by verse, and tell us, definitively, what it is all about. For while it contains its histories of past prophets, it is no history book; it contains invocations and petitions offered to the Divine, but it is no book of prayer; there are within its pages a smattering of 'legal' verses, yet it is no law book; and while it tells us how the Creator fashions the cosmos and makes the world turn, it is no treatise on cosmology. It is all of those things and yet it is none of those things: more than any other book can it truly be said of the enigmatic Koran that it is far more than simply the sum of its component parts.

Nevertheless, the fact remains that when it comes to the ques-tion of overall definition, the Koran is impossible to pin down. The disjointed nature of the book, together with its often difficult lit-erary forms and conventions, have led some critics to dismiss it as incoherent and ultimately unreadable. Even those versed in Arabic will agree that trying to discover what the Koran says about the numerous subjects it covers is not the easiest of tasks. The subjects it covers are not discussed consecutively; nor, as we have already noted, do they follow any particular kind of order. To see what the

Koran has to say on a subject, the reader has to search through its verses with the help of a concordance, or, less helpfully, a subject index, and then piece together its disparate references into a coherent whole.

A number of scholars within the Muslim tradition have focused on the question of the themes or contents of the Koran. Having surveyed the most important of these works, I have come up with what I believe is a list of the seven main themes of the Koran. These themes will all be revisited in Chapter 3 in the sections on 'fundamentals of belief'. They are:

(i)   God, Divine Unity and the question of belief and unbelief
(ii)   The 'prophetic narratives': the mission of the apostles preceding Muhammad
(iii) The career of Muhammad in Mecca and Medina
(iv)   The hereafter
(v)   Man and the 'Creator–created' relationship; angels, jinn and the dilemma of earthly existence
(vi)   The 'cosmic phenomena verses'
(vii) The 'legislative verses': laws and guidelines; ethical precepts and moral teachings

THEME 1: GOD AND DIVINE UNITY

The Koran is at pains to point out that while God is remote in the sense of being completely dissimilar to His creation, He is nearer to man than his jugular vein. In emphasising God's immanence, the Koran highlights that God is a Creator who is constantly and continuously engaged in the creative act. The God of the Koran did not create the heavens and the earth in six days and then 'rest' on the seventh; He continues to create it at each instant. Indeed, one can describe His creative act as 'continuous creation' – the second-by-second annihilation and re-creation of all matter. We shall return to the discussion of God as creator in Chapter 3.

The Koran does not employ any rigorous philosophical arguments to prove the existence of God. Indeed, the Koran does not attempt to prove the existence of God at all. Rather, in keeping with the mission of the prophets who preceded Muhammad, the Koran sets out to prove not that there is a God, but that God is one.

The Koran wishes not only to demonstrate that God is one, but also to reveal to man those aspects of the Divine which are accessible to the human intellect. While God in his absolute essence is unknowable, He can be glimpsed, as it were, through the 'veil' of His creation.

> Do they not look at the camels, how they are made? –
> And at the sky, how it is raised high? –
> And at the mountains, how they are fixed firm? –
> And at the earth, how it is spread out?
>
> (88:17–20)

Repeated exhortations to 'ponder', 'deliberate' and 'meditate upon' the various 'signs' scattered throughout the cosmos are not made merely in order for man to acquire knowledge of his universe for the sake of knowledge. Rather, he is encouraged to study the universe around him in order to know better the Creator of that universe. For it is only by knowing God that one can learn to love God, and it is only through loving God that one can be moved to obey Him. Man cannot love both self and God. Muslims would join with Christians in the prayer to God which asks that 'Thy Kingdom come, Thy will be done.' But for God's kingdom to come, man's imaginary kingdom must go; and for God's will to be done, man's will must be subservient. The emphasis of the Koran on Divine Unity, and on the importance of submission, is there precisely in order to show how such a kingdom may come about, be it in this life or the life to come.

THEME 2: THE 'PROPHETIC NARRATIVES'

The second major theme in the Koran is the story of how God's message of unity and submission has been received by various communities in the past, told through a series of quasi-historical accounts that we may call 'prophetic narratives'. These accounts tell how, in almost every society known to man, men of outstanding spiritual vision have, chosen by God, risen among their own people to warn of the dangers of henotheism and disbelief, to lead them to the path of Divine Unity and thus secure salvation. Muslim tradition tells us that 124,000 divinely appointed messengers have been sent to various communities across the globe since the time of Adam – considered by some to have been a 'messenger' in his own right. The Koran tells us about no more than two dozen such men by name, most of whom will be familiar to the Western reader from his or her knowledge of the prophets and patriarchs of the Old Testament.

That the Koran should recount the stories of Judaeo-Christian messengers such as Abraham, Moses, Joseph and Jesus should not come as a surprise, given the claim that Muhammad is said to have come as their natural successor, chosen by God not to contradict their messages but to bring them to their logical conclusion. The religion of Judaeo-Christian messengers and all of the messengers mentioned in the Koran was, after all, one and the same: the religion of *islām*, or submission to God. The mission of all of these men was, the Koran asserts, to warn men of the folly of worshipping idols, to preach the message of Divine Unity, and to impart to them the vision of a lasting peace made possible only by embracing belief in that unity, and by surrendering one's will to the will of God. Throughout the Koran, Muhammad is reminded time and time again of his spiritual lineage:

> We have sent thee inspiration, as We sent it to Noah and the Messengers after him: we sent inspiration to Abraham, Isma'il, Isaac, Jacob and the Tribes, to Jesus, Job, Jonah, Aaron, and Solomon, and to David We gave the Psalms.

> (4:163)

Other Biblical figures whose stories are recounted in the Koran are Adam (and Eve), Zachariah, John and Mary, mother of Jesus. There is also mention of prophets native to the Arab peninsula and other areas who do not appear in the scriptures of other religions, while some scholars have also identified one particular prophet, Dhu al-Kifl, as the Buddha.

As far as the prophetic narratives are concerned, the Koran is highly *referential*: it assumes that its readers are familiar with the stories of past prophets, and so dispenses with most of the extraneous detail. This approach reveals two important things about the Koran and the milieu into which it was introduced. It shows us that the original audience of the Koran was, like Muhammad himself, far more familiar with the stories of the Bible than many Muslim apologists would have us believe. And second, it confirms the high esteem in which the Koran holds not only the messengers of the past, but the scriptures which emerged to embody their message.

The prophets who appear in the Koran have numerous features in common. They are all 'men of the people', emerging from their own communities as seers and challengers of the status quo, ready to dedicate their lives to the same goal: the guidance and shepherding of humankind back to the pristine monotheistic ideal – the knowledge, love and worship of the One true God. The attempt to secure eternity, be it on the terms of man or on the terms of God, is the sub-text which informs most of the prophetic narratives which appear in the Koran.

THEME 3: THE MUHAMMADAN MISSION

The Koran does not contain anything even closely resembling a biography of Muhammad. Nevertheless, despite the fact that they are not arranged chronologically, careful study of its verses does allow one to build up a sketchy picture of Muhammad which allows us some insights into his character, his role as God's Messenger, and the difficulties he faced in carrying out his mission.

The Meccan verses are understandably the most laconic, with few references to Muhammad over and above general indications of his status as God's Messenger, and reassurances that his messages from God are not a sign of incipient madness.

Other Meccan verses offer Muhammad support and consolation, guaranteeing him success in the end if only he is prepared to suffer the slings and arrows of Meccan intransigence and carry his mission through as God has intended.

A considerable number of verses revealed in Medina chart Muhammad's ever-changing fortunes as he grappled with the complex social dynamics of the new community-state.

The main players in the Medinese drama were the Muslims themselves, be they migrants (muhājirūn) from Mecca or the helpers (ansār) who welcomed them to Medina; the unbelievers, including the Quraysh of Mecca; the Jews and Christians, grouped together as 'people of the Book'; and the munāfiqūn or 'hypocrites', a large group of individuals who professed Islam nominally, but who sided in private with the 'forces of unbelief', forming a kind of 'fifth column' that caused Muhammad untold grief.

The Koran chronicles the most significant of the Prophet's campaigns against the Quraysh, such as Badr and Uhud, referring to minor battles indirectly, in the context of Muhammad's general mission to oppose what the Muslims saw as the tyranny of unbelief. The gradual revelation of the Koran was such that verses were often revealed as events unfolded, sometimes to presage them but, more importantly, to explain or justify them once they had happened.

Underpinning all of the verses which refer to Muhammad is the assertion not only that Muhammad is a mere mortal, like all other mortals, but that his mission, like the mission of all of the prophets who have gone before him, is merely to warn:

> For me, I have been commanded to serve the Lord of this city, Him Who has sanctified it and to Whom [belong] all things: and I am commanded to be of those who bow in Islam to God's Will, – And to rehearse the Qur'an: and if any accept guidance, they do it for the good of their own souls, and if any stray, say: 'I am only a Warner.'
>
> (27:91–92)

THEME 4: THE HEREAFTER

Like the Torah in Judaism and the Gospels in Christianity, the Koran affirms the reality of life after death, and the continuation of human existence in the 'hereafter', where man will be confronted with the truth of all that he has done, be it good or bad, while on earth. Almost a quarter of the Koran is given over to eschatological matters such as bodily resurrection after death, divine judgement and the requital of man's deeds in either heaven or hell.

The Koranic approach to the afterlife can be broken down into four main sub-themes: the incredulity of the sceptics and the non-believers with regard to the possibility of life after death; death, resurrection and return; the final judgement; and the rewards and punishments of heaven and hell as a consequence of one's deeds while on earth.

In several places and in various ways, the Koran recounts how, since time immemorial, man the sceptic has scoffed at the idea of life after death:

They say: 'What! when we are reduced to bones and dust, should we really be raised up [to be] a new creation?'

(17:49)

The Koran responds by invoking the same creative power responsible for creation in the first place. Whether man be made of iron or stones, it says, or of flesh and bones, the fact remains that He who gave man life in the first instance will surely be able to bestow life again once man has returned to earth:

Then will they say: 'Who will cause us to return?' Say: 'He who created you first!'

(17:51)

Various aspects of the actual phenomenon of death and the physical resurrection of the body are outlined throughout the Koran. The moment of death is the moment when the soul is separated from those things to which it has become habituated during its earthly sojourn. Consequently, the less one is attached to the 'life of the world', the easier one's passage from this life to the next; the more one is mired in the materiality of the here-and-now, the more difficult it will be to progress to the hereafter. Hence the Koranic assertion that the souls of the wicked are 'torn out' by the angels of death, while the souls of the righteous surrender peacefully, submitted as they are to the reality of the divine which underpins all existence.

This so-called 'Last Day' is presented by the Koran in a series of colourful and highly emotive vignettes: at an appointed 'hour' known only to God, a series of apocalyptic events will occur, signalled by an almighty 'trumpet blast', whereupon the cosmos as we know it will undergo a complete transformation.

During the judgement that ensues, all that man has ever said, done or thought will be made apparent to him, be it good or evil, and however apparently trivial or inconsequential:

Then shall anyone who has done an atom's weight of good, see it! And anyone who has done an atom's weight of evil, shall see it.

(99:7–8)

The result of the judgement will be the entry of all humankind into a state of eternal existence which befits the way individuals lived their lives and responded to God's message while on earth. A discussion of verses describing heaven and hell will appear in Chapter 3, in the section on belief in the hereafter.

The fact that almost a quarter of the Koran is concerned with the issue of the hereafter shows quite dramatically the importance of the concept of everlasting existence in Islam. Indeed, for the Koran, each human individual possesses an eternal spirit that is clothed with a corporeal shell and allowed a very brief sojourn in this finite world, simply in order that the spirit – like a fish taken out of water – may come to know its true source. Conceptually, the hereafter is not seen as more important than the world, for without the world, the hereafter would be meaningless. However, the large proportion of verses which deal with the hereafter do tend to reflect the primacy in Islam of everlasting life over the all-too-fleeting life of man on earth.

THEME 5: MAN IN THE KORAN

This theme concerns the relationship between the Creator and the creation, at the pinnacle of which stands God's supreme work of artistry, man himself. Man's duty on earth is to realise his true nature, and to serve as a representative of the Divine on earth. As God's most wondrous creation, man has the ability to reflect myriad 'attributes of perfection' which characterise the absolute Ground of all being. These include power, wisdom, knowledge, mercy and forgiveness. The danger is that man – part spirit, part matter – may choose to attribute to himself all of the attributes of God which he finds reflected in him. Should he choose this route, he has no option but to deny God and to affirm the sovereignty of his own soul. This stark choice – between self-worship and God-worship – is the 'test' with which man is burdened during his short sojourn on earth. Belief and unbelief, then, are the result of a choice, and the state of each soul in eternity depends on how that choice is made.

THEME 6: THE 'COSMIC PHENOMENA VERSES'

There are a large number of verses in the Koran in which various natural processes and cosmic phenomena are discussed – some in considerable detail – and posited as proofs of the existence of the benevolent omnipotence of God. The constellations of stars in the heavens, the existence of mountains and seas on earth, the falling of rain on dry earth, the diversity of colours and races, the alternation of day and night – all of these are seen as indications of a merciful Creator who not only brings man into the world, but who nurtures and cares for him constantly by providing him with all of the things necessary for his continued existence.

> Behold! in the creation of the heavens and the earth; in the alternation of the night and the day; in the sailing of the ships through the ocean for the profit of humankind; in the rain which God Sends down from the skies, and the life which He gives therewith to an earth that is dead; in the beasts of all kinds that He scatters through the earth; in the change of the winds, and the clouds which they Trail like their slaves between the sky and the earth; – [Here] indeed are Signs for a people that are wise.
>
> (2:164)

Some Muslim apologists cite the 'cosmic verses', as proof of the miraculous nature of the Koran, for some of these appear to describe phenomena which modern science discovered only recently: the 'big bang', for example, is held to have been foreshadowed by the Koran. However, this would appear to be missing the point: the Koran does not cover these phenomena solely in order to draw attention to them in their own right. Rather, the Koran sees the cosmos as a vast showcase of 'signs', each one pointing to God. It is surely no coincidence that the Arabic word for 'sign' – *āya* – also means 'verse'. Not only, then, are created beings 'signs' of God's creatorship but also 'verses' in the vast 'book of creation', there to be read and understood. The main function of the so-called 'cosmic verses', then, is to draw attention to the artistry of God and make manifest His 'beautiful names', presumably in the hope that man will interpret them correctly and conclude that 'there is no god but God.'

THEME 7: THE 'LEGISLATIVE VERSES'

The Koran is not a law book, and one cannot find in it the kind of lengthy corpus of religious laws that one finds, say, in the Old

Testament. Rather, the Koran provides a broad ethical framework in which believers are encouraged to operate, and which serves as a basis for the regulation of private and public life. The absence of legal detail would suggest that while the spirit of the law is for God to outline, the letter of the law is for man to work out for himself, according to time and circumstance. The idea that 'Islam legislates for every facet of human life', a mantra espoused by those who claim that since Islam is a whole way of life, it regulates human behaviour down to the most minute of detail, can be found nowhere in the Koran.

Apart from the numerous moral and ethical precepts which appear in the Koran, there are, however, a number of practical rules and instructions given in order to help man regulate his personal and social life, from guidance on when and how to perform certain acts of worship, such as prayer and fasting, to directives on issues such as marriage, divorce, inheritance and other social transactions. The 'legislative verses' from which practical 'Islamic laws' are derived are actually very few in number; more will be said about them in Chapter 4.

PRESERVATION AND TRANSMISSION OF THE KORAN

There are two main schools of thought with regard to how the Koran was preserved in writing and transmitted from generation to generation: the 'traditional' school, whose arguments are based on evidence afforded by the *hadith*; and the 'critical' school, spearheaded by those for whom the *hadith* hold little or no value as historical sources. Each accommodates a wide range of approaches and views. The 'traditional' school includes 'liberals' – those, for example, who are willing to question the authenticity of *hadith* – as well as 'conservatives', who are less likely to depart from orthodox views on the historical value of the prophetic traditions. Similarly, while the 'critical' school has pockets of 'hardcore', neo-Orientalist scholars who dismiss the *hadith* entirely, it also has a growing number of less doctrinaire scholars who are still ready to call the *hadith* into question, but who stop short of discrediting the Muslim approach altogether, and actively seek common ground with their ideological 'opponents'. However, despite the different approaches within each school, and the overlap between them, how one approaches the issue of the preservation and transmission of the Koran depends largely on one's acceptance or rejection of those early historical accounts which have come to us via the Traditions of the Prophet, the *hadith*.

THE TRADITIONAL MUSLIM ACCOUNT

While the existence of conflicting reports among the Traditions makes our task more difficult, it is possible to wade through the large amounts of anecdotal evidence which has reached us via the *hadith* and piece together the traditional Muslim account how the Koran was preserved and transmitted. The story is as follows. The preservation of the received revelations and their collation into a single text known as the Koran took place in three main stages: during the lifetime of the Prophet; during the caliphate of Abu Bakr; and during the caliphate of Uthman.

THE KORAN DURING THE LIFETIME OF MUHAMMAD

While the Koran as we know it did not emerge as a single text until long after Muhammad's death, evidence from the Traditions suggests that most, if not all, of the Koran was written down during his lifetime. While Muhammad's alleged illiteracy is still the subject of debate, the Traditions indicate that he dictated the revelations to various scribes, and played no part himself in recording God's utterances for posterity. Writing was still a relatively novel phenomenon in Bedouin society, and few of Muhammad's followers possessed the skill. One who did, however, was the Prophet's chief scribe, Zayd b. Thabit, and it is he who is credited with having recorded in writing the lion's share of the Koran. The materials on which the revealed verses were written were diverse and included animal hides, bones and palm fronds, as well as parchment. Other scribes also played their part, but the vast majority of Companions contributed to the preservation of the Koran by memorising it, word for word, verse for verse, chapter for chapter.

The *hadith* reports of people travelling to Medina to see the Prophet and to learn about Islam, and of their being given copies of various passages of the Koran to read and ponder. Also according to the *hadith*, Umar, Muhammad's future father-in-law, accepted the new faith after reading verses from the *sūra* which he found members of his immediate family reciting from a piece of parchment.

Evidence of the existence of a written Koran during the lifetime of the Prophet comes also from the famous 'Farewell Sermon', given by Muhammad shortly before his death. In it he declared that he was bequeathing his community two things: the 'book of God' and the Prophetic *sunna*. It is possible to argue that the reference to the 'book of God' here implies that the Koran was available at this point as a single, written document.

Nevertheless, there are a number of Muslim scholars who readily admit that it is possible that the Prophet died with God's revelation to him completed, but with the Koran existing only as scattered verses written on bone, leather and parchment, and in the hearts and memories of men.

SEQUENCING THE REVELATION

It is also alleged that the Prophet himself was responsible for marking the division of the revelations into 'verses' and 'chapters', as well as the general sequencing of all that was revealed. According to Uthman, the Prophet would have his scribes insert freshly revealed verses into existing chapters on the basis of subject matter. Whether Muhammad made any pronouncements concerning the sequencing of the chapters and the order in which they should appear is open to question, particularly when one considers that the ordering of chapters is relevant only when the text concerned is a coherent unity, rather than a loose assemblage of scattered materials, which is exactly what it was during the lifetime of the Prophet.

In short, then, from the evidence of the *hadith* it is fair to assume that, by the time of the Prophet's death, most, if not all, of the Koran existed in written form, albeit on a number of different materials rather than as a single, self-contained document. Tradition also holds that the Koran – all of the Koran – also existed in the memories of the Companions, whose oral transmission of the book would prove invaluable when the collation of the disparate materials into one document actually took place.

THE COLLECTION OF THE MATERIALS UNDER ABU BAKR

The Battle of Yamama, fought in 633, a year after the death of the Prophet, was the catalyst which prompted the first political leader of the Muslim community, Abu Bakr, to bring together all of the materials on which the Koran was written and collate them into a single text. The reason for this was the high number of Muslim casualties, particularly among those who were well known for the fact that they had memorised the Koran. Realising that the transmission of the Koran from generation to generation would be in jeopardy if all those who had memorised it were wiped out, Abu Bakr decided that the best thing to do would be to have a single, written volume, put together from all of the different materials upon which the revelations had been recorded. The man upon whom this responsibility was devolved was none other than Zayd b. Thabit, the Prophet's chief scribe.

Initially, Zayd was reluctant, particularly since the production of a single text had not taken place during the lifetime of Muhammad himself. Zayd's prevarication implies that he considered the collation of the Koran tantamount to an unacceptable 'innovation', and it was not until he was reassured several times by Abu Bakr that he accepted the task. Having brought together all of the materials upon which the revelations had been recorded, Zayd collated them into one manuscript. This was deposited in the house of Abu Bakr, and when he died it was given to 'Umar, and after 'Umar to the latter's daughter, Hafsa.

It is also reported, however, that several of the Companions had used the scattered Koranic materials independently to collate their own 'single-document' copies of the Koran. Members of the Prophet's immediate family such as Ali and Aisha were said to have their own written collections, together with Zayd b. Thabit, the Prophet's scribe, and Companions such as Ibn Mas'ud and Ubay b. Ka'b. For all intents and purposes, all of these collections are copies of the same Koran, or at least collations of the same material used by Zayd in the manuscript handed down to Hafsa. However, although their source material was more or less identical, they include many variations in content, sequencing and spelling.

The existence of different collections of the Koran shows us how seriously the task of recording the revelation, was taken, and how enthusiastically it was embraced. All the more reason, then, for our regret that none of the alternative readings has survived.

THE FINAL STAGE OF THE PRESERVATION OF THE KORAN: THE 'UTHMANIC RECENSION'

By the time of the third Caliph, Uthman (r. 644–656), the Muslim empire was expanding and the number of copies of the Koran in circulation was rising accordingly. However, as the spread of the Koran continued, regional differences in how the book was read began to appear. Eventually, to avoid the possible emergence of radically different, and possibly even contradictory, 'versions' of the same book, Uthman decided once and for all to 'set the Koran in stone', as it were, and produce a definitive text from the manuscript in Hafsa's possession.

The job was entrusted to Zayd b. Thabit and three other scribes. Copies of the definitive text were then sent to the main centres of learning across the Muslim empire, to replace the gradually differing Korans that were in circulation, which were apparently destroyed. Hafsa's manuscript was returned to her and later destroyed, lest it become the cause of even more disputes. The Koran finalised by Uthman would later be accepted unanimously by Muslim scholars as a true and precise reflection of the revelations sent by God to Muhammad.

The Koran in use today is generally believed to be identical in all respects to the document which emerged from the third Caliph's endeavours, which later came to be known as the 'Uthmanic recension'. Muslims believe that in the past fourteen hundred years, neither a word has been changed nor a letter displaced, and that the Koran in their possession today is identical in every respect to the original message as received by Muhammad from God.

WAS CARLYLE RIGHT AFTER ALL?

Critics, such as Carlyle, describing the Koran as lacking 'shape', 'coherence' and 'internal unity', are not few. However, they are, with very few exceptions, individuals who have tried to read the Koran in translation and so we must consider with the utmost

caution any disparagement of the Koran that is based on translations in English, or, indeed, any other language than the original
Arabic.

Criticisms of the Koran as lacking 'internal unity' are often
made by those who attempt to read it from cover to cover, as
though it were a novel that possessed a beginning, a middle and an
end. Yet to judge one work according to criteria applicable to another
is to misjudge, and criticisms levelled accordingly have to be treated
with extreme caution.

Whether one feels able to 'approach' the Koran depends largely
on one's attitude to claims made regarding its provenance. Those
who approach as non-Muslim believers in other scriptures will
approach it with the assumptions and preconceptions of the non-
Muslim believer; those who approach it as atheists will approach it
with the assumptions and preconceptions of the atheist, and so on.
What one 'gets out of' the Koran reflects what one is prepared to
'put in'. As a Muslim sage once said.

> If you want support for your belief in predestination and look for it in
> the Koran, you will find it. Similarly, if you want support for your belief
> in free-will, you will find that too. You will find anything you *want* to
> find, if you look long and hard enough: after all, a jaundiced man
> thinks that everything is yellow.

This pertains to the Muslim believer in the Koran as much as it
does to anyone else, for believers too bring their own set of
assumptions and prejudgements.

The notions of 'shape', 'coherence' and 'approachability' are
relative: what we mean by them depends on the context. To determine whether the Koran has 'shape' depends on the yardstick by
which we intend to judge it. Whether the Koran is 'coherent'
depends on the factors we believe constitute 'coherence'. And the
'approachability' of any text depends, among many other things,
on precisely how and why we wish to 'approach' it in the first
place.

The only way that the reader may judge whether the Arabic
original warrants the same kind of criticism that was levelled by
Carlyle at the translation would be to learn the Arabic of the Koran
to a level that would qualify one to pass judgement on its literary

quality. For surely it is those discerning enough to tell whether Arabic prose and semi-rhyme possesses literary excellence, shape and coherence who are the ones whose judgement of the Koran *as literature* is to be valued, rather than those who not only read the Koran in another language, but whose ideological or political agenda render them blinkered from the outset?

Furthermore, 'literary excellence' is a relative, wholly human construct that ultimately has little or no bearing on the message that a piece of writing is meant to convey, particularly if that message claims to be divine revelation, vouchsafed to man in order to secure his salvation.

THE KORAN AS THE CORNERSTONE OF THE 'ISLAMIC SCIENCES'

The importance of the Koran as a catalyst for the development of the so-called 'Islamic sciences' – law, theology, exegesis and the like – cannot be underestimated.

Intellectual interest in all aspects of the Koran meant that a range of disciplines known as the Koranic 'sciences' was able to develop in tandem with the growth of the Muslim community. Each of the intellectually oriented members of the nascent Muslim community would, in accordance with his personal ability or preference, busy himself with a certain aspect of the revelation. For example, the Prophet's son-in-law, Ali, is said to have been the first person to teach the correct pronunciation and method of recitation of the Koran; this he did by codifying the rules of Arabic grammar, or so it is claimed, and clarifying the language for future generations.

Indeed, Muslims trace all branches of what they term the 'Islamic sciences' back to the Koran. Undoubtedly, the Koran was one of the underlying reasons for Muslim success in the arts and sciences during the early medieval period. The emphasis of the Koran on the importance of knowledge, and the absence in the Islamic tradition of any notion of irreconcilability between religion and the pursuit of science, meant that Muslims were able to make astonishing progress in all areas of learning. Examples of the cultural, scientific and technological advancements made by medieval Muslim civilisation in comparison with the relatively backward Christian West abound, and the point has even been made that it is possible that neither the Renaissance nor the Enlightenment would have happened had Muslim scholars, sages and scientists not paved the way some several centuries earlier. However, the Koran was only one contributory factor. It may have emphasised the importance of the acquisition of knowledge, but the discovery of technique, and the further application of knowledge that is uncovered thanks to technique, are wholly human endeavours, and to explain these we cannot only rely on the Koran.

Yet the problem is not simply the risk of overlooking non-Koranic causes of Muslim progress. The problem is the risk we run of unintentionally 'secularising' knowledge by dividing it artificially into the 'Islamic' and the non-Islamic. Many Muslim writers, particularly those concerned with the contemporary debates about the so-called 'Islamicisation' of knowledge, fall into this trap.

IS THERE SUCH A THING AS 'ISLAMIC' KNOWLEDGE?

Both Muslims and non-Muslims alike continue to talk about 'Islamic law' or 'Islamic theology' as though these terms actually signify something. They do not. For the qualifier 'Islamic' implies that whatever is so described carries the kind of divine sanction that renders it immutable and definitive. To describe a law as 'Islamic', for example, is to say that it is representative of Islam and thus somehow sanctioned by God. Yet in reality, law as a discipline is a human endeavour, and as such a wholly fallible one.

The same applies to all of the other disciplines held up as examples of 'Islamic' sciences. The term 'Islamic theology', for example, connotes a particular way – the 'Islamic' way – of talking about God, rather than what it actually is: a collection of techniques, arguments, proofs and precepts used – successfully or unsuccessfully – by Muslims to advance certain arguments and ideas about God. As such, we can talk in terms of 'Muslim theology' or, to be more precise, 'Muslim theologies', but not 'Islamic theology'. In fact, the term 'Islamic theology' is not only misleading, but it is also positively harmful, for it reinforces the misconception among Muslims and non-Muslims alike that there is an 'orthodox' theology in Islam, the techniques and conclusions of which really ought not to be questioned.

I hope this short digression will have cleared up the misconceptions surrounding terms such as 'the Islamic sciences'. Maybe we can now rephrase the sub-heading of this section and talk not about the 'Islamic sciences' but about the 'Muslim world of learning', at the very heart of which does indeed lie the cornerstone that is the Koran.

EXEGESIS AND TRANSLATION

We end this chapter on the twin issues of exegesis (Koran commentary) and translation, for it is through these that the Koran has been made known: a long tradition of scholarly commentary on the Koran has allowed generations of Muslims to understand the meanings of the Holy Book, and the translation of the Koran into hundreds of different languages has enabled non-Arab readers of the Koran to sample a flavour of the Islamic revelation.

That there are many types of exegesis reflects the fact that there are many different ways of approaching and understanding the Koran. The Koran itself talks of some verses being 'straightforward' and others being 'metaphorical' or 'allegorical'. One of the tasks of the exegete is to interpret both the 'straightforward' and the 'metaphorical' in the light of both the context in which they were revealed and the current understanding and mindset of the age. The Koran, it is said, is multi-layered, and it is the job of the exegetes to tease out these layers and make manifest the multiplicity of meanings which are hidden there. As such, exegesis is possibly the most important – and as a result, the most contested – of the 'Islamic sciences'.

Translation of the Koran is an even thornier issue, with many of the more traditionally minded Muslims believing that the Koran cannot, and should not, be translated. It is true that the Koran cannot be translated and remain the Koran, just as it is true that a translation of *War and Peace* will always be a translation, and not the real thing. In the case of the Koran, of course, there is the added feature of its perceived inimitability: how can one translate a work, every word of which is deemed miraculous? Nevertheless, there are numerous translations of the Koran, in virtually every language in the world. Some are better than others, but none of course can approach the original. As long as there are translators to do the job, the Koran will be translated. And so long as one is aware that it will never be more than an approximation of the meaning of the original, one should be able to read a translation with total impunity. After all, should the 'word of God' be restricted to those who speak Arabic?

FURTHER READING

There are several excellent works which aim to guide their readers through the Koran, outlining its themes, explaining its historical and cultural context, and throwing light on its historical and cultural context. One of the most learned and accessible of these is Farid Esack's *The Qur'an: A Short Introduction* (Oneworld, 2002). For those in search of slightly more substantial academic fare, Neal Robinson's magisterial *Discovering the Qur'an* is hard to beat, touching all of the bases covered by Esack, but also addressing some of the thornier controversies surrounding the Koran, including its contested provenance. However, Robinson's work is the fruit of years of assiduous research and, unlike Esack's, is not the kind of book that can be read in a few sessions.

3

BELIEF

There are hundreds of references in the Koran to the question of belief, particularly in contradistinction to its opposite number, unbelief. Belief, it is asserted, is the result of a choice, and one which must be made in the full light of knowledge and awareness: it must be arrived at through investigation, not emulation. While all men are born with the capacity to believe, and are surrounded by myriad signs and indications which confirm the necessity of belief, some choose instead to deny, opting for the inevitable ignominy that follows on from a life lived in unbelief.

In the Koranic worldview, belief may increase or decrease: it can never be static. The knowledge which underpins belief must be continuously increased if belief is to be maintained, and the submission which follows on from belief constantly renewed if belief is to be perfected. Yet most people, the Koran declares, do not believe. And most of those who are believers are often found wanting in their belief. However, the rewards of true belief can be found in the perfect bliss that is everlasting life in the presence of God.

Belief, then, runs like an ever-present leitmotif throughout the Koran, and stands at the very centre of the Islamic revelation. But what *is* belief, what are its requirements, and what is it that believers believe *in*?

BELIEF AND ITS REQUIREMENTS

Put at its simplest, belief in the Koranic view is the assertion of the intellect, and the conviction of the heart, that there is no god but God; that Muhammad is His messenger; and that all men will be tried on the Day of Judgement before being resurrected into eternal life, there to be 'rewarded' or 'punished' in accordance with their spiritual state on earth.

The principal requirement of belief in the Koranic sense of the word is that the individual should attain to a state of perception and reflection in which he sees the cosmos not as a collection of 'natural' phenomena, but as 'signs' (*āyāt*) which make known the One Creator. All of the 'natural world' is claimed by the Koran to point to Him. Intellect is the prerequisite of belief: the use of reason has to be applied to the 'signs' in order for belief to obtain.

Belief, known in Arabic as *imān*, includes internal submission (*islām*) of the intellect and the heart to the truth of the thing believed in. And belief should, if it is sincere, engender external submission, in the form of outward expressions of faith such as prayer and fasting. It is this outward expression of faith, this external show of submission, that is included in the term 'Islam'. However, as the Koran is quick to point out, not all believers reach the stage of external submission; and not all of those who submit externally are true believers. While belief and practice should go hand-in-hand, many individuals attain one but not the other. This issue will be explored more fully in Chapter 5.

Belief, then, is crucial to our understanding of the Koranic worldview. However, exactly what is it that would-be Muslims are encouraged or expected to believe *in*?

THE 'FUNDAMENTALS OF BELIEF'

According to the Koran, there are five things in which a believer is to cultivate, develop and maintain belief: God; angels; prophets; the 'revealed books' or scriptures; and the hereafter. Some add to these belief in 'Divine decree and determining'.

Traditionally, these six 'articles of faith' have been grouped together under three main categories, known as the 'fundamentals of belief'. These are: belief in Divine Unity (*tawhid*); belief in

prophethood (*nabuwwa*); and belief in resurrection and the hereafter (*ma'ād*).

THE FIRST 'FUNDAMENTAL OF BELIEF': DIVINE UNITY

GOD IN THE KORAN

> God! There is no god but He: the Living, the Self-subsisting,
> Eternal. No slumber can seize Him nor sleep. His are all things
> in the heavens and on earth. Who is there can intercede in His
> presence except as He permitteth? He knoweth what [appear-
> eth to His creatures as] before or after or behind them. Nor
> shall they compass aught of His knowledge except as He will-
> eth. His Throne doth extend over the heavens and the earth,
> and He feeleth no fatigue in guarding and preserving them for
> He is the Most High, the Supreme [in glory].
>
> (2:255)

As we have seen, the central message of the Koran is not that God
exists, but that *God is one* – which is why the first fundamental of
religion is 'Divine Unity' and not 'Divine existence'. However, in
demonstrating Divine Unity, the Koran also paints a vivid picture
of the Creator so that man may augment his conceptual knowledge
of God's oneness with a more immediate awareness of God's
'character', or the 'names' and 'attributes' by which He makes
himself known in the creation. For it is only through uncovering
the truths and realities concerning God that man may love, worship
and obey Him, and in doing so fulfil the requirements of his role as
Divine vicegerent on earth.

The word 'God' – Allah – is mentioned approximately 3,000
times in the Koran, and there are countless passages in which He is
described in terms of various 'attributes of perfection'. To enumerate these would be pointless, for contrary to the popular Muslim
tradition, the 'names of God' do not number ninety-nine, but are in
fact innumerable: wherever there is 'an attribute of perfection',
such as life, beauty, wisdom or power, God is said to possess it
infinitely and absolutely.

Thus, the Koran asserts, He is omniscient, omnipotent and
omnipresent. He has always existed and will always exist, and the

entire cosmos of created beings depends on Him and Him alone for its existence. He is the First, the Last, and the Ground of all being. He is immanent but yet transcendent; no eye can perceive Him, yet wherever one looks, there is His 'face'. He is beyond space and time, yet is the Creator of all things which exist in space and time. He is the uncaused Causer of all causes, who stands above all matter and materiality. His power and knowledge extend to all things, and all things will return to Him in the end.

The Koran does not attempt to prove the existence of God, taking for granted that all men are believers in an originator of all being, regardless of how they describe Him. What the Koran is at pains to demonstrate is not the existence of God, but that God is *one*. Readers who wish to know more about how God is portrayed in the Koran are referred here to the Koran itself; we now turn to the heart of the matter and look at the key issue of Divine Unity.

DIVINE UNITY AND THE 'ONENESS' OF GOD

The main focal point of the Koranic worldview, and the cornerstone upon which the whole edifice of Islam has been constructed, is the notion of *tawhid* or the 'oneness' of God. There is, as many Western writers have pointed out, an uncompromising monotheism at the heart of the Islamic endeavour which distinguishes Islam from other major religions. This is not to say that, in theory at least, the oneness of God is any less a reality in Christianity and Judaism than it is in Islam. In practice, however, the emphasis on Divine Unity in Muslim theology far outweighs the attention paid to this concept by theologians of other faiths.

That there is only one God, and that all created beings are attributable to Him alone, is to express the concept of *tawhid* at its simplest level, uncluttered by the jargon of the theologians, who argued and debated the nature of Divine Unity for several centuries after the death of Muhammad. We shall attempt to strike a balance, providing an overview of *tawhid* which avoids over-simplification on the one hand, but which eschews the mystifying verbiage of the medieval Muslim theologians.

The word *tawhid* is translated either as 'unity' or 'oneness', as though these are synonymous. As we shall see shortly, they are not. The fact that there are subtle differences between the notions of Divine 'oneness' and Divine 'unity' is often hidden and mis-understood by both non-Muslims and Muslims.

Put simply, the oneness or *ahadiyya* of God can be understood when one looks at any single manifestation of Divine artistry, such as the human eye, for instance, or the embryo in the womb. The beauty, harmony and interconnectedness of all the constituent parts of the eye, for example, point to the impossibility of its being brought into existence by either blind chance or a collective of creators, for the unity of creation and purpose that it exhibits points to a single Source – One who is in possession, in the absolute sense, of all of the attributes of perfection which are made manifest in the created entity.

Unity or *wāhidiyya* can be understood when the cosmos is looked at as a whole, through the interconnectedness of its con-stituent parts. When one looks at a single human eye and concludes that its Creator is One, the next logical step is to attribute the creation of *all* human eyes to the same Creator. One can extra-polate from this and extend the reasoning to everything which exists in the cosmos. On account of their unity and inter-connectedness, Whoever created the seed must also have created the rain that is sent to nurture it, and the sun which is placed there to give it warmth, and the flowers which grow from it, and the wind which is sent to disseminate the flower's new seeds.

Thus the One who creates the tiniest of atoms must, according to this argument, be the One who creates the whole cosmos, on account of the inextricable links which exist between all beings in existence. To see God in terms of both *ahadiyya* and *wāhidiyya* helps to explain the principle of diversity within unity – and unity within diversity – which underpins the cosmos. Also, by focusing on the uniqueness of every created thing, it avoids the tendency to think in terms of a 'conveyor-belt creation', or a cosmos which is set in motion by God, but which then runs of its own accord.

CONTINUOUS CREATION

Linked closely to the twin concepts of *ahadiyya* and *wāhidiyya* is the notion of 'continuous creation'. The Koranic conception of God is as a Creator who is never absent from His creation, and Who nurtures and tends to every atom in existence continuously. The

God envisioned by the Koran is not a 'God of the gaps'; rather, He is one who manifests Himself constantly through His creation. Everything which exists is held to be dependent on His Will at each and every instant, and should God, for any reason, withdraw His creative power from a thing, it would immediately cease to exist.

A corollary of this is that causality – the principle of cause and effect which we all take for granted – is seen by the Koran to be but a necessary illusion: a veil, as it were, which covers the true Source of all being, namely God. The reasoning behind this is complex, but put simply it is a question of knowledge and power. The French philosopher Malebranche, who also believed that causality was an illusion, had a famous argument he used to illustrate his position. 'No man,' he declared, 'is able to lift his arm.' How can man claim to create an action if he does not know how it works, or what is needed to effect it? Malebranche concluded that the only part of the action which belongs to man is the *intention* to lift it: once he intends to lift it, God creates the action for him. The action concerned is just one constituent part of a cosmic whole, in which everything works together in harmony. In short, 'man proposes, God disposes'.

Muslim thinkers go one step further. Not only does God create all things, but He does so continuously. For created matter, which, since it is contingent on another for its existence, possesses neither omnipotence nor omniscience, is unable to create anything itself. Indeed, it cannot exist for longer than an instant, unless it is supported by the One who created it in the first place. Thus the Islamic notion of 'continuous creation' holds that God creates and re-creates all things at all times, bringing things into existence, annihilating them, and bringing them back into existence, all within the twinkling of an eye while maintaining the illusion of the permanency of matter.

THE CARDINAL SIN OF *SHIRK*, OR ASSOCIATING 'PARTNERS' WITH GOD

> Do they indeed ascribe to Him as partners things that can create nothing, but are themselves created?
>
> (7:191)

In the eyes of the Koran, and the religion of Islam, no sin is greater, or more deserving of punishment, than the sin of *shirk*, or associating 'partners' with God. Translated variously as 'polytheism' or 'idolatry', *shirk* involves attributing power – or, indeed, any of the attributes of perfection – to created beings or abstract forces other than God himself.

In the context of pre-Koranic societies, the sin of *shirk*, or ascribing 'partners' to God, finds expression most prominently in the worship of idols – statues, images or effigies constructed to represent gods, goddesses, spirit beings and other objects of worship which were venerated alongside God or in His place. Examples of such deities abound in other cultures too.

Modern theologians are usually eager to point out that idolatry is no longer a matter of primitive practices such as the actual veneration of statues or images. Now, rather than bow down physically before gods created from wood and stone, man bows down metaphorically before the idols of money and power and fame, sex and celebrity. The gods of the modern and post-modern eras may not be as instantly recognisable as the idols of the past, but their function is identical and the dangers they represent to the human soul are seen as being every bit as acute.

The Koran makes it quite clear that *shirk* is not something from which believers in God are immune. Again, to translate the word *shirk* as 'idol-worship' or 'polytheism' without qualifying those translations is to risk misunderstanding the concept entirely. For example, *shirk* is a subtle form of 'idol-worship', but it does not only mean to worship 'idols' in place of God: it can also mean to worship idols *alongside* God. Unbelief (*kufr*) involves 'covering' the truth or denial of God. One who refuses to worship God will, given the innate human propensity for worship, inevitably venerate something else in the place of God – the self, nature, money or whatever. However, while from one perspective the unbeliever is worshipping 'idols' in place of God, the very fact that God exists regardless of whether or not the unbeliever affirms His existence means that, he or she is in fact worshipping those idols alongside God, albeit unwittingly. In this sense, the unbelief or *kufr* of the unbeliever is compounded by the unwitting *shirk* which is involved in the act of denial.

Lest any of the Muslim believers assume that only unbelievers can be guilty of *shirk*, the Koran makes it quite clear that *shirk* is as much of a snare for those who believe in God as it is for those who deny Him. In fact, the Koran goes so far as to claim that most men are unbelievers, and of those who do believe in God, most also believe in His 'partners'. For many devout Muslims, this verse is difficult to accept, and because the connotations are so grave, many prefer to interpret it as something pertaining to believers at the time of the Prophet.

THE ISSUE OF DIVINE POWER AND HUMAN FREE WILL

According to the Koran, no man can be born or die, no leaf can fall from a tree, no neutron can orbit the nucleus of an atom without its place in the cosmic scheme of things being ordered and structured in accordance with a 'predetermined measure': a plan or blueprint which exists timelessly in the realm of divine knowledge, and upon whose coordinates and values the nature, duration and effect of any entity's existence in time and space are based. In other words, the 'plan' upon which each being is 'constructed' exists in the supra-material realm, as part of God's timeless, eternal knowledge; the 'construction' of that being in time takes place in strict accordance with the 'specifications' of the plan. This applies to the whole of the 'seen' or 'manifest' world: the material world of creation, or the cosmos that we see before us and of which we are a crucial component. Nothing that exists, then, exists randomly, by chance or as the result of accident: everything is measured, planned, determined and decreed by God.

The main criticism levelled against belief in 'Divine decree and determination', which some hold to be the sixth 'article of faith', is that it posits a world which is like a machine, where everything is determined in advance and, more importantly, where there is no room for human freedom. In a world where everything is preordained, how can man be said to possess choice in any meaningful sense of the word? If God knows all our actions in advance, how then can we be said to be free? For example, if God knew before I existed that I would go to hell, why did He create me in the first place? More importantly, why punish me for something over which I have had no control from the outset? Indeed, does reward and punishment make any sense at all if the outcome of one's life on earth is already known?

Champions of free will respond by saying that while God knows in advance that our actions will be free, His knowledge does not compel us to do wrong. To know is not to compel: God knows that we will go to hell, for sure, but He also knows that we will go to hell *entirely of our own accord*. In other words, He knows that we will go to hell because He knows of all the wrong decisions and bad choices we will make that will take us there.

The critics counter this by saying that if God knows in advance that we will make the kind of bad decisions that will lead us to hell, why did He not have the foresight not to create us at all? The counter-argument is that the idea of God knowing anything 'in advance' is to bring God 'into time'. God is beyond time: for Him, the past, present and future are all as one. Therefore God does not 'predetermine' man's fate in the way that we imagine.

Furthermore, to refrain from creating someone simply because that person is likely to make the wrong choices is in fact to call into question not only the whole concept of free will but also the purpose of divine punishment. Divine punishment, argues the defence, is a manifestation not only of justice but also of compassion, for it is possibly the only means through which the unregenerate may come to know their Creator and ultimately gain salvation once his or her dues have been paid.

Opinions on this issue in the world of Muslim theology were polarised at a very early stage, with one group espousing the idea of total predetermination (*jabr*) and another championing the idea of free will. The Shi'ites, and to a lesser extent groups such as the Ash'arites and the Maturidites, concluded that the truth of the matter lay somewhere between compulsion and free will. A famous saying emerged amongst these groups: 'It is neither compulsion nor free will, but something between the two.' The theological arguments forwarded to justify this position are complex but they can be summarised as follows.

Following the Muslim theological argument to the extent that reason allows, it seems that as far as the past is concerned, we should see ourselves as 'predestined'. For in order to reach the place we are at present, from one point of view an inestimably large number of events have *had* to take place. This is understandable on the simple level of genealogy. In order that I may exist, for example, my parents had to exist; in order that they might come into existence, four more people – my grandparents – had to exist, and so on. We must conclude that in order for me to exist, the whole of mankind had to be created. It is not difficult, then, to believe in 'destiny' or the 'predetermination' of events once those events have passed and become part of our history. As many a sage has said, 'What hits us could not have missed, and what passes us could not have hit.'

However, as far as the future is concerned we should think the road as being well and truly open. For we have been endowed with the freedom to choose between alternative paths of action. Despite the fact, some may argue, that our choices are often coloured by habit, upbringing, addiction or even genetic predisposition, the fact is that the underlying principle is the same: we can accept something or reject it. In any case, if there are mitigating circumstances – situations in which, for example, our ability to choose is somehow hampered or stymied completely by forces beyond our control – God is surely more compassionate than to ignore the fact that we are acting under external compulsion.

Yet to say that we are 'predestined', even if only in respect to past actions, Muslims are at pains to stress that we are not 'compelled'. Indeed, the notion of 'compulsion' makes sense only if one is free to begin with, for only the truly free can be compelled to do anything: to compel the compelled is tautological nonsense, and forces us to look for another term capable of explaining the predestined way we feel when we look at our situation from a certain perspective.

BELIEF IN ANGELS (MALÀ'IKA)

Belief in the existence of beings known as angels is common to most of the world's religions, but only in Islam has it been accorded the status of 'article of faith', second only, some claim, to belief in God. Despite the integral role that angels play in the Koranic cosmology, medieval Muslim theologians have very little to say on the subject, while modern scholars – with a few notable exceptions – tend either to avoid it completely or to explain it away in somewhat apologetic terms, as though the Koranic vision of the angelic host really is of questionable relevance to a modern, highly politicised and science-friendly religion such as Islam.

It is not difficult to understand why some might think that the subject of angels is a rather difficult one with which to engage on an intellectual level. In the West, the portrayal of angels as corporeal beings with recognisably human attributes is largely a Judaeo-Christian construct, and is at odds with the picture painted of angels by Muslim theological tradition, and with the role played by angels in the cosmic hierarchy outlined by the Koran.

THE CONCEPT OF ANGELS IN THE KORAN

In accordance with the principle of continuous creation, outlined earlier, things which are created cannot themselves create: power belongs only to One. Similarly, knowledge – and with it, consciousness – cannot be attributed to inanimate creation in any meaningful sense of the word. And that which lacks power and knowledge cannot be said to have any discernible sense of purpose. But if we dismiss inanimate particles as unconscious, and their functions as purposeless, how do we account for the myriad wondrous new shapes and forms they bring into being? It would appear that only by bringing 'angels' into the equation can we begin to make sense of this dichotomy.

For angels are 'bearers' of the Divine 'commands'. According to the Koran, when God decrees that a thing come into existence, all He has to do is say 'Be!' and that thing appears. The angels are, in one sense, the 'mirrors' which are held up to the Divine Essence so that the attributes of God may 'shine' into them directly. Man, who cannot perceive God directly, knows Him only through the reflection of the names that he views in the 'mirror' provided by the angels. The angels, then, act as the interface between God and man.

Angels possess consciousness but not free will: their obedience is unwavering, but it is never blind. The apparent consciousness of an otherwise seemingly blind, inanimate being is actually the consciousness of the angels, who 'bear' the creational commands which make up that being's external existence.

Facing God directly, the angel, equipped with the ability to reflect one or more of the Creator's 'names', accepts God's command and proceeds to 'bear' it. They carry it from the unseen realm and display it in the manifest realm, or the realm where the names of God are given a sort of material existence in the form of created beings.

The existence of angels helps to explain why matter behaves with such apparent purposefulness while at the same time exhibiting absolute ignorance and dependence. Yet there is more to Koranic angelology than merely serving to explain why material causes do not actually create anything. For the reflection of God's names onto the 'angels' brings about nothing less than the material world of which we are part. They are like so many prisms which catch the white light of God and refract it into the myriad colours of material existence, so that humankind may come to know and comprehend His true Source. Angels are there not because God needs them, but because we need them.

THE SECOND 'FUNDAMENTAL OF BELIEF': PROPHETHOOD

Reason, Muslims argue, can take man only so far, for there are domains which are not accessible to intellect alone. Belief in God involves belief in the Unseen Creator.

While man is able to use his intellect and powers of reason to deliberate upon the workings of the cosmos and reach the conclusion that there is a Creator, intellect alone cannot discern the purpose of creation, the nature of the Creator, the path he should tread and the way he should tread it – for this man needs an explanation from God himself.

The central function of prophethood, then, is to provide a means whereby God may address man through the channel of human speech, in a language or languages that man is able to understand easily. A God that does not talk to His supreme creation – man – in a language that man can understand is unimaginable. Thus the concept of Creator and the notion of prophethood as one of the means by which that Creator is made known go hand-in-hand.

Communication between Creator and created does not occur directly, however: not even the prophets are direct recipients of the Divine word, which transcends time and space and is thus inaccessible to finite, material, earthbound creatures like human beings. According to the Koran:

> It is not fitting for a man that God should speak to him except by
> inspiration, or from behind a veil, or by the sending of a messenger to

reveal, with God's permission, what God wills: for He is Most High, Most Wise.

(42:51)

Prophethood makes known to man the will of God, and serves to provide answers to all of the big questions and existential dilemmas that face man in his life on earth.

ATTRIBUTES OF THE PROPHET

Prophets not only communicate the message but also serve as exemplars, showing their communities how to live in conformity with God's will.

The Koran does not offer any answer to the old question of whether a prophet is a prophet by nature or by nurture. Prophet-hood is not something that is given on merit alone: it cannot be earned, deserved or won through endeavour or competition. But it is equally inconceivable that prophets be solely the result of nature too. To be a prophet 'from birth', as it were, would seem to fly in the face of reason, for the inevitability of one's prophethood would render the idea of piety, moral excellence and personal worthiness redundant: such a man would be endowed with all of these things from the outset simply because prophethood demands them, and not because he has developed them while striving for spiritual growth.

There is a compromise solution, of course, and that is to suppose that God 'chooses' to bestow prophethood upon the person in a community through whom God can best communicate His message to humankind. In order to serve as this channel, the chosen one has to be introduced to the spiritual truths and realities which transcend this material world, and endowed with gnosis – that is, knowledge of God that man receives directly from God Himself, rather than obtaining it through personal intellectual endeavour. Thanks to the function of revelation, his communion with God is constant and direct, enabling him to communicate God's word to other men with complete inerrancy, while retaining his humanity and, more importantly, the fallibility that goes with it.

The 'special assistance from God' that a prophet receives elevates him into one whose words become characterised by truth and constancy, by integrity and trustworthiness. As he progresses spiritually, the prophet may even become the recipient of 'evidentiary miracles' – actions which are beyond the ken and ability of ordinary human beings, and which serve as confirmation of their role as Divine ambassador. The greatest miracle of Muhammad, according to Muslims, is the Koran itself: a timeless, inimitable message of unsurpassed eloquence, produced by a simple, unlettered desert Arab.

PROPHETIC INFALLIBILITY

Many Muslims believe that prophets are endowed with something known in Arabic as 'isma, which is often translated into English as 'infallibility'. What this means in practice is open to debate. For some, prophetic infallibility means that prophets are immune from committing major sins; for others, it means that prophets are immune from all sins, major or minor.

The reason that some claim total immunity from sin on the part of the prophets is not difficult to grasp. The responsibilities of prophethood are considerable, and would not be entrusted to someone who was as fallible as everyone else. The problem with the popular understanding of 'isma or 'prophetic infallibility' is that it transforms the human messenger figure into little more than an angelic automaton. For a man who is unable to sin cannot be called human in any meaningful sense of the word, and a man who is not human in the way that others are human cannot be a prophet. The real merit of prophethood lies in the moral excellence of the prophet, and where there is no ability to do wrong, there can be no moral excellence. One of the ways in which prophets distinguish themselves from other men is through the refinement of their moral characters, an endeavour which can take place only if the commitment of sin remains an ever-present possibility.

The prophets whose stories appear in the Koran are all portrayed as men of outstanding moral character, yet almost all of them appear to have made mistakes at various points in their careers. Moses, for example, killed a man out of anger, while Jonah was imprisoned in the belly of a whale on account of his chronic impatience with God. While none of them is recorded as having ever committed a major sin, the prophets of the Koran appear as flawed, credible beings who are all the more believable because of their foibles and their shortcomings.[1] Men are far more likely to empathise with fallible human beings like these than with the infallible automatons of popular Muslim tradition.

The doctrine of 'isma, then, needs to be reconsidered. Rather than see the prophets as individuals who were unable to sin, we should see them perhaps as men who were perfectly capable of sinning, but who chose not to, cushioned as they were by the heightened sense of restraint that accompanies faith at this level. To rob a man of the ability to sin is not only to disqualify him for prophethood but also to negate him as a member of humankind.

BELIEF IN 'THE BOOKS'

Another little-known and even less understood 'article of faith' is belief in the 'books' brought by the prophets who preceded Muhammad. The word 'books' here denotes those messages communicated by God to His messengers which were written down and disseminated in the form of scripture. As we saw in the previous section on 'messengers', not all prophets with a mission from God actually produce divinely revealed scriptures in support of their claims: not all apostles were at the same time messengers.

Muslim tradition puts the number of nabi – prophets – in the region of 124,000. Of these the Koran mentions fewer than three dozen; among which no more than a handful can lay claim to the title of rasūl or 'messenger', i.e. the bringer of scripture. The Koran mentions five prophets who were blessed with written records of the messages they brought. These are Abraham, Moses, David, Jesus and Muhammad. Abraham's revelation is referred to as suhūf which literally means 'pages', but which denotes any type of divinely revealed message that is committed to writing and recorded for posterity. To the prophet David is attributed the Zabūr or Psalms, while Jesus is seen as the bringer of the Injil or Gospels. And Muhammad is, of course, the channel through which the final revelation, the Koran, was communicated to humankind.

The Koran is seen as the jewel in the crown of God's messages revealed to humankind, confirming those earlier scriptures. Many Muslims believe that the Koran is superior because the other scriptures have, in the course of time, become corrupted. However, a thoughtful comparison of all three main scriptures reveals nothing that could be construed as contradictory or incongruous, and there are far more points of convergence than one might imagine. After all, it would seem rather pointless of the Koran to emphasise belief in previous scriptures if those scriptures were to be found wanting.

THE THIRD 'FUNDAMENTAL OF BELIEF': RESURRECTION, JUDGEMENT AND THE HEREAFTER

Belief in a realm after death, where man is judged with regard to the deeds he has committed while on earth, and where he is rewarded or punished accordingly, is shared by almost all of the world's major religions, and certainly by the three most widespread of the monotheistic faiths. Details of the 'hereafter' differ from one religious tradition to the next, but on the fundamentals they are more or less in agreement: death is not the end of life, and once man has died he will be 'raised up' again; once he has been raised up, he will be asked to account for the time he has spent on earth; and once he has been 'judged', he will enter a realm where he will be treated in accordance with the way he has conducted himself in his first, earthly life.

ISLAM: FAITH FOR THE HEREAFTER OR RELIGION OF THE HERE-AND-NOW?

Before we look at what belief in the 'world to come' actually entails for the Muslim believer, we should try first to contextualise the issue with regard to the popular perception of Islam as a rather legalistic faith that appears to be more concerned with the here-and-now than the hereafter.

The prominence of law and jurisprudence in the Muslim world of learning, the interconnectedness of 'religion and state' in modern Muslim political theory, and the rise of 'Islamism' in the past fifty years have all served to compound the much-vaunted belief that Islam is a 'this-worldly' religion. While the view of Islam as a largely earthbound faith is not totally without foundation, the over-politicisation of Islam in the past quarter of a century has served – for some at least – to strip the supra-material heart out of the faith, leaving a husk of rules, regulations and socio-political precepts that now form the basis of *Islam the ideology*, rather than *Islam the path of submission to God*. In many parts of the Muslim world, Islam – or, rather, 'political Islam' or 'Islamism' – is just another discourse of power, vying for supremacy with all of the other discourses of power operating within the socio-political and economic system.

The reasons behind the transformation of Islam into a quasi-political ideology are numerous, and will be discussed in greater depth in Chapter 6. The Islamic revelation, however, must on occasion be separated conceptually from the religion which has emerged as a response to it, for at times, what passes as 'Islamic' is often at variance with what appears to be Koranic.

MAN THE ETERNAL

For the Koran, man's appearance on earth represents only a fraction of his overall existence. Man's sojourn on earth is like a temporary break in the loop of existence, necessitated by the fact that it is only by stepping outside the loop that man is able to understand that he is inside a loop in the first place.

Man's life in this world is necessary because it enables him to understand the concept of eternity, for which he has been created. But it also serves as a training ground in which he is prepared for the eventual transition, via death, to his permanent abode in the world to come, the realm of the 'hereafter'. The preparation comes in the form of a life-long 'examination', in which man is 'tested' by God in order that his potential as God's 'vicegerent' be realised and the extent of his knowledge, love and worship of the Creator be made known. The world is thus like a metaphorical field, which one is encouraged to cultivate with knowledge, belief, submission and good deeds, in order to be able to reap the abundant harvest of eternal joy – proximity to God – in the world to come.

Viewed as such, this world would appear to be every bit as important as the world to come, simply by virtue of the fact that one's position with regard to God in the hereafter depends very much on the nature of one's relationship with God in the here-and-now. Consequently, to claim that Islam is a 'this-worldly' religion is to disregard the fact that this world and the next are both parts of the same continuum of existence, albeit with very different terms of reference as far as their innate natures and external conditions are concerned.

The Koran appeals to human reason in its various attempts to demonstrate the reality and rationality of the hereafter, and the resurrection and judgement which proceed it. The Koran insists that its followers deliberate upon God's 'signs' before assenting to the truths indicated by them. Indeed, nowhere is the idea of blind acceptance of these fundamental principles sanctioned or tolerated: while the final leap is indeed ultimately a leap of faith, the run-up, as it were, is solely a matter for the intellect and the faculty of reason.

How, then, does the Koran attempt to demonstrate the plausibility of the resurrection and the events which follow on from it?

The Koran uses the 'first creation' of man – the fact that every individual has been brought into the world – to show that what has happened once can happen again, especially if it happens according to the creative will of God, for Whom all things are possible:

> See they not how God originates creation, then repeats it: truly that is easy for God. Say: 'Travel through the earth and see how God did originate creation; so will God produce a later creation: for God has power over all things.'
>
> (29:19–20)

The Koran also alludes to the fact that the phenomenon of resurrection is prefigured in this world: 'mini resurrections' occur in the natural world all of the time, from the partial death of trees in winter and their resuscitation the following spring, to the constant 'death' and 'revivification' of the cells of the body. The Koran uses the example of the desert, whose parched dead earth springs to lush green life with each merciful drop of rain:

> It is He Who sendeth the winds like heralds of glad tidings, going before His mercy: when they have carried the heavy-laden clouds, We drive them to a land that is dead, make rain to descend thereon, and

produce every kind of harvest therewith: thus shall We raise up the dead: perchance ye may remember.

(7:57)

THE KORANIC VISION OF THE HEREAFTER

The fact that the Koran on numerous occasions juxtaposes 'belief in God' with 'belief in the Last Day' shows exactly how central the question of the 'hereafter' is to the Islamic worldview. Apart from being a 'fundamental of faith', the 'Last Day' also constitutes one of the six 'articles of belief', with almost a quarter of the Koran devoted to eschatology. It is now time to consider the Koranic view a little more closely, so that we can build for ourselves a picture of the events which, followers of the Koran believe, await us all.

THE INEVITABILITY OF DEATH

Death is treated matter-of-factly by the Koran as something that comes to all human beings.

Every soul shall have a taste of death.

(3:185)

Death is not the taboo subject among Muslim believers that it often can be in Western secular societies, and it is accepted as a wholly natural and inevitable stage in man's existential journey. Death merely marks a transition between two qualitatively different modes of existence, in this case the material life of the 'seen' world and the supra-material life of the 'unseen' realm.

Death is nothing to fear, the Muslim sages tell us, given that our bodies are constantly in flux, constantly 'dying' from one state and 'being born' into another. Examples of death and rebirth, as we have already seen, abound throughout the cosmos. The poet Rumi captures the quintessentially Islamic view of death beautifully in one of his mystical verses:

I died as a mineral and became a plant;
I died as a plant and became an animal;
I died as an animal and became a man.

> What is there to fear? When have I ever become less by dying?
> And as man I shall die once more, to soar
> With the blessed angels, but even from angelhood
> I must pass on: Everything perishes save His Face
> And when I have given up my angel soul
> I shall become that which no mind has ever grasped
> So let me not exist! For non-existence proclaims in organ
> tones:
> 'From Him we come and to Him we shall return.'

Furthermore, death is something which Muslim believers are encouraged to contemplate frequently, in order to foster constant awareness that one is dependent for life at every instant on God. Meditation upon death should be offset with celebration of life, and man is enjoined by the Koran to live his life balanced between mindful fear of the consequences of his own acts and hopeful trust in God's mercy as the means of his salvation. A famous adage, attributed to the Prophet's cousin Ali, among others, advises man to 'live each day as though it is your first, but also as though it is your last'.

THE 'INTERMEDIATE REALM' OR PURGATORY

The Koran does not go into great detail about the actual process of death, but confirms that at the moment when life ceases, the supra-material aspect of the individual is separated from the body. The body, which is simply the corporeal shell used to house man's spiritual essence during his lifetime, is committed to the earth, symbolising man's physical return to the minerals and elements used in his original material creation. From the time that each individual dies until the 'end of the world' and the general resurrection, man's spirit is said by the Koran to reside in a realm known as *barzakh* – the isthmus or 'partition' between this world and the next, known more commonly as the 'intermediate world' or 'purgatory'. According to Prophetic Tradition, each individual spirit has full awareness as it awaits its resurrection and the final judgement, and is given a taste of the kind of existence it can expect to lead once it has been 'judged' at the divine tribunal of the resurrection.

THE 'END OF THE WORLD'

At some unspecified point in the future, the universe as we know it will cease to exist. Ushered in by a series of awesome cosmic occurrences – the terrifying catastrophes of the 'end days' – an event described by the Koran variously as 'the Hour', 'the Day of Noise and Clamour' and the 'Great Calamity' will occur. Popularly termed the 'end of the world', in actual fact the apocalypse will herald the total transmogrification of the cosmos into what the Koran terms 'a new creation'. The cataclysmic drama that unfolds will mark the transition from one world – the world we know now – to another world, the world of the hereafter.

The Koran paints a vivid picture of a world that will be seen to spin out of control before dissolving in a series of literally earth-shattering cosmic dramas. The celestial bodies will leave their orbits and collide with each other, collapsing into nothing and robbing the heavens of light and warmth. On earth, the mountains will be scattered about by the cataclysm 'like carded wool'. Seas and oceans will surge up and boil over, flooding the land and carrying all along with it. The 'great calamity' will take man by utter surprise, and those who do not die immediately will soon envy the dead.

The 'end of the world' will be ushered in by what the Koran describes as a 'trumpet' blast, signifying the end of the causal, material realm as we know it:

> The Trumpet will [just] be sounded, when all that are in the heavens and on earth will swoon, except such as it will please God [to exempt].
> (39:68)

Following the 'trumpet blast', it is traditionally believed that all living things will die, although if 39:68 is to be understood literally, there remains the fascinating possibility that some creatures may be exempt from annihilation at this point.

There then follows a second 'trumpet blast'. This is the call that summons the dead back to life and ushers in the resurrection. At this point, the graves will open and the dead will rise up again, their physical bodies restored. Trembling uncontrollably with fear they will ask:

> 'Ah! Woe unto us! Who hath raised us up from our beds of repose?'
> (36:52)

THE FINAL JUDGEMENT

Then the whole of humanity will be led to the 'plain of resurrection' where man's life on earth will be assessed and the 'final judgement' will take place. This 'day of reckoning' – the duration of which will be a thousand years in human estimation, but which will appear to pass in the twinkling of an eye – will be the day when divine justice comes to the fore and manifests itself openly. For while man's stay on earth was characterised by a certain conflation of good and evil, on the day of judgement a clear distinction will be made between the two. On that day, man will be shown the true nature and significance of everything that he ever did, said or thought. It is a realm in which man is unable to deny his Creator and where all things bear witness to the truth and reality underpinning all existence.

Once everyone's deeds have been weighed in the 'scales' of divine justice, the assembled multitude will be sorted into three groups: the 'companions of the left hand'; the 'companions of the right hand'; and the 'foremost of the foremost'. The 'companions of the left hand' are those whose denial of God has destined them for perdition: their destination is the realm commonly known as 'hell'. The 'companions of the right hand' are those whose submission to God has destined them for salvation: their destination is the realm commonly referred to as 'heaven'. The 'foremost of the foremost' are those whose spiritual station is such that they transcend designations such as 'heaven' and 'hell': their destination is union with God Himself, in a realm that is beyond all description and comprehension.

THE KORANIC PORTRAYAL OF 'HEAVEN' AND 'HELL'

The richly figurative depictions of 'heaven' and 'hell' are among the most vivid and dramatic in the whole of the Koran.

HEAVEN

The Koranic portrayal of heaven centres on a highly idealised image of a 'garden' or 'gardens':

> [Here is] a Parable of the Garden which the righteous are promised: in it are rivers of water incorruptible; rivers of milk of which the taste

never changes; rivers of wine, a joy to those who drink; and rivers of honey pure and clear. In it there are for them all kinds of fruits; and Grace from their Lord.

(47:15)

The 'garden' is the setting in which the regenerate soul lives out eternity – a timeless realm where all that one desires is possible. The inhabitants of the 'garden of bliss' will know neither sorrow nor weariness, for 'heaven' is a realm in which the divine attributes manifest themselves with no lack or defect: the grief that comes from the absence of beauty, knowledge, power – or, indeed, any of the divine names – cannot exist there, for with the perfection that flows from the unhindered manifestation of all of God attributes, all are satisfied and none is left wanting. Unknown in the realm known as 'heaven' are the limitations and restrictions of the previous existence on earth, for in the hereafter the veils of causality and materiality are lifted: all one has to do is will a thing and it will come into existence, without the need for physical endeavour.

The 'garden of bliss', then, represents the apotheosis of peace (salām) that results from submission (islām), and the culmination of a certain type of spiritual endeavour while on earth.

HELL

The Koranic portrayal of the abode referred to as 'hell' is uncompromising in what can only be described as its relentless savagery.

Those who fail the final judgement and are destined for hell will, having been made aware of the truth, be consumed instantly with regret:

The Day that the wrong-doer will bite at his hands, he will say, 'Oh! would that I had taken a [straight] path with the Apostle!'

(25:27)

The unregenerate then kneel down in shame and beg to be given another chance, claiming that if they are allowed to return to earth, they will live their lives as true believers. Their claims will be rejected, and they will be marched ignominiously to their ultimate destination in one of the various realms of eternal perdition. There, amidst a fire whose fuel is 'men and stones' (i.e. 'idols'), he will be given to eat from the accursed 'tree of Zaqqum' which grows in Hell and which, presumably, is the embodiment of all that is signified by lack, negation and 'other than God', including the sins of man and the recalcitrance of the unregenerate soul. This bitter, unsatisfying repast:

> Will be the food of the Sinful, –
> Like molten brass; it will boil in their insides.
> Like the boiling of scalding water.
> [A voice will cry]: 'Seize ye him and drag him into the midst of
>   the Blazing Fire!
> 'Then pour over his head the Penalty of Boiling Water,
> 'Taste thou [this]! Truly wast thou mighty, full of honour!
> 'Truly this is what ye used to doubt!'
>
> (44:44–50)

The punishment of 'hellfire' will be a protracted one, with continuous tortures of the most unimaginable kind:

> Those who reject our Signs, We shall soon cast into the Fire: as often as their skins are roasted through, We shall change them for fresh skins, that they may taste the penalty: for God is Exalted in Power, Wise.
>
> (4:56)

Boiling water, blazing fire, unimaginable darkness and the incessant screams of the damned provide an astonishingly graphic backdrop against which the drama of eternal perdition is played out according to the Koran. Yet on numerous occasions we read that Hell is nothing more than the embodiment of man's own intransigence, and that if a soul enters hell, it does so – in one very important sense at least – entirely of its own accord.

SOME MISCONCEPTIONS AND OBSERVATIONS CONCERNING THE KORANIC HEAVEN AND HELL

There is a Prophetic Tradition which claims that 'God is as one thinks of Him.' This simply means that the human mind can conceive only what it can conceive, and that it will never be able to expand to the point where it can encompass the Divine as it truly is: after all, is it possible for the finite to comprehend the Infinite, or the relative the Absolute? God, it would seem, fills man's perception of Him with as much of His image as man can encompass mentally, spiritually and emotionally. The goal of Islam, therefore, is to teach man to broaden and sharpen his perception so that he is able to attain the clearest and fullest image of God possible.

Because there are countless different degrees and levels of belief, faith, submission and perception, it is clear that God will be not be understood or envisioned the same way by everyone. The same is true of 'heaven' and 'hell', which, Muslim teaching confirms, will correspond for the most part to our own expectations. The only constant is the fact that there will be two very different modes of existence in the life to come: a state in which belief in God and submission to His will is 'rewarded' with bliss; and a state in which denial of God is 'punished' by grief, regret and alienation.

In order to emphasise the bliss or nirvana that is the culmination of true faith and submission, and the abject misery that follows on from denial and intransigence, the Koran externalises them as material abodes with very physical pleasures and pains. For the eighth-century Arab, surrounded by harsh, arid desert, the Koranic vision of 'heaven' as a place filled with abundant greenery and ever-flowing streams of sweet water must have had an unimaginable resonance. Similarly, what could have been more redolent of abject misery than the Koran's depictions of 'hell'? Given that the Koran addresses every individual on his or her level of understanding, there is nothing to suggest that its portrayal of 'heaven' and 'hell' has to be comprehended in the same way by everyone. If one believes that 'hell' will burn, then either physically or metaphorically, it will burn; if one believes that there are really 'rivers of milk and honey' in heaven, then who is to say that such things will not exist? For the believing Muslim, it is all a matter of perception.

Yet perception is connected to one's degree of belief, to the depth of one's faith, and to the extent of one's submission to God. As belief, faith and submission increase, it is held, the perception becomes more refined and the vision of God – and of 'heaven' and 'hell' – becomes clearer and closer to the Truth. The truly enlightened soul, it is said, transcends both the desire for heaven and the fear of hell. An example of this can be found in an anecdote concerning the famous female mystic, Rabi'a:

> One day, someone saw Rabi'a running frenziedly through the streets. In one hand, she carried a blazing torch; in the other, a pail of water. Amazed by this bizarre sight, someone stopped her and asked her what she was doing. 'This torch,' she cried, 'is to set fire to the gardens of Heaven. And this water is to put out the flames of Hell. Only then will we worship God for His own sake, rather than work for rewards as a mercenary works for his wages.'

It would seem, then, that the ultimate goal for the Muslim believer is not to focus on the pleasures of heaven or the pains of hell, although their importance as incentives should not be underestimated. The true goal, however, should be the vision of, and union with, God Himself – man's true reward for a life lived in faith and righteousness.

NOTE

1   The case of Moses involves manslaughter rather than murder, and is thus not technically speaking a major sin.

FURTHER READING

Few, if any, books are dedicated solely to the issue of belief in Islam, apart from those works on Muslim theology which consider issues of belief to be part of their remit by default. None of these is to be recommended, however. In my opinion, there is only one work in English which covers the central principles of belief satisfactorily, and that is William Chittick and Sachiko Murata's excellent *The Vision of Islam* (Continuum International, 1995). This is a lucid and eloquent exposition of the fundamental beliefs of Islam, covering faith, practice, spirituality and the Muslim view of history with consummate skill and considerable literary flair.

4

PRACTICE

ISLAM AND THE CONCEPT OF RIGHTEOUS ACTION

Apart from the moral values and ethical norms which, one assumes, are expected to go hand-in-glove with belief in God, and to which believers are encouraged to aspire, the Koran also talks of the need for 'righteous deeds', presumably as an external expression of belief in God and, more importantly, submission to God's will. Indeed, the 'key to salvation' in Koranic terms lies not in belief alone, but in belief which is complemented by righteous action: there are numerous verses in the Koran where the two things – 'faith and works', for want of a better term – are mentioned in the same breath:

> Those who believe, and do deeds of righteousness, and establish regular prayers and regular charity, will have their reward with their Lord: on them shall be no fear, nor shall they grieve.
>
> (2:277)

> But those who believe and do deeds of righteousness, We shall soon admit to Gardens, with rivers flowing beneath, – their eternal home.
>
> (4:57)

To those who believe and do deeds of righteousness hath Allah promised forgiveness and a great reward.

(5:9)

The kind of 'righteous deeds' that spring immediately to mind in
the case of Islam are prayers and fasting, or the pilgrimage to
Mecca – specific rites and rituals of worship that many would list
under the term 'religious acts'. However, while the Koran does
mention specific practices such as these, it focuses much more on
the development in each individual of an *attitude of submission* in
all that he or she does. The goal, as far as the Koran sees it, is not to
'do Islamic acts', but rather to make all of the acts one does Islamic.

For the Koran does not accept the false human construct of a
division between acts that are deemed 'religious', such as prayer,
and acts that people somehow assume to be 'secular' or 'neutral',
and quite clearly not 'religious' in the usual sense of the word, such
as eating and drinking, going to the shop or making love. For the
Koran, all acts are sacred so long as they are undertaken sincerely
for the sake of God and in His name, whether they are outward
expressions of worship, such as ritual prayer or fasting, or whether
they are seemingly mundane acts such as study, going to the lavatory or sleeping: the key, for the Koran, is not to perform 'sacred
acts', but to make all acts sacred. By making all acts sacred, one
makes one's whole life sacred.

Islam is, therefore, designed to be a 'whole way of life', although
clearly not in the way that many Muslim apologists mean. Making
Islam one's whole way of life does not mean trying to apply as
many 'Islamic laws' to one's life as possible. In fact, it has little to do
with 'Islamic laws' at all, *per se*. For there are many areas of man's
day-to-day existence for which neither the Koran nor the *sunna*
legislates in the sense of prescribing precise rules and regulations to
be followed. What the Koran does appear to offer, however, is a
recipe for the cultivation of an attitude of conscious and willing
submission which, if nurtured carefully, will colour everything one
does with the spirit of *islām*.

This attitude of submission will be explored in greater depth in
Chapter 5. The topic to which we now turn our attention is that of the
so-called 'pillars of Islam' – those specific acts of worship and parti-
cularised expressions of submission for which the religion is renowned.

THE FIVE 'PILLARS OF ISLAM'

THE FIRST PILLAR: *SHAHĀDA*, OR 'PROFESSING ISLAM'

The word *shahāda* literally means 'testimony' or 'evidence', and refers traditionally to the act of 'bearing witness' to the existence of God and the prophethood of Muhammad that one performs upon accepting Islam as one's chosen approach and way of life. The spoken formula, pronounced in Arabic and uttered in the presence of witnesses, translates as 'I bear witness that there is no god but God, and that Muhammad is His Messenger.'

Profession of the *shahāda* gives one entrance into the community or *umma* of Islam, and implies that one has attained belief in God and is now ready to embrace those normative behaviours or practices now expected of one as a Muslim. As such, the *shahāda* is an important psychological mechanism, for in theory it signals the transition from one state of being to another, and indeed from one way of seeing to another: in becoming a Muslim, or 'one who submits', one reorients oneself totally and attributes all one is, and all one has, to God rather than to self, or to nature, accident or blind fortune, with all that such a change in attitude implies. In this sense, the *shahāda* is a one-sentence crystallisation of all of the beliefs outlined in the previous chapter: belief in God, in the prophethood of His final messenger, Muhammad, and in all of the acts of submission – internal and external – that this belief entails.

There are two misconceptions that need to be cleared up with regard to the 'profession of Islam'. First, while the *shahāda* is usually understood to be a one-off declaration of intent, it actually implies an intellectual, emotional and spiritual approach to the world and to everyday life that needs to be nurtured constantly and continuously. As such, it is something which is to be renewed periodically as one moves through life towards the inevitable meeting with one's Creator. Second, declaration of the *shahāda* should not be seen as something which 'converts' to Islam alone must do. Unfortunately, an inordinately large number of seemingly devout Muslims labour under the misconception that 'accepting Islam' is something that only a former non-Muslim can do, and that they are 'born Muslim' and thus deserving of Islam by birthright. Even the most cursory glance at the Koran and its stance on the question of belief and submission should be enough to convince the reader that Islam is something which is to be attained through conviction, not through force of geographical or genealogical circumstance. One is a Muslim as the result of a conscious choice, and thus it is incumbent on all Muslims, regardless of whether they are 'born Muslims' or 'converts', to make the *shahāda* part of their mental make-up. The issue of 'geographical Islam' will be dealt with in greater detail later on in the chapter.

THE SECOND PILLAR: *SALĀT*, OR CANONICAL PRAYER

Arguably the most important – and for non-Muslims by far the most recognisable – outward expression of devotion in Islam is the *salāt* or canonical prayer, which is incumbent on all believers once they have reached puberty. Although the *salāt* is not the only form of prayer in Islam, the bowings, prostrations and recitations which make up the practice offer the believer a tangible means of communing with the Creator on a regular basis. Indeed, the centrality of *salāt* to the devotional life of the Muslim believer can be understood from the words of Muhammad himself, who is reported to have said:

> Prayer is the pillar of religion; to neglect it is to prepare the downfall of religion. If a man performs the five prayers, in a proper state of purity and at the times prescribed, they will be a light and a proof for him on the Day of Resurrection. But he who misses them will be resurrected along with Pharaoh and Haman.

Like various other rites in Islam, *salāt* is said to have been practised by earlier prophets such as Abraham, Ishmael, Moses and Jesus. The form of their particular *salāt* is not specified, although the Koran does claim that later generations neglected the practice: by the time that Muhammad revived it, it had become nothing more than the 'whistling and clapping' of the pagan Meccans as they circled their idols in the *ka'ba*. The prayers of the great patriarchs may indeed have been lost to the later generations of Arabs, but the tradition of prayer was clearly preserved by the Peoples of the Book. Indeed, in the prayers of today's Orthodox Jews and Eastern Orthodox Christians, one sees enticing glimpses of some of the movements included in traditional Islamic *salāt*, suggesting the kind of common origin posited by the Koran.

References in the Koran to the *salāt* performed by both Moses and Jesus indicate that the notion of *salāt* as prayer in the most general sense of the word was not unknown to Muhammad at the outset of his prophetic career in Mecca. Indeed, as we have already seen, Muhammad was himself given to introspection and meditation long before he was called to prophethood, and it is not inconceivable that he too was given to the performance of some kind of ritual prayer; however, whether it was the same as the *salāt* performed today we can never know. Similarly, we can never know whether or not Muhammad and the early Meccan converts to Islam prayed individually or in congregation before his mission became public. The first indication that some form of devotional rite was current among the followers of Muhammad in Mecca comes in *sūra* 96, one of the earliest chapters to be revealed, in which those who prevent others from praying are rebuked. The command to establish regular prayer at various intervals throughout the day comes towards the end of Muhammad's career in Mecca, on the eve of the *hijra* to Medina:

> Establish regular prayers – at the sun's decline till the darkness of the night, and the morning prayer and reading: for the prayer and reading in the morning carry their testimony.
>
> (17:78)

According to the *hadith*, the actual number of daily prayers was fixed by Muhammad during his fabled 'night journey' or *mi'rāj*. However, the above verse and others such as 11:114 and 20:130 are interpreted by Muslim exegetes and jurists as indicating the particular times – five in all – during a 24-hour day that the *salāt* is to be performed.

The names of the five daily prayers reflect the time of day at which they are said. They are:

- Morning prayer (*salāt al-subh*). This may be performed at any time between the break of dawn and sunrise.

- Midday prayer (*salāt al-zuhr*). This may be performed at any time between the beginning of the sun's descent from its zenith and the point when the shadow of an object becomes the same length as the object itself.
- Late afternoon prayer (*salāt al-asr*). This may be performed at any time between the end of *salāt al-zuhr* and the setting of the sun.
- Early evening prayer (*salāt al-maghrib*). This may be performed at any time between sunset and the disappearance of daylight.
- Evening or night prayer (*salāt al-ishā*). This may be performed at any time between the disappearance of daylight and the beginning of daybreak. Prophetic tradition deems it more meritorious, however, to perform the night prayer before midnight.

Just as they differ on all manner of jurisprudential issues, the various schools of jurisprudence often have slightly different regulations with regard to the nuts-and-bolts of canonical prayer, including the times at which prayers should be performed, where prayers may or may not be offered, what the individual can or cannot wear, and so on. Most of the Shi'ite jurists, for example, allow their followers to combine the midday prayer with the late afternoon prayer, and the early evening prayer with the night prayer, in effect reducing the number of times that one prays during the day to three. While this is not disallowed by the Sunni majority, most jurists insist that the five prayers be kept separate.

Since prayer times are determined by the movements of the sun, they vary not only from season to season but also from day to day. In modern Muslim societies, prayer times are printed in daily newspapers, while most mosques and Islamic societies in the West publish timetables month by month.

THE ADHĀN OR 'CALL TO PRAYER'

In most Muslim countries, and in some Muslim communities in the West, each prayer time is announced by the *adhān*, first introduced in Medina by the Prophet. The *adhān* is traditionally called out from the minarets of mosques, and in modern societies is also broadcast from the radio. Individuals performing the *salāt* in a place where no *adhān* can be heard are recommended to repeat it themselves before praying. The first *muezzin* or 'announcer of prayer' was Muhammad's freed Abyssinian bondsman, Bilal, who summoned the community to their devotions with the famous cry of *Allāhu akbar* or 'God is the greatest of all'. The full *adhān* is as follows:

> God is the greatest [of all] – *repeated four times*
> I bear witness that there is no god but God – *repeated twice*
> I bear witness that Muhammad is the Messenger of God –
> *repeated twice*
> Hasten to the *salāt* – *repeated twice*
> Hasten to prosperity – *repeated twice*
> God is the greatest [of all] – *repeated twice*
> There is no god but God.

PREPARING FOR PRAYER: TAKING ABLUTION

Personal hygiene is of supreme importance in Islam, and there are many situations for which Muslims are required to attain ritual purity or *tahāra*. Ritual purity is achieved through either of two forms of ablution, depending on the circumstance. These are the 'greater ablution', or *ghusl*, and the 'minor ablution', or *wudū*.

The 'major ablution' becomes necessary prior to *salāt* for men if they have had a seminal emission, regardless of the cause; for women if they have just completed menstruation or have given birth in the last forty days; and for both men and women if they have had sexual intercourse where full penetration takes place. Islamic jurisprudence prescribes two ways of performing the major ablution, the more common of which is to wash the whole of the body under clean, running water. To perform the major ablution before the Friday congregational prayers (see below) is also deemed meritorious, even if one is not, strictly speaking, ritually impure as a result of recent intercourse, childbirth and the like.

If the circumstances which require the 'major ablution' are absent, then it is the 'minor ablution' or *wudū* which must be performed prior to *salāt*. The minor ablution consists in the ritual washing of the mouth, nose, hands and forearms, face, head and feet in accordance with the *sunna* of the Prophet and in the particular manner recommended by the individual's chosen school of jurisprudence (*madhhab*). There are minor differences between the five main schools, but in essence they amount to very much the same practice. There are a number of things which 'void' the state of purity that *wudū* confers, such as the passing of urine, defecation, vomiting or breaking wind, in which case the ablution has to be repeated before the next performance of *salāt*. Some jurists also deem the minor ablution necessary before touching the Koran, while brushing the teeth is also seen as a highly meritorious act, highly recommended by the Prophet.

In the absence of water, or in cases where water may be injurious to the health, the practice of *tayammum* is prescribed. This is a kind of 'dry ablution' in which the individual wipes his or her face and hands with pure soil, sand or stone, depending on what is accessible at the time.

Apart from the ritual purity required for prayer, personal hygiene is of paramount importance to Muslims, who consider *tahāra* to be 'part of faith'. This includes using water rather than paper after defecating; rinsing dishes after they have been washed; showering after a bath to remove all traces of dirty bathwater; shaving under the arms and in the genital areas in order to prevent the build up of odour, and so on. Interestingly enough, the habit of frequent bathing, and the use of soap and perfume, are said to have been brought to the West by returning Crusaders, who had adopted these practices from Muslims in the Holy Land.

WHERE TO PRAY AND WHAT TO WEAR

There is no prescribed dress code for prayer: so long as what they wear is clean and modest, Muslims may dress as they please when they stand to perform the *salāt*.

Similarly, there are very few places in which Muslims are not allowed to pray: according to a Prophetic Tradition, the whole world is a 'place of prostration' or *masjid* – the Arabic word for mosque – and so long as one faces Mecca, one can pray virtually wherever one likes. To pray in the local mosque is regarded traditionally as being more meritorious than praying at home, although for the Koran it is the intention underlying the prayer which is important, and not where the prayer is performed.

Each prayer is made up of a number of 'units', known in Arabic as *rak'a*. The morning prayer has two *rak'a*; the midday and late afternoon prayers have four each; the early evening prayer comprises three *rak'a*; and the late evening prayer has four. Each unit consists of a recitation from the Koran, which is performed while standing; a ritual bowing or *rukū*; and a prostration or *sujūd*. During the bowing and the prostration, various prayers are uttered. The *rak'a* is then repeated until the required number of units – two, three or four, depending on the time of day – is completed. At the end of the two-*rak'a* prayer, the individual kneels and recites another series of supplications, including the invocation of blessings on all righteous believers and of benedictions on the Prophet. This is known as the *tashahhud* or 'bearing witness'. The *tashahud* marks the end of the prayer. In the three-*rak'a* prayer of early evening, a shortened version of the *tashahhud*, performed seated, follows the second *rak'a*, whereupon the individual rises and performs another complete 'unit' before sitting for the final *tashahhud*. In a four-*rak'a* prayer, the short *tashahhud* following the first two units is itself followed by two more units, whereupon the individual performs the full *tashahhud* and thus completes the prayer.

While the Koran is silent on the issue of language, it is taken for granted among Muslims that the canonical prayer should be offered in Arabic. Intention, however, is all, and while non-Arab Muslims are learning to perform the *salāt* in the language of the Prophet, they may offer their prayers in whichever language they choose, so long as the spirit of the original is preserved.

Canonical prayer is deemed incumbent on the Muslim believer whenever he or she reaches maturity. While the *salāt* is seen as a lifelong commitment, there are situations in which it may be either shortened or suspended temporarily. Muslims on a journey and who find it inconvenient to pray a full four-unit prayer, for instance, may shorten it to two units; those who are incapacitated in some way may offer the prayer sitting or lying down.

Those who are unable to pray within the specified time are, like those who miss prayers altogether, expected to make up for the loss by offering the prayer later – and preferably as soon as he or she is able.

Menstruating women are debarred from performing *salāt* until all traces of blood have disappeared. Then, after a full ritual ablution, they are allowed to pray once more, without any obligation to make up the number of prayers missed. Traditionally, menstruating women have also been debarred from touching the Koran, although there appears to be no sound scriptural basis for such a prohibition.

CONGREGATIONAL PRAYER

To offer prayer in the company of other Muslim believers is held by Prophetic Tradition to be more meritorious than offering the prayer alone. Congregational prayer (*salāt al-jamā'a*) is the term applied to any prayer which is performed by at least two people in unison, with one acting as *imām* or prayer leader. There is no upper limit to the number of people who may pray together, and in some of the larger mosques in the Middle East, huge congregations can often be seen, particularly at times of fasting and festival. The prayer leader stands at the front and initiates the prayer; the others stand behind him and 'follow' the *imām*'s movements.

Women and men may form part of the same congregation, but tradition has tended to dictate a modified form of segregation, in which women stand in rows behind the men, presumably to preserve their modesty when bending and prostrating. Tradition also dictates that the prayer leader be male, although women are allowed to lead the prayers in congregations where no men are present. However, there are contemporary scholars who believe that a woman may lead a mixed congregation, particularly if she is more knowledgeable in matters of jurisprudence, or more proficient in Arabic, than the male candidates for prayer leadership.

FRIDAY PRAYERS

> O ye who believe! When the call is proclaimed to prayer on
> Friday [the Day of Assembly], hasten earnestly to the
> Remembrance of God, and leave off business [and traffic]: That
> is best for you if ye but knew!
>
> And when the Prayer is finished, then may ye disperse through
> the land, and seek of the Bounty of God: and celebrate the
> Praises of God often [and without stint]: that ye may prosper.
>
> (62:9–10)

The Friday congregational prayer, prescribed by the Koran, is held
by the Sunni majority to be incumbent on all adult males; women
may attend if they wish, but are usually advised to pray at home.
The Koran, as can be seen from the verse cited above, does not
make any distinction between men and women with regard to Friday prayer attendance, showing once again that it is often cultural
tradition that wins out over Koranic reality. Among the various
Shi'ite denominations there is no firm consensus with regard to the
Friday prayer: some deem it obligatory at all times; others see it as
recommended but not ritually incumbent; and a minority claims
that Friday prayer is held in abeyance until the return of the
Mahdi.

The Friday congregation prayer consists of a sermon or *khutba*,
and two units of prayer, performed behind the *imām*. The sermon
is in two parts: a short, formulaic introduction in which the *imām*
praises God, invokes blessings on Muhammad and on the Muslim
community in general, and recites verses from the Koran which
enjoin belief and God-awareness on all humankind. Following a
short break in which the *imām* sits, the second half of the sermon
begins. This part of the sermon is traditionally didactic in nature,
with the *imām* lecturing briefly on a fundamental belief, say, or a
pillar of Islam. In certain Muslim communities, the tenor of the
Friday prayer sermon has changed considerably in the past fifty
years, with highly politicised prayer leaders taking advantage of the
large numbers attending Friday prayer to put their ideological
messages across. The politicisation of the Friday prayer sermon was
very much in evidence in the run up to the Iranian revolution of

1979, and politically oriented sermons can still be heard in many parts of the Muslim world today.

The sermon over, members of the congregation are free to disperse, although some stay behind to perform supererogatory *salāt*. In accordance with the Koranic injunction, those who have attended the Friday prayer may go about their business as normal, indicating that in Islam there is no concept of a 'sabbath' or 'day of rest' as there is in Judaism or Christianity. Nevertheless, in most Muslim countries, Friday is a designated holiday, and with Thursday afternoon forms part of the weekend.

OTHER KINDS OF SALĀT

Supererogatory *salāt*, that is, prayers which are not actually incumbent, but which are performed by some believers as a further expression of devotion, include the *tahajjud* or night prayer, and a whole host of *salāt* known as *nāfila*, which are said either prior or subsequent to the canonical prayers. Modifications on the daily *salāt* are also used in ritual prayers for the dead; prayers which are offered at times of great cosmic consequence, such as in the middle of an earthquake or at the start of an eclipse; and prayers offered on the occasions of Eid al-Fitr and Eid al-Adhā, the celebrations following Ramadan and the *hajj* respectively. Shi'ite devotional life includes a veritable treasury of different kinds of *salāt* for different occasions,

NON-CANONICAL DEVOTIONS

The *salāt* – whether in its canonical or supererogatory sense – is not the only form of devotion open to a Muslim believer: as we shall see in Chapter 5, there are many other ways in which a Muslim can, should he or she so wish, commune with God. Believers are free, and indeed encouraged, to talk to God and call on Him whenever they wish and in whichever manner they choose, so long as it is broadly in keeping with Islamic etiquette or *adab*. Non-obligatory devotions of this kind are known collectively in Arabic as *du'ā*. Frustratingly, like *salāt*, this word is often translated into English as 'prayer', and thus there are many who confuse the two. In reality, a *du'ā* is literally a 'calling on' God, and as such should be translated as 'invocation'. However, there are also devotions described as *du'ā* which non-Muslim Westerners would understand more readily as 'supplications' or 'meditations', and thus a hard and fast translational rule is probably best avoided.

What the ritual of *salāt* is to public worship, the spiritual exercise known as *du'ā* is to private devotion. The *du'ā* may be offered at any time and in any place, depending on the needs and desires of the individual. Furthermore, ritual ablution is not necessary before offering this kind of devotion, and women are not debarred from offering *du'ā* during menstruation. And unlike the *salāt*, private spiritual exercises of this type do not have to be performed in Arabic.

The Koran does not prescribe a particular form that a *du'ā* should take, although through history certain formulaic *du'ā* have emerged, and there is a huge amount of devotional literature in the Muslim world which documents the *du'ā* of certain pious individuals: the recorded supplication and meditations of the Shi'ite imams, for example, stand out in this regard.

THE SPIRITUAL SIGNIFICANCE OF SALĀT

The central notion underlying both *salāt* – whether in its canonical or non-canonical forms – and *du'ā* is communion with God. For the Muslim, to commune with God, in the Koranic sense of the term, means many things. It means to express one's total and utter impotence before One who is omnipotent; it means to communicate all of one's inner and outer needs to One who stands in need of nothing; it means to give praise to the One who is responsible for all things at all times, and who, as such, is deserving of all praise; it means to ask for guidance in all matters, states and affairs, from One who is omniscient, and whose guidance never fails; and it means to express one's devotion to the One who is Lord, God and Creator of all things at all times, ever present with His creation at each instant, and who, as such, is the only One deserving of human devotion.

The goal of human life is to achieve such communion at all times, in order that man may realise his true nature as the supreme manifestation of God on earth. However, man is a creature prone to forgetfulness, and it is the institution of canonical prayer – the five-times-a-day performance of *salāt* – that is designed to wake him up from the dream of this 'worldly life' and restore him, however briefly, to normalcy. As such, the *salāt* is an emblem, signifying the state of submission, worship and love to which he should aspire at every instant, and not just when the *muezzin* calls. Not without justification, then, has the *salāt* been described as the 'ascension of the believer'.

THE THIRD PILLAR: FASTING

The ninth month of the *hijri* lunar calendar is Ramadan, a period of thirty days during which practising Muslims the world over suspend their usual routines and break away from day-to-day habits by subjecting themselves to a regime that is designed not only to have far-reaching effects on their everyday lives during the month of Ramadan, but also to bring about a qualitative transformation on the level of mind, body and spirit during the rest of the year. For the month of Ramadan is the month of fasting or *sawm*, the third 'pillar of Islam'.

THE KORAN AND FASTING

There are few religious traditions in which some kind of fast is not held to be obligatory or, at least, deemed meritorious: one thinks of the Jewish fast of Yom Kippur, for example, or the period known in the Christian Church as Lent, the forty-day fast that precedes Easter. Fasting was first made incumbent on the Muslim community following Muhammad's migration to Medina, in a series of Koranic directives the nature of which suggests quite explicitly that the practice was not unknown to the desert Arabs:

> O ye who believe! Fasting is prescribed to you as it was prescribed to those before you, that ye may [learn] self-restraint, –
>
> (2:183)

In keeping with Islam's insistence that its spiritual ideals and practical injunctions accord with the monotheistic traditions that have gone before, the Koran, in the only Meccan reference to the practice, tells us how Mary 'vowed a fast' to God shortly before Jesus was born:

> So eat and drink and cool [thine] eye. And if thou dost see any man,
> say, 'I have vowed a fast to [God] Most Gracious, and this day will I
> enter into not talk with any human being.'
>
> (19:26)

In prescribing the fast to the new community of Muslims, the
Koran seems to be advocating not so much a wholesale replication of
other religious traditions but a continuation of the general concept
of fasting, with details regarding the number of days, or the particular
time and manner of the fast, to be supplied partly by Divine decree
and partly in accordance with Prophetic practice. This is what appears
to have happened with regard to most of the practices which have
pre-Islamic origins, but which were taken up by the new community
and 'Islamicised': the *hajj*, as we shall see, is a striking example. In
the case of fasting, the Koran supplies little detail on the practical
issues involved, and even less on the spiritual whys and wherefores,
suggesting that the initial addressees of the Koran must have been
well acquainted with the concept already. This is not difficult to
understand, given the fact that the desert Arabs had lived for centuries with Jews and Jewish traditions in their midst.

Koranic regulations covering the Ramadan fast are confined to
three or four verses in the second chapter, *al-Baqara*, most of
which was revealed shortly after the migration to Medina:

> [Fasting is] for a fixed number of days; but if any of you is ill, or on a
> journey, the prescribed number [Should be made up] from days later.
> For those who can do it [With hardship], is a ransom, the feeding of
> one that is indigent. But he that will give more, of his own free will, – it
> is better for him. And it is better for you that ye fast, if ye only knew.
>
> (2:184)

Having established that the fast is to be carried out for a 'fixed
number of days', and suggesting ways in which those unable to fast
may compensate, the Koran then stipulates that the ninth month of
the lunar calendar – the month in which the Koran itself was
revealed – be devoted in its entirety to the practice:

> Ramadan is the [month] in which was sent down the Qur'an, as a
> guide to humankind, also clear [Signs] for guidance and judgment

[between right and wrong]. So every one of you who is present [at his home] during that month should spend it in fasting, but if any one is ill, or on a journey, the prescribed period [should be made up] by days later. God intends every facility for you; He does not want to put you to difficulties. [He wants you] to complete the prescribed period, and to glorify Him in that He has guided you; and perchance ye shall be grateful.

(2:185)

Along with eating and drinking, sexual intercourse is also proscribed during daylight hours. Come sunset, however, the life of the fasting Muslim regains a semblance of pre-Ramadan normality as restrictions on food, drink and sexual relations between married partners are lifted until sunrise of the following morning.

EXEMPTIONS AND EXCEPTIONS

From the Koran it is clear that fasting is only for those who are able, physically, to undergo the hardships that the practice involves. Those who are chronically ill, for example, or for whom fasting has been ruled out on other medical grounds, are not required to fast. Those whose illness is temporary are expected to compensate by making up the number of missed fasts once the illness is over. Menstruating women are also exempted from the fast, but are expected to make up for the missing fasts before the following Ramadan.

THE RAMADAN FAST IN PRACTICE

Cultural differences notwithstanding, Ramadan unites the Muslim world through the shared experience of fasting, propelling all of its members – theoretically at least – towards the same spiritual goal. Virtually no-one who lives in a Muslim society can remain unaffected by the fast, which tends to regulate the mood and pace of family and social life for thirty days each year. In many Muslim communities, the fast is not only a religious rite, but also something of a socio-cultural event, and many of those who pay little more than lip-service to Islam during the rest of the year often endeavour to fast for at least a few days during Ramadan. Muslims would generally agree that there is something about the fast that inspires the spiritual even in those nominal Muslims, for whom religion is merely a cultural badge rather than an orientation of choice.

In the not too dim and distant past, during a typical month of Ramadan in the Muslim world, everything would slow down, most shops would open for only a few hours, and most of those with the financial wherewithal would have retreated somewhere quiet to get away from it all. Restaurants would close, or would cover their windows with newspaper in order to shield passers-by from the view of food being prepared for the evening meal. Today, while the pace of life throughout the Muslim world does become perceptibly slower during Ramadan, modern metropolises have generally assimilated it into the general current of everyday life, with as little disruption as possible to business and commerce – both key to the participation of Muslim nation-states in a globalised economy.

To describe a typical Ramadan fast day would be impossible, as all communities differ, at least in the detail. In general, those fasting tend to rise an hour before the break of dawn, the point at which the prohibitions of the fast become binding. The pre-dawn meal, known as *suhūr* or *sahari*, usually prepared the day before, is heated and eaten. Supplications are offered and those who wish may also offer supererogatory *salāt*. The call to morning prayer signals the beginning of the fast, and none of the actions which invalidate the fast are allowed again until the call to early evening prayer.

Since the month of Ramadan is part of the lunar calendar, which is only 355 days long, the annual fast moves back by either ten or eleven days each year. This means that Ramadan moves back through the seasons, taking approximately thirty-three years to run through all four seasons. The fact that Ramadan is to be experienced in all seasons is seen by some as evidence of the divine wisdom which underpins it. Muslims seem divided as to whether a summer fast is harder than a winter one, even in those geographical areas where there is greater seasonal variation of temperature. In Britain, for example, it is difficult to gauge whether the long days of summer, where the fast can last up to twenty hours at some latitudes, are more onerous than the shorter days of winter: in summer, thirst is a problem; in winter, it is the desire for warm food to ward off the cold that proves difficult. Above certain latitudes, of course, where there is virtually no daylight in the winter and hardly any darkness in the summer, it is impossible to know when to begin the fast and when to break it. In such situations, any Muslims wishing to fast usually abide by times operating in Mecca, or in the nearest large town or city where the fast is a practical possibility.

During the day, most who are fasting attempt to go about their business more or less as normal. Fasting would appear to be somewhat easier in communities where most of the people are doing the same thing, and where the sense of shared purpose is often palpable. Muslims living abroad often encounter difficulties during Ramadan, particularly if those with whom they work or study are not familiar with the issues surrounding the fast. Most large towns in the West have either mosques or Islamic societies which arguably become more active during Ramadan than at other times of the year, partly in response to the needs of those Muslims who may need to draw on group support during this month. Many mosques and Muslim charitable societies arrange group meals during Ramadan, allowing people to take their morning meal, and to break fast, together.

The call to early evening prayer, just after sunset, signals the time for the fast to end. Most people break their fast with something light before prayer; then the evening meal is eaten, preferably in the company of others. In Muslim countries, the breaking of the fast is a joyous occasion: after prayers, the streets fill with people, some out to eat, others simply to soak up the carnival atmosphere that often pervades big cities whose residents have been hungry and thirsty all day. Unfortunately, some seem to forget that the month is partly about self-restraint, and spend most of the evening eating to excess, often consuming more than they would under normal circumstances. Most eat moderately; in fact it takes quite a lot of effort, after a long day's fast, to eat even a moderately sized meal, let alone too much.

Praying in congregation is considered particularly meritorious during Ramadan, and special supererogatory prayers known as *tarāwih* are performed nightly during the month in mosques and private houses. The second half of Ramadan is seen as particularly auspicious, for tradition holds that this was when the Koran was first revealed. People attend the mosque as often as they can, and some actually retreat there for the full ten days to pray and meditate.

The sighting of the new moon at the end of Ramadan brings the fast to a conclusion, and the first day of the next lunar month is devoted to one of the biggest festivals in the Muslim calendar, the *Eid al-Fitr*. Families and friends congregate to celebrate: a special *salāt* is performed in congregation, a big meal is usually taken together, and gifts are exchanged. The final obligation at the end of Ramadan on all of those who have fasted is the donation of a small sum of money – the *fitriya* – to the deserving poor.

MISSED FASTS

Those who become ill during a fast day are required to break their fast; they may begin to fast again when they are well, and are expected to make up the required number of missed days when Ramadan is over.

There is no consensus with regard to travelling during a fast. Some jurists claim that, just as the canonical prayers are shortened during a journey in order to alleviate hardship, fasting while on a journey is invalid because of the practical difficulties it may cause. Islam is, after all, a religion that is opposed to the imposition of hardship or difficulty for its own sake. For the most part, to fast or not during a journey is left increasingly to the discretion of the individual.

While no-one is forced to fast, those who miss a fast day intentionally find that Muslim jurisprudence is uncompromising in its range of penalties: for every day of fast that is voided intentionally, the individual must fast for sixty consecutive days once Ramadan is over; alternatively, he or she must feed a certain number of deserving poor for a certain number of days, in accordance with the stipulations of the particular school of law that he or she follows. Again, no-one can be forced to comply with such regulations, which are always a matter of personal belief and private conscience.

FASTING AT OTHER TIMES

Fasting is a meritorious act in Islam whenever it is practised, and many Muslims will fast at various times during the year, over and above the obligatory fast of Ramadan. Fasting, with its implicit attack on man's animal appetites and carnal cravings, is seen as another way of purifying the self and bringing the recalcitrant soul into line. As such, it is also seen as a means of expiating one's past sins, and growing stronger in self-knowledge and God-awareness. Some days are considered more auspicious for fasting than others: the first three days of every lunar month, for example, or the tenth of Muharram (the first month of the lunar *hijri* year), which, as the Jewish 'Day of Atonement', was singled out as a particularly important fasting day by Muhammad himself. The Prophetic *sunna* identifies many other points on the lunar calendar when fasting is said to be of particular importance, and in fact the only day on which fasting is prohibited – and then according to Prophetic Tradition rather than the Koran – is the post-Ramadan feast day known as *Eid al-Fitr*.

THE SPIRITUAL SIGNIFICANCE OF FASTING

The practice of fasting is said to bestow numerous physical benefits on those who undertake it. The purpose of fasting, however, is not to benefit the body, although this may be a welcome side effect. The purpose, as with all Divine commands, is to carry out God's will as a believer who wishes to grow in self-knowledge, God-awareness, worship and love.

THE FOURTH PILLAR: 'SPENDING FOR THE SAKE OF GOD'

> The parable of those who spend their substance in the way of God is that of a grain of corn: it grows seven ears, and each ear has a hundred grains. God gives manifold increase to whom He pleases: And God cares for all and He knows all things
>
> (2:61)

The fourth 'pillar of Islam' is described by Western writers variously as 'alms', 'charity' and even 'religious tax'. None of these designations really defines what lies at the heart of this fourth pillar, which is best – although by no means perfectly – described here as 'spending for the sake of God'. For the broad Arabic term used in the verse quoted above – *infāq* – covers not only the donation of money to the poor, but also the giving of one's self – one's time or one's talents perhaps, one's physical skills or one's intellectual powers. There are many ways in which one can spend for the sake of God, including the dedication of one's whole life to a particular cause, as in the case of the prophets.

The principle of spending 'for the sake of God' or 'in God's cause' is perhaps best understood if we first see how the Koran views personal wealth and private property. Despite attempts by certain political ideologues in the 1950s and 1960s to portray the Koran as some kind of blueprint for a socialist utopia, it is not opposed to the idea of private ownership, the pursuit of profit, or even the accumulation of wealth. What the Koran is at pains to emphasise, however, is that the intention of the individual must be pure, and that wealth and possessions are to be used in God's name and for His sake. For according to the Koran, all of man's worldly possessions – including his own self – are given to him on loan, as it were, to be used in as wise and 'God-oriented' a manner as is possible. To 'spend for the sake of God' from one's wealth and possessions is, in a sense, to give back to God what was His all along, but which was bestowed on man as part of the 'divine trust' of earthly existence.

The practice is there principally as a means by which man may realise his indebtedness to God and his responsibility to his fellow man. It is also in essence a spiritual practice, for it serves to remind man that he owns nothing – neither his own self nor the material things he appears to possess – and that everything is loaned to him by the True Owner of all creation. Muslims believe that such sacrifices are ultimately to man's benefit as they will be turned to his advantage in the world to come.

THE THREE FORMS OF CHARITABLE GIVING

The concept of 'spending for the sake of God' was systemised early on into three particular forms of charitable giving, all of which still exist today. These are *sadaqāt*, the giving of which is voluntary; and *zakāh* and *khums*, the payment of which the Koran makes incumbent on all believing Muslims.

SADAQÂT. The word *sadaqât* – usually translated as 'alms' – was used to denote charitable giving in the broadest sense of the term, and covered obligatory as well as supererogatory acts of charity.

> Alms [*sadaqât*] are for the poor and the needy, and those employed to administer the [funds]; for those whose hearts have been [recently] reconciled [to Truth]; for those in bondage and in debt; in the cause of God; and for the wayfarer: [thus is it] ordained by God, and God is full of knowledge and wisdom.
>
> (9:60)

Today, *sadaqât* almost always denotes charitable giving that is voluntary rather than obligatory. As such, all Muslim believers are encouraged to give as much as they can to good causes, and particularly to the deserving poor. The giving of *sadaqât* is seen as meritorious in itself on purely practical grounds. However, the spiritual importance of voluntary giving should not be overlooked, with many Muslims believing that the donation of *sadaqât* on a regular basis attracts divine favour and repels misfortune.

ZAKÂH. The word *zakâh* (or *zakât*) describes the form of charitable giving which the Koran deems incumbent on all believing adult Muslims with adequate financial means at their disposal. While there are minor differences according to the school of jurisprudence to which one adheres, in general *zakâh* involves the annual donation of 2.5 per cent of one's net worth to the *bayt al-mâl*, or 'community treasury'. The word *zakâh* is derived from the Arabic verb *tazakka*, which means 'to purify': the payment of *zakâh* is, therefore, one prescribed way in which Muslims may in a sense purify or make sacred their wealth and possessions by giving a small proportion of them away in God's name and for His sake. Among those most devoted to God, the Koran asserts, are those who

> spend their wealth for increase in self-purification, and have in their minds no favour from anyone for which a reward is expected in return.
>
> (92:18–19)

The spending of wealth for the sake of God renders pure not only one's possessions but also one's self – provided of course that one gives with the intention of pleasing God, and not for the sake of attracting attention by giving openly and conspicuously. In the payment of *zakāh* – the giving freely of one's self and one's wealth – one is encouraged to abnegate one's own imaginary ownership and to acknowledge the True Possessor of all things.

The social importance of zakāh.   This important exercise in spiritual purification is the primary goal of *zakāh*, but clearly by no means its only objective. Many commentators have interpreted this particular 'pillar' as the cornerstone of social justice in the early Muslim community – hence the erroneous translation of *zakāh* as 'religious tax'. For the *zakāh* is to be used first and foremost for the needy, in order to alleviate the problem of poverty, if not to extirpate it completely. Traditionally, *zakāh* was also used for the 'propagation of the faith', to free slaves, to relieve people of inordinate debt, to help travellers in need, and for a variety of other uses sanctioned by scholars of jurisprudence. The centrality of *zakāh* to the economic and welfare system of any Muslim society cannot be underestimated. The main forms of wealth on which *zakāh* is levied according to Muslim jurisprudence include gold and silver, livestock, agricultural produce, stocks and shares, currency and other liquid assets. Those with no net assets at the end of the year are not expected to pay anything.

KHUMS.   The word *khums*, which means 'a fifth', was originally a tax based on 20 per cent of the war booty that was given by Muslims to Muhammad and his family. After Muhammad's death, many believed the tax to be defunct, although later jurists – particularly those of the Shi'ite persuasion – interpreted the *khums* as a tax to be levied on profits of various sorts.

The *khums* is still an important financial consideration in Shi'ism, particularly since it provides the Shi'ite clergy, who are the traditional administrators of the tax, with an important source of income.

Traditionally, the tax was levied on the following items:

(i)   surplus income
(ii)   lawful wealth or property that is mixed with the unlawful

(iii)   riches obtained from mines
(iv)   riches found as treasure
(v)   riches obtained from sea-diving
(vi)   booty obtained in *jihād*
(vii) lands obtained from non-Muslims

Today, *khums* is payable on many kinds of earnings: income from commerce, industry and agriculture; net profit from business; salaries; savings, and on such things as unused clothes and food and luxury goods. The *khums* is calculated only after one's needs have been met, and household and/or commercial expenses have been deducted. The tax is also deducted from gifts, lottery wins, and money bequeathed in wills. In Shi'ite communities, partly for reasons already mentioned, the *khums* is arguably a far greater focus of both jurisprudential and popular attention than *zakāh*, although from the point of view of their shared spiritual goal – the purification of one's possessions, and, by extension, the purification of the self – they are more or less identical.

THE FIFTH PILLAR': THE HAJJ, OR PILGRIMAGE TO MECCA

> Pilgrimage is born of desire and belief. The desire is for solution to problems of all kinds that arise within the human situation. The belief is that somewhere beyond the known world there exists a power that can make right the difficulties that appear so insoluble and intractable here and now. All one must do is journey.
>
> (Alan Morinis, *Sacred Journeys: The Anthropology of Pilgrimage*, Greenwood Press, 1992, p. 1)

The idea of the 'sacred journey' is a universal one: the concept of pilgrimage – the temporary physical movement of the individual from the 'this-worldly' to the 'other-worldly' while still on earth – is common to all of the world's major religions. Every tradition has its own notion of what constitutes 'sacred space', and how that space should be approached – both metaphorically and literally. And so each cultural setting is home to its own particular form of sacred journey, with rites and rituals suited to the lives, beliefs and desires of those individuals operating within it. The sacred journey is alive today as it was in the Middle Ages, with religious pilgrimages accounting for the largest regular gatherings of humans on the planet. The *hajj*, the annual pilgrimage to Mecca, and fifth 'pillar of Islam', attracts in the region of two million Muslims from all corners of the globe.

THE HAJJ BY DEFINITION

While the *hajj* is commonly defined simply as 'pilgrimage to Mecca', it is in actual fact a relatively complex set of rites and rituals that are performed at set times and in fixed locations in and around the city of Mecca. The performance of *hajj* is incumbent on all Muslims past the age of puberty, provided that they have the financial means and the physical wherewithal to undertake the journey. The pilgrimage and its attendant rites take place during the first two weeks of Dhū al-Hijja, the twelfth month of the lunar *hijri* calendar. There is also a non-obligatory version of the pilgrimage to Mecca known as *umra*, which can take place at any time of year. Like the supererogatory prayers known as *nāfila*, or the voluntary alms known as *sadaqāt*, the *umra* is meritorious in its own right as an act of devotion over and above what is required canonically.

PRE-ISLAMIC MECCA AND THE HAJJ

Arabs believed that Mecca was a sacred place long before the advent of the Koran and the mission of Muhammad.

At the centre of Mecca stands the most enigmatic structure in Muslim architecture, the *ka'ba*. The *ka'ba* – which in Arabic means 'cube-like building' – is approximately 12 metres long, 10 metres wide and 15 metres high; it sits on a platform and is draped in a veil of thick black brocade known as the *kiswa*. Built of grey stone and marble, the structure is oriented so that its four corners align approximately with the cardinal points of the compass. Embedded in the eastern corner of the *ka'ba* is the mysterious 'black stone' (*hajar al-aswad*). Set in a silver surround, the stone is said to be meteoric in origin: pilgrims to Mecca endeavour to kiss the stone as they encircle the *ka'ba* as part of the pilgrimage rite. The burial place of Abraham's wife, Hagar, and her son, Ishmael, is said to lie beneath the north-west wall, while opposite the east corner is a stone with footprints in it said to be those of Abraham himself.

The link between Abraham and Mecca is an important one, for it is he – together with his son, Ishmael – who is said to have raised the foundations of the *ka'ba* in the first place. The Koran relates how Abraham was ordered to purify 'God's house' (*bayt Allah*) – another term for the *ka'ba* – in order that the righteous may worship there. The *ka'ba* was to be a sanctuary and a place of retreat for the whole of humankind, and the 'station of Abraham' – the stone with the patriarch's footprints – was to be a place of prayer and prostration.

Muslim tradition, backed by the Koran, thus asserts that the rites of *hajj* were introduced by Abraham himself. However, as monotheism became corrupted, the original *hajj* fell into desuetude, although important features of it remained as part of what would later become a very different kind of pilgrimage altogether: the pilgrimage of the Meccan henotheists.

The Arabic word *hajj* shares its roots with the Hebrew word *hag*, which in turn derives from the verb 'to circle': the most salient example of a Jewish *hag* is the 'Feast of Tabernacles', which involves the circumambulation, seven times, of an altar. The pre-Islamic pilgrimage of the henotheistic Arab nomads seems to have combined elements of Jewish ritual with their own pagan or animistic practices. The *ka'ba* was a pagan sanctuary and the 'black stone' a cultic object of veneration, drawing in worshippers from all over the peninsula.

Around the *ka'ba* were ranged some 360 idols carved from wood or stone, representative perhaps of the days of the solar year. These idols were dedicated to deities such as Venus, or to Quza, the god of thunder responsible for fertilising the earth. Other idols were the goddesses Lat, Manat and al-Uzza, whom the Arabs believed to be the 'daughters of Allah'. For at the heart of the pantheon was the mysterious Semitic god Allah – a shortened form of *al-ilāh*, which simply means 'the god'.

THE KORAN AND THE HAJJ

Understandably, the Meccan sections of the Koran focus more on the concept of pilgrimage, while the more practical aspects are covered by those verses revealed in Medina, where pilgrimage had become 'Islamicised' and, towards the end of the Prophet's career, more accessible. As with all of the 'pillars', the Koran's overview of the *hajj* never goes into precise detail, and so for insight into the minutiae of the *hajj* as it is performed today, one must look to the *hadith*.

THE RITES AND RITUALS OF THE HAJJ

The canonical pilgrimage or *hajj* takes place over a seven-day period in the month of Dhū al-Hijja, the twelfth month of the lunar *hijri* year.

On the 7th of Dhū al-Hijja, the pilgrims don the *ihrām*, the symbolic garb that one must wear before one is allowed to enter the *haram* or sacred precincts. The male *ihrām* consists of two white sheets, unadorned by seams or stitching, one of which is fastened around the waist to form an ankle-length robe, and the other which is draped around the shoulders, leaving the head uncovered. For women, any simple garments which fulfil the criteria of modesty can pass as *ihrām*, so long as the arms, legs and hair are covered; interestingly enough, women are forbidden to wear full veils while performing the *hajj*, and must leave their faces exposed.

Being in a 'state of *ihrām*' is not just about correct attire, however, and before one can enter the *haram*, one must also cleanse oneself ritually. For men this means cutting the hair, shaving the face and depilating the body. While in a 'state of *ihrām*', both male and female pilgrims must wash with water only, eschewing the use of soap. Perfume is also forbidden, as is the combing of hair and beards, or the wearing of shoes that are stitched. Pilgrims in *ihrām* must also abstain from sexual relations, or any behaviour that is likely to excite the passions and lead to sexual desire. Hunting while in a state of *ihrām* is also forbidden. In fact, pilgrims must refrain from killing all living creatures, however small and seemingly insignificant, and plants too must be neither cut nor uprooted.

On the morning of the 8th, after the morning prayer, the *hajj* proper begins. Pilgrims enter the *masjid al-harām*, where they perform the *tawāf* or circumambulation: this consists of seven anticlockwise circuits of the *ka'ba*, begun at the eastern corner, where pilgrims invariably endeavour to show their respect by kissing the 'black stone'. The pilgrims are usually so numerous, however, that reaching the *ka'ba* is often impossible, and pilgrims have to be content to circle it at a distance. Returning pilgrims describe how they were literally knocked off their feet while performing the *tawāf*, and carried around the *ka'ba* almost without touching the ground. The circumambulation of the *ka'ba* is seen by some to represent the centrality of the Divine and the dependence of all created beings upon It. Others have likened the encircling of the *ka'ba* to the frenzied fluttering of moths around the flame, a dance of love in which the lover is ready to sacrifice itself for the sake of the Beloved. Time-exposure photographs taken of the ritual circumambulation reveal the pilgrims as a misty blur, similar to the rings that encircle Saturn, or a haze of subatomic particles whizzing around the nucleus of an atom. In the words of one pilgrim, 'To enter the *masjid al-harām* and to be caught up in this whirlpool of devotion literally takes the breath away: it is like drowning, but in a sea of love.' Pilgrims conclude this rite by offering two units of *salāt*, performed at the 'Station of Abraham'.

The circumambulation over, pilgrims then perform a rite known as *sa'i*. This literally means 'exertion', and consists of walking at speed, and usually running, between the two small hills of Safa and Marwa, situated near to the *ka'ba*. The *sa'i* is performed in emulation of the trials and tribulations of Hagar, the mother of Abraham's son, Isma'il (Ishmael). Hagar and her son were allegedly abandoned in the desert by Abraham on account of the jealousy shown by his wife, Sara. In a frantic search for water to quench her son's thirst, Hagar ran back and forth between the two hills, until the well of Zamzam was revealed by God to save them. Pilgrims complete the *sa'i* by taking a little Zamzam water, which is also said to have healing properties.

At midday on the 8th the pilgrims move several miles to a place called Mina, where they remain until the morning of the 9th, performing their canonical prayers in the normal way and continuing to fulfil all of the conditions of *ihrām*. On the morning of the 9th, after the morning prayer, the pilgrims move approximately nine miles east to the plain of Arafat, where they pitch their tents and set up camp. This precedes a rite known as *wuqūf* or 'standing': from noon until sunset the pilgrim stands before his Creator,

calling upon His Names and beseeching Him humbly for forgiveness. The 'standing' at Arafat is a particularly auspicious occasion
for pilgrims, who believe that their entreaties will be heard more
readily here than in any other place on earth. A sermon is also
preached at Arafat, in commemoration of Muhammad's famous
'farewell sermon' delivered during his final pilgrimage. The
'standing' at Arafat is one of the three rites that are incumbent on
pilgrims, and without which one is deemed not to have completed
the *hajj* properly.

At sunset the pilgrims decamp and move on foot to Muzdalifa, a
narrow mountain pass outside Mecca, where they perform the two
evening prayers and then spend the night out in the open, communing with God under a clear desert sky. At sunrise the pilgrims
move into the valley of Mina, where they perform the ritual
'stoning of Satan'. This rite, which involves throwing a number of
small pebbles at the largest of three stone pillars, symbolises
renunciation of all evil and wrongdoing and is performed in recognition of Abraham's stand against Satan when the latter tried to
dissuade the patriarch from obeying God and sacrificing his son.

The 'stoning of Satan' over, those pilgrims with the financial
wherewithal are encouraged to sacrifice a sheep, a goat or a camel,
again in recognition of Abraham's trial. It is then recommended
that male pilgrims shave their heads; females do not shave their
heads, but have a few centimetres of their hair trimmed as a symbolic gesture.

Over the next two or three days, pilgrims move between Mina
and Mecca, performing more circumambulations and symbolic
stonings. When pilgrims arrive in Mecca for the final time, they
put on their ordinary clothes and prepare to leave, their *hajj*
completed.

THE NON-OBLIGATORY PILGRIMAGE OR UMRA

Muslims are required to attend the *hajj* once in their lives. However, pilgrimage to Mecca at times of the year other than the period
of *hajj* is considered to be highly meritorious. Known as *umra*,
which simply means 'visit', this supererogatory pilgrimage repli-
cates many of the *hajj* rites. The *umra* was originally a pre-Islamic
ritual which took place at the beginning of spring. The henotheistic

Arab nomads would sacrifice animals and perform naked circum-ambulations of the *ka'ba*, moving in a clockwise direction to emulate the movement of the sun. Needless to say, when the *hajj* was 'Islamicised', the *umra* too was transformed: worshippers were instructed to circle the *ka'ba* anticlockwise, thus severing the link to those solar cults from whom the practice had been adopted, and clothes were to be worn at all times.

THE SPIRITUAL SIGNIFICANCE OF THE HAJJ

As with any pilgrimage, or indeed with any religious rite or prac-tice, it may be argued that one gets out of the *hajj* as much as one puts in. And one puts in according to intention: the Koran insists that man is not judged by the number of righteous deeds that he performs, but by the substrata of sincere belief that underpins them. Those who perform prayers to be seen by others, for instance, will receive according to their intention: they will, indeed, be seen. The benefit of an action performed in so cavalier a manner is presumably a material one only: there can be little, if any, spiri-tuality connected to an act that is performed, as it were, as part of a show of piety. In fact, the Koran reserves its strongest reprimands for those whose actions are underpinned not by a love for God and a desire to obey him, but for personal gain.

The *hajj*, like congregational prayer, is a highly public event, and the honorific title of *hāji*, which those who have completed the *hajj* confer upon themselves, instantly indicates fulfilment of one of the most important obligations in the Islamic canon. Opportu-nities for self-aggrandisement exist at every turn where the fulfil-ment of religious commands is concerned, and so it would be churlish to think that everyone who attends the *hajj* does so with intentions that are wholly free from self-interest. In this respect, Muslim scholars have traditionally prescribed caution. They say that a sincere believer who performs the *hajj* will return from his pilgrimage like a newborn child, with all his sins forgiven, but that one who attends the *hajj* with ulterior motives is likely to return with worse character than before.

Ulterior motives are numerous, and may range from the see-mingly innocuous – to preserve family honour, for example – to the nefarious: Mecca, it would seem, is at times of pilgrimage a haven for petty thieves, and many are those pilgrims who fall foul of pickpockets, scam-merchants and confidence tricksters during their short stay in Mecca and its environs. Places of pilgrimage the world over are renowned for having as much chaff as they do wheat. Mecca is no different. Some say that it is the inhospitable nature of this parched desert city, together with the hardships involved in travelling there, that add to the sacredness of the experience. After all, a treasure, they say, is often guarded by poisonous snakes and scorpions: to reach the treasure, one must be prepared to make sacrifices.

The pilgrimage to Mecca today may not be as arduous as it was before the advent of the motor car or the aeroplane, and when facilities to house pilgrims during the two-week event were so basic as to be non-existent. However, pitfalls for the unwary still exist – and not just in the form of petty criminals on the make. One returning pilgrim described Mecca as 'a huge shopping mall with minarets', and decried the fact that most of his fellow pilgrims seemed more focused on buying cheap electrical goods and designer clothes than on the significance and inner meaning of the rituals. The large yellow M sign, situated several hundred metres from the holy precinct, confirms the general 'McDonaldisation' of the *hajj* experience, as it jostles with billboards advertising Pepsi-Cola and Toshiba. While facilities to house the pilgrims have improved in recent years, there is still a huge disparity between rich and poor. The fact, of course, that both Mecca and Medina – Islam's most sacred sites – lie within the oil-rich kingdom of Saudi Arabia, home to a royal family renowned for consumption so conspicuous that it beggars belief, is also, for some at least, a serious downside to the *hajj* experience. Arguments that Mecca should be released from the grip of the Saudi kingdom and given its own Vatican-like autonomy are often forwarded, but have so far come to nothing. After all, does it really matter who is officially responsible – in the political sense – for the *hajj*? Surely it is the intention of the pilgrim that is important, rather than the pilgrimage itself? And so long as the intention is fuelled by a desire for spiritual growth, the negative aspects of the Meccan experience would appear to matter little, if at all.

But what is the spiritual meaning of the *hajj* for a Muslim? The pilgrimage to Mecca means different things to different people and one tends to get out only as much as one puts in, particularly as far as intention is concerned. Nevertheless in one very important way, the *hajj* is the same as all other religious pilgrimages the world over: it is a journey undertaken in quest of a place or a state that the pilgrim believes to embody an ideal. The journey to Mecca is both physical and metaphorical: physical in the sense that one moves through time and space, leaving one's homeland behind; and metaphorical in the sense that one moves upwards, hopefully, in an ascension towards God, leaving one's self behind.

Whatever his or her starting point is, a Muslim's journey to Mecca is by definition a homeward one: it is, even if one has never been there before, a 'return', just as Muhammad returned there victoriously after his self-imposed exile in Medina. To return is to re-turn, to 'turn again': just as a Muslim turns towards Mecca five times a day wherever in the world he may be, once during his life he gets to turn again, but this time to the very hub of his spiritual world, the 'house' of God Himself. And thousands of miles they flock to circle this 'house', only to find it empty! The *ka'ba* is a six-sided figure encompassing empty space, just as the six directions – north, south, east, west, up and down – point to everything and yet point to nothing. The emptiness of the *ka'ba* symbolises the fact, reiterated time and time again, that God is not like His creation; indeed, there is 'nothing like unto Him'. The attributes of God cannot be imagined; He cannot be limited to a 'house' or confined within a space, however sacred.

The rites of *hajj* contain other potent symbols which remind the Muslim believer of his or her relationship with God, and the fact that one day, all things will be returned to Him. The physical journey from one's homeland is a reminder that one must eventually leave this world forever; the donning of the shroud-like *ihrām* acts as a reminder not only that all men are equal in their nothingness before God, but that man will be dressed in a shroud when he is dead, and will meet his Maker shorn of the ability to dissemble behind clothing and status. The vast crowds camped out on the plain of Arafat, and under the clear desert sky at Muzdalifa, bring into mental view the tumult of the Resurrection, when all will be gathered together for judgement.

Arguably the most potent symbol, however, is the rite which takes place at the very end of the *hajj*: the sacrifice of a sheep, to commemorate the trial of Abraham. Abraham had been commanded to sacrifice his son and, after much agonising and many 'dark nights of the soul', was on the verge of doing so when God commanded him to untie the boy from the sacrificial altar and slaughter a sheep instead. The story of Abraham – the founder of the *ka'ba* – permeates the whole of the *hajj* experience. For Abraham's story is a story of submission – and it is submission which is at the heart of Islam. Indeed, 'submission' is the literal meaning of the word *islām*.

WHY FIVE PILLARS?

Why are there *five* pillars in Islam? Why not six, or ten, or twenty-five? More importantly, why are there any pillars at all? This is a question posed more often than not by those who consider themselves believers and/or Muslims, but who perform none of the external acts of worship known as the 'pillars of Islam'.

To a certain extent, such objections are not without justification. As the Koran points out in no uncertain terms, it is not God that stands in need of worship, but man himself: if man has been asked to fast and pray, it is because such acts are necessary in some way for man, not for God, who – according to the Koran – is exalted far above the need for His creatures' worship.

In what sense, then, are the acts of worship represented by the 'five pillars' necessary for man himself? First, as actual physical acts, they are probably of little intrinsic value, although many Muslims will attest to the health benefits to be had from fasting, for example, or the economic benefits that accrue from a well-executed system of *zakāh*. It goes without saying, however, that the material benefits of such acts matter even less in the Koranic scheme of things: what is important is that 'deeds of righteousness' follow on naturally as just one of the many external manifestations of belief. It is belief in God that should fuel one's desire to pray and fast, rather than mere habit or, worse still, the desire for any material benefit that such acts might bring.

Necessity, then, is an issue not of material benefit but of psychological and spiritual need. However, one should not think that prayers, fasts, the payment of alms and the pilgrimage to Mecca are ends in themselves, for they are not. From the verses of the Koran it becomes clear that the five pillars of Islam are simply means to an end. In the Koranic view, the external acts of worship such as the obligatory five-times-a-day prayer, or the fast of Ramadan, are in a sense mnemonic devices: they embody actions, behaviours and ritual performances which are designed to bring about remembrance, to remind man – who, according to the Koran, was created to be inherently forgetful – of the true state to which he is always expected to aspire: a state of peace based on the knowledge, love and worship of God, and submission to the Divine will in all things and at all times.

THE FIVE PILLARS AS EMBLEMS

In this sense, one can look at the pillars primarily as emblems. The canonical prayer, for instance, is emblematic of the prayerful attitude that a Muslim believer is expected to cultivate at all times and in all situations. To bow before God at least five times a day acts as a reminder that one should avoid bowing before others at all times; to prostrate oneself before God at least five times a day is seen as a symbol of the submissiveness to the Divine will that one is encouraged to bring to all areas of one's life beyond the prayer mat, and so on.

Similarly, fasting, alms and pilgrimage can be seen as emblems which point to deeper truths and realities than is at first evident from the actual acts themselves: fasting, for example, can be seen as a reminder that man is dependent on God for all things at all times, while the payment of alms may serve to remind man that he cannot dispose of what he appears to own in the way that he wishes, and that he is responsible at all times not only to God but to those less fortunate than himself.

With regard to the symbolic nature of the pillars of Islam, there are as many interpretations as there are Muslim scholars and thinkers to interpret them. The bottom line, however, is that the pillars of Islam function like the pillars of a building: they uphold it and, as such, are a means to an end: they are not the building itself, but without them, the building would cease to exist.

OTHER ISLAMIC PRACTICES

The five 'pillars of Islam' embody the practical expressions of submission made incumbent by the Koran. However, they do ·not represent the only rites, rituals and behaviours expected of the Muslim believer. As we shall see in the rest of this chapter, there are few areas of life which are not regulated in some way by what are perceived by Muslims to be the laws of God.

While the 'five pillars' are concerned largely with man's relationship with the Creator, there is a huge body of laws which cover man's relationship with his fellow men. Some of these laws are derived directly or indirectly from Koranic commands; others are based on the *sunna* or practice of the Prophet. Put simply, there are two basic categories of 'law': commands which cover acts of worship, or *ibādāt*; and commands which cover interpersonal and social relations, or *mu'āmalāt* (lit. 'transactions').

The *ibādāt* laws cover all outward expressions of worship, such as prayer, fasting, pilgrimage and the like, while the *mu'āmalāt* laws cover things such as marriage, inheritance, divorce, commercial contracts and the like. Muslim jurists in the second and third *hijri* centuries separated all acts, be they *ibādāt* or *mu'āmalāt* into five categories or legal values, as follows:

The *obligatory* acts, known in Arabic as *fard* or *wājib*. Readily recognisable examples of the obligatory are those outward expressions of submission commanded explicitly by God in the Koran, such as the ritual prayer or the fast of Ramadan. As we have seen, all of the so-called 'pillars of Islam' are obligatory acts, although they are by no means the only ones.

The direct opposite of the obligatory act is the *forbidden*, known in Arabic as *harām*. This category covers everything prohibited explicitly by God in the Koran, such as the consumption of alcohol and pork, the spilling of innocent blood or adultery, and so on. Only those things forbidden explicitly by God in the Koran are *harām*, and a Koranic verse warns man clearly not to prohibit that which God has allowed. Contrary to popular opinion, there are relatively few forbidden acts in Islam, particularly when compared, say, with the long lists of the forbidden that one finds in the Old Testament.

Between these two extremes, there are three other classifications. A *mustahabb* (lit. 'preferred') act is one that is *recommended*: it is not obligatory, but to perform it is better than not to perform it. For example, after the canonical *salāt*, it is *mustahabb* to perform a certain number of units of non-canonical *salāt*; however, while one will presumably be rewarded for this extra show of obedience, one will not be reprimanded if one leaves it out. The most important *mustahabb* act is male circumcision. This is not prescribed explicitly by the Koran, and so technically is not obligatory. It is, however, accorded great significance as an Abrahamaic legacy that all prophets have followed, and most Muslims consider it indispensable. Female circumcision, on the other hand, has no sanction in Islam.

Other *mustahabb* acts, of which there are possibly thousands, include paying visits to friends and neighbours; keeping one's room tidy; performing the supererogatory night prayer; buying souvenirs for one's family when on a journey, and so on. Indeed, everything that the Prophet ever did over and above what was strictly *fard* or obligatory is considered by Muslim jurists to be *mustahabb* or recommended, which is why many Muslims endeavour to emulate the Prophet's practice or *sunna* in all that they do. Thus they try to eat as he ate, to sleep as he slept, and even to perform ablutions or to ease the call of nature as he did.

Then there is, the classification known as *makrūh* or *discouraged*. This covers those acts which have not been forbidden, but which, according to interpreters of the *sunna*, are best avoided. Examples of *makrūh* acts include sleeping after the sun has risen, urinating in stagnant water, eating food while in a state of ritual impurity, and many hundreds – if not thousands – more. In short, anything discouraged by the Prophet is deemed *makrūh*, although no punishment is prescribed for those who commit such acts.

The final classification is known as *mubāh* or *permitted*. This is the largest category, for it includes all acts in man's personal or social life that have not been forbidden expressly by God. In other words, so long as something is not *harām*, it is permitted. Examples of *mubāh* acts are innumerable in everyday life. For instance, one may choose to live and work where one pleases, and to marry whom one likes. One may choose to study or to work in whichever area one desires. A society may choose the political system it thinks best, and apply the socio-legal regulations it feels work most efficiently. In fact, so long as it has not been forbidden explicitly, any act that a Muslim believer does is, depending on his or her sincere intention, considered both 'Islamic' and sacred, whether it be praying, eating, making love or using the lavatory. In Islam, everything is allowed – so long as it has not been forbidden by Koranic dictate.

Living in accordance with what they perceive to be Islamic law means that Muslim believers will endeavour to regulate their lives in a way that accommodates their understanding of the fivefold categories outlined above. Some endeavour to carry out not only all of those acts deemed obligatory, but also as many as possible of the recommended acts as well, while avoiding the forbidden absolutely and abstaining from the discouraged as far as is humanly possible. Others carry out the obligatory and avoid the forbidden, but do not pay much attention to the recommended or the discouraged. Again, what is important is the intention involved, and the fact that God judges not the act but the sincerity with which it is carried out.

THE REGULATION OF SOCIAL LIFE

The category of *mu'āmalāt* or 'transaction' laws is the one to which we must turn if we are to understand many of the regulations covering social life in the Muslim experience. Immediately recognisable areas in which such laws operate are those related to family matters, such as marriage, divorce, inheritance and the rights of children. To enter into a lengthy discussion on these issues is beyond the scope of a work such as this, and the reader will be guided to further reading at the end of the chapter. Furthermore, there are quite often differences of opinion on many aspects of these laws between different Muslim jurists, depending on the school of jurisprudence to which they are affiliated.

Non-Muslim readers of this book will recognise some of the regulations regarding Muslim family and social life from their own acquaintance with Muslim friends or colleagues, or possibly from the media. However, what one sees on television or reads in newspapers – and even in some of the less discerning textbooks – does not often square with reality. Issues such as polygamy and the rights of women, for example, are controversial at the best of times, but doubly so when marred by an abject ignorance of the facts on the part of those who debate them. Let us look at a few examples.

POLYGAMY

Polygamy was not abolished outright by the Koran; instead, a man would be allowed to take more than one wife only if he could guarantee to treat his wives with complete fairness. The idea was that by making it difficult in theory for a man to take more than one wife, in practice the institution would die a natural death. The same is true of slavery, which was not outlawed directly, but which was discouraged to the extent that it would later atrophy and disappear naturally.

What Islamic law obviously does not regulate or codify is the large number of moral and ethical precepts which appear in the Koran, such as injunctions to treat one's parents honourably, or to avoid greed and waste – propositions which, it may be argued, are all obligatory, but which, since they are not readily quantifiable, fall outside the scope of formal jurisprudence. As such, these acts are matters which are connected to the level of one's belief and the state of one's personal conscience – none of which is measurable in the sense that external acts such as prayer or fasting can be measured. And as we have seen on several occasions, it is not the external act that is important, but the intention that underpins it.

MARRIAGE

Marriage in Islam is a civil contract concluded between two adults, who must marry in front of two witnesses. The marriage ceremony is simple and there need be no third party to officiate, although traditionally there is usually a notary to record the event. Historically, marriage has been treated by Muslims more as a union of two families than a union of individuals, and arranged marriages have been – and still are – *de rigueur* in many parts of the Muslim world.

However, the reality of the matter is that neither a man nor a woman can be forced into marriage: the Koran states explicitly that there can be 'no compulsion' in any matters such as these. Men and women are free to marry whomever they wish – so long, of course, they do not contravene the prohibitions which prevent couples enjoying certain degrees of blood relationship from marrying:

> Prohibited to you [For marriage] are: – Your mothers, daughters, sisters; father's sisters, mother's sisters; brother's daughters, sister's daughters; foster-mothers [Who gave you suck], foster-sisters; your wives' mothers; your step-daughters under your guardianship, born of

your wives to whom ye have gone in, – no prohibition if ye have not gone in; – [Those who have been] wives of your sons proceeding from your loins; and two sisters in wedlock at one and the same time, except for what is past; for God is Oft-forgiving, Most Merciful.

(4:23)

Man and wife are equal partners before God in a Muslim marriage, and Muslim wives retain their own surnames as a sign of individuality. A dowry is paid to the bride directly by her husband, and this becomes her personal property, to which the man has absolutely no right. In all financial matters, man and wife are treated as individuals, each with rights over his or her own property. While Muslim societies have often been characterised by the tendency of some males to treat women in general, and their wives in particular, as their own private property, nowhere in the Koran is such an attitude encouraged.

DIVORCE

Divorce is allowed in Islam, but only as a very last resort. Contrary to popular opinion, women are as free to initiate divorce proceedings as men, and may insert clauses in their marriage contracts to guarantee the right to divorce in the future should certain circumstances obtain. In theory, pre-nuptial agreements in Muslim society predated their Western counterparts by several centuries.

INHERITANCE

According to the Koran, two thirds of one's estate is to be reserved for inheritance; the other third is put aside for debts and bequests. Originally, an estate was divided up in accordance with the perceived needs of the deceased's inheritors, with sons being granted double the amount left to daughters – presumably on the grounds that daughters would later marry and be provided for by their husbands. While such inheritance laws may still apply, there is nothing to prevent Muslim jurists from using discretion in cases where, for example, the daughter or daughters of the deceased can be shown to be as financially deserving as her brothers. In those circumstances, estates can be – and often are – divided equally among close kin. The full list of those entitled to inherit can be found in the Koran (4:7–11).

MODEST ATTIRE: AN ISLAMIC 'DRESS LAW'?

Much controversy exists, both in and outside of the Muslim world, over the issue of modest dress in Islam. The Koran discusses the issue briefly, advising both men and women to behave with decorum towards each other. Part of this decorum is expressed as 'lowering the gaze' – averting one's eyes – physically and metaphorically – from anything that might lead one astray and open the road to wrongdoing, fornication in particular. The Koran goes one step further by asking women not to expose those parts of their bodies which may incite desire in others, such as the breasts: apparently, pre-Islamic Arab women were wont to uncover their breasts when out and about, contributing no doubt to the rather laissez-faire approach to sexual relations which existed before the advent of the Koran. The verse at the heart of the controversy is:

> And say to the believing women that they should lower their gaze and guard their modesty; that they should not display their beauty and ornaments except what [must ordinarily] appear thereof; that they should draw their veils over their bosoms and not display their beauty except to their husbands, their fathers, their husband's fathers, their sons, their husbands' sons, their brothers or their brothers' sons, or their sisters' sons, or their women, or the slaves whom their right hands possess, or male servants free of physical needs, or small children who have no sense of the shame of sex; and that they should not strike their feet in order to draw attention to their hidden ornaments. And O ye Believers! turn ye all together towards God, that ye may attain Bliss.
>
> (24:31)

The word translated as 'veil' in the above verse denotes in fact any kind of covering that can be drawn over the breasts to keep them covered. Some commentators have extrapolated from this to include the hair as something which must remain covered, which is why many Muslim females opt for either an all-embracing veil, or a combination of scarf and loose-fitting clothes, leaving only the face and hands exposed.

There is no explicit command in the Koran for women to cover their hair, although many do on account of the ambiguity of the word 'veil', and the caution advised by generation after generation of Muslim jurists. In even stricter milieus, such as Saudi Arabia where the ultra-conservative Wahhabi denomination holds sway, women appear in public clad not only in veils but also in mask-like face veils, which expose only the eyes to the outside world. Such women are free, of course, to dress like this if they wish, but will not find any justification for it in the Koran.

WOMEN'S RIGHTS IN GENERAL

A mix of patriarchy, cultural tradition and conservative exegesis of the Koran have, in certain parts of the Muslim world, tended to work to the detriment of women, who have traditionally been unable in practice to take advantage of the equal rights which the Koran in theory accords them. Men and women are different, yet equal, and enjoy the same existential status before God. In the egalitarian ethos of the Koran and, surprisingly enough, in the early community-state of Medina, women were basically given all of the rights enjoyed by men, with few if any exceptions. And where there were exceptions, these were dictated purely by context rather than by theory. If, for example, the Koran talks about women being dependent on men financially, it is in those cases where the man works and the woman stays at home. According to modern exegetes, such provisions are contextual rather than normative: when women work, they are no longer dependent on their men for support, and when a woman works but her husband does not, the shoe goes onto the other foot and the woman may become responsible for the man. There is an inherent flexibility in Muslim jurisprudence which allows verses to be re-examined and re-interpreted in the light of changing circumstances: verses which deal with polygamy and slavery, and the sole verse which appears to disfavour women, are among them.

FURTHER READING

Most of the general introductory books on Islam contain sections on the question of orthopraxy and the 'pillars of Islam'. Neal

Robinson's aforementioned *Islam: A Concise Introduction* has some very insightful chapters on prayer, fasting, pilgrimage and alms, while Imam Ghazali's *Inner Dimensions of Islamic Worship* (The Islamic Foundation, 1983), an eleventh-century treatise on the spiritual realities which lie at the heart of Islamic practice, provides a fascinating Muslim perspective on the 'five pillars'.

5

SPIRITUALITY

IN SEARCH OF 'ISLAMIC SPIRITUALITY'

A Muslim sage once recounted how a young man once approached him joyfully, saying: 'Thank God that I have come to believe in Islam, for I feel that I have finally come home.' The sage said nothing but merely smiled. 'I didn't have the heart to tell the young man that to accept Islam is indeed to "arrive", but it is to arrive at a temporary stopping-place, not one's final destination.'

The cryptic response of the Muslim sage reveals, when deconstructed, the existence in the Islamic tradition of a whole world of meaning beyond the formal profession of belief in God and external submission to God's laws. The creation of human beings took place not merely that they should affirm the existence of a Creator and bow down to His laws through various rites and rituals: God is not merely a principle that is to be accepted, or a giver of laws who is to be obeyed. While the God of the Koran is infinite, absolute, theoretically unfathomable and ultimately unreachable in the very real sense of those terms, He can be understood through His creation and, more importantly, His reality can be gradually 'uncovered' by man, who is able to approach God and become ever more aware of what He is simply by virtue of the fact that he is created *in imago Dei*, or in the image of God. In the cosmology of the Koran, man is the reflection whose purpose in life is to perceive and understand the Reflected.

Islamic spirituality is not about becoming more God-like. In fact it is the very reverse. It is about realising that those attributes in man which appear to make him like a God belong in reality to another. The journey of man towards God, then, is not about becoming more like Him. It is about 'purifying' oneself of all possible claims to 'Godlikeness' and making room for Him to reveal Himself through us. It means not acting like Him, but acting in His name; it involves not being like Him, but manifesting or revealing Him. For that to happen, one has to clear out the 'clutter of the self' – the imaginary ownership we exercise over our own attributes – so that His 'image' may be reflected in the mirror of the soul.

In the Koranic worldview, God is the Ground of all being, the One who created man to be His 'vicegerent' or representative on earth, in order that man should know, love and worship Him. And in order to know God, man must first solve the mystery of his own existence. For, according to the Prophetic Tradition:

Whoever knows his own self, knows his Lord.

The chief objective of man's life on earth, according to the Koran, is to 'journey' towards the knowledge, love and worship of God through a continuous process of affirmation and submission, as outlined in the previous chapter. The objective of the journey towards God is to move ever onwards towards communion with Him as the Ground of all being, in Whom we are all reflected, and Whom we all reflect. In order to do that, man must strive for something described as 'God-awareness'. It entails reading and interpreting the myriad 'signs' which exist in one's own self, and in the cosmos around us, and which indicate the countless names and attributes of God, so that knowledge, love and worship of God may be nurtured. God is infinite and absolute, and so the truths concerning Him to which these 'signs' point are literally without number: an endless objective entails a potentially endless quest, one in which man must journey onwards without ceasing, rather than risk moving backwards and away from the ultimate destination.

The quest to 'know' God has at its heart the quest to 'know' oneself, for as we shall see shortly, at the heart of Islamic spirituality lies the principle of 'purification of the soul'. While this may connote notions of harsh personal penances, privations and mortification, it involves nothing of the sort, although it has to be said that the 'spiritual journey' to God as envisaged by the Islamic tradition is not an easy one; nor is it something that all believing Muslims can embrace. Nevertheless, it is open to anyone who wishes to transcend the purely material aspect of his or her creation and discover in reality Who he or she really is.

The idea of 'purification of the soul' which lies at the heart of Islamic spirituality entails the gradual surrender of all human claims to sovereignty, and to realise that it is God and not man who is the real Centre of the human universe. It involves the realisation that all that we appear to be, have and own come from an Other; and that all of the attributes of perfection – knowledge, beauty, wisdom, power and so on – that we believe make up our human selves belong in reality to Him, and must be 'surrendered' while we are here on earth. To invoke the Biblical phrase, the journey involves the gradual realisation that the 'kingdom of God' is within us, and that to know who He is, it is necessary to know who and what we are. More precisely, it is by knowing what we are *not*, that we come to know what He *is*.

THE HIDDEN FACE OF ISLAM?

There are some for whom the very existence of a facet of Islam describable as 'spirituality' comes as rather a surprise, given the religion's hard-edged profile as an ideology and 'way of life' that appears to be more about the Islamic state than the Islamic state of mind. 'Islam has no gentleness, no compassion, no *spirituality*', a Christian student once remarked to one of my Muslim colleagues. 'Where is the Islamic equivalent of the Sermon on the Mount, or the "turning of the other cheek"?' My Muslim colleague looked nonplussed at first, but within minutes had quoted several verses in the Koran where unconditional forgiveness is encouraged, and had located at least two substantial passages that are similar in tone and tenor to Christ's famous sermon. 'However,' he said, 'I'm not quite sure what any of this has to do with the existence or absence of

Islamic spirituality.' The student's response was immediate. 'It has everything to do with spirituality,' she said. 'You have just proved that the Koran *does* talk about forgiveness and compassion, and all of the things preached by Jesus. But no-one ever hears about this side of Islam: the only things that Muslims seem to care about are law and politics. If Islam had a developed spiritual side, surely things such as forgiveness and compassion would be emphasised: those values are, after all, the product of spiritual awareness.'

The average Western reader may be unaware of the inner dimensions of the Islamic revelation, but even a cursory study of the Koran will reveal that it addresses, first and foremost, the question of man's relationship with his Creator, and how the human soul and spirit within must respond to the questions that such a relationship poses. If, by spirituality, one means the attempt to commune with God directly, the Islamic tradition is as rich as any other; one only has to look. And we intend to do exactly that.

For a glimpse of the 'spiritual' face of Islam, traditionally it is to Sufism that people have looked. Sufism, like Islam, is also notoriously difficult to pin down and define, although we have no option but to attempt this if we are to understand anything at all about one of the most pervasive channels through which the realities of Islamic spirituality have been communicated. So in our search for Islamic spirituality we shall look first at Sufism.

We shall then look at a contemporary non-Sufi Islamic movement which, in total contradistinction to all other Islamic movements, sees a return to the spirituality inherent in belief in God as the Muslim's only hope of redemption: unlike other contemporary expressions of Islam, it is concerned not so much with an Islamic *state* as an Islamic *state of mind*. I understand it to be primarily a spiritual movement, and one which is gaining tremendous support throughout the Muslim world, particularly in Turkey and Central Asia.

Finally, we shall take a glimpse at something that is neither movement nor school of thought, but rather an expression of spirituality that transcends all considerations of religious or denominational difference, and that is the practice of invocation or *du'ā* – 'calling on the names of God' – which we in the Western world often term 'prayer' or 'talking to God'. The practice of *du'ā*, particularly in the sense of communing with God by invoking His 'most beautiful Names', is one that the Muslims – Shi'ites in particular – have elevated to something of an art form.

SUFISM

Sufism, like Islam, is difficult to pin down. Sufism is sometimes translated as 'Islamic mysticism', but this description is rather vague. The word 'mysticism' is problematic, and few words in the English language have been used as loosely and as meaninglessly. Sometimes it is used as an equivalent for the inner truths which hide beneath the surface of religion, or the 'esoteric' – another term that is misunderstood and, as a consequence, much maligned. Sometimes, mysticism is used to describe the occult or the quasi-magical quackery of New Age philosophy or new religious movements. And sometimes, 'mysticism' is used to describe the 'sense of the mysterious' felt by those who claim some kind of 'spirituality' but who are unable to identify it as pertaining to any religion in particular. Sufism has little, if anything, to do with these. Consider four classical definitions, given by Sufis themselves:

> Sufism is being with God, without any attachments.
>
> (Junayd)

> Sufism consists of abandoning oneself to God in accordance with God's will.
>
> (Ruwaym b. Ahmad)

> Sufism is about not possessing anything, nor letting anything possess you.
>
> (Samnun)

> Sufism means attaining every exalted quality and leaving behind every despicable quality.
>
> (Abu Muhammad al-Jariri)

Almost as perplexing as its definition is its origins. No-one really knows where it came from, or how it came about. Some claim that Sufism was a natural follow-on from hanifism – the pre-Islamic monotheism of desert hermits in Arabia; others believe that it postdates

Islam, arising as a response to the stuffy and rather legalistic religion of the orthodox jurists. Others claim that Sufism is simply the Islamic strand of *sophia perennis* – the eternal wisdom which underpins all religions. Its etymology is equally unclear, although it is possible that Sufism took its name from the coarse woollen material, known in Arabic as *suf*, that was worn by its adherents.

EARLY SUFISM

Early Sufism, arising in the eighth and ninth centuries, may be described as a natural 'interiorisation' of Islam. It was in a sense an attempt to commune with God directly, and to pursue the spirit, rather than just the letter, of the law. The early Sufi should be seen as one who recognised that true knowledge is knowledge or gnosis of God, which in turn can be reached only through the acquisition of self-knowledge: the realisation of what man *is not*, in order to attain knowledge of what God *is*. In this sense, the emphasis for the Sufi was on belief (*imān*) and internal submission rather than on the external religion of Islam. As such, it was in the early Sufi that Koranic spirituality found its particular embodiment and expression. External religion – the performance of rite and ritual – was not eschewed, however. In fact, one of the most salient features of early Sufi teaching was its emphasis on the importance of ritual practice and adherence to the *shari'a*, the channel through which the *external* expression of Islam is made manifest. Early Sufism, then, preserved the harmony that is supposed to exist between the internal and external aspects of the faith.

The designation 'early Sufism' is an important one, for with the passing of time the phenomenon underwent many changes: from being a term used simply to describe an individual's sincere and private spiritual quest, and the techniques employed to facilitate the journey, Sufism became a blanket expression which came to cover many different forms of organised 'ways' and 'paths' to the truth.

The gradual institutionalisation of Sufism took place in three distinct stages: from the stage of the individual's personal submission to God, through the stage of communal surrender to the dictates of an 'Order' or *tariqa*, and finally to the stage of surrender to a person – a sheikh or guru – in what is known as the *ta'ifa* stage.

THE SUFI 'ORDER' OR *TARIQA*

The word *tariqa*, literally meaning 'way' or 'path', symbolises the spiritual journey towards God, and is used to describe the grouping of a number of disciples (*murids*) around a leader or *shaykh*, to whom they pledge allegiance as their spiritual guide. The *shaykh* is generally considered to be the spiritual heir of the founder of the Order, who in turn is believed to have inherited his authority from other saints, sages and mystics before him, in a line or 'chain' (*silsila*) of spiritual authority stretching back to the Prophet Muhammad. Each Order thus has its own spiritual lineage, which each individual is able to trace back through his Order's founder to the founder of Islam himself. The fact that most of these 'chains' have Ali b. Abi Talib as the link which connects them to the Prophet has led a number of writers to misidentify Shi'ism as the ultimate source of Sufi wisdom. That Ali b. Abi Talib is a crucial component in the spiritual makeup of both Shi'ism and Sufism is undeniable, but hardly proof that one is responsible for the other. Indeed, historically speaking, Sufism has been a largely Sunni phenomenon; while Sufi Orders identifiable as being Shi'ite in outlook have existed, these were the exception and not the rule.

In the gradual institutionalisation of Sufism lay the seeds of its decay. With time, the once spontaneous spirituality of the individual became subordinated to conformity and group experience. With the rise of the *shaykh* as spiritual guide, individuality often gave way to blind imitation, and the transformation of sincere disciples into spiritual slaves. The spread of the Sufi Orders across the Muslim world, especially during the thirteenth and fourteenth centuries, and the interaction of diverse cultural and religious traditions, meant that innovative practices began to creep in, working at variance with the original aims of Sufism and creating sects and factions that were totally removed from the pristine spirituality of the early adepts.

It is for this reason that from the early medieval period onwards we are able to talk in terms of the parallel development of two types of Sufism. The first is mainstream or 'high' Sufism. This was the form of Sufi belief and practice that remained more or less faithful to the ideals of the early Sufis, and before them the *hanifs*. It was typified by highly orthodox Sunni orders such as the Mawlawiyya, centred in Anatolia, and the Naqshbandiyya, centred in Transoxania. The second type of Sufism to emerge was 'folk' Sufism, present in orders such s the Bektashiyya and the Hurufiyya, whose rituals and practices were highly questionable, not only in the eyes of the orthodox Muslim jurists who saw all forms of Sufism as suspect, but also in the view of the 'high' Sufi adepts themselves.

FOLK SUFISM

'Folk Sufism' owes little if anything to the wisdom of the early Sufis or the leaders of the 'high' Sufi Orders, and even less to the spiritual teachings of the Koran. Its origins are obscure, but it evolved on the geographical fringes of the Muslim world, amongst the largely nomadic Muslims in remote rural areas where the teachings of Islam were conflated with a variety of beliefs and practices taken from Hinduism, Buddhism, gnostic Christianity and shamanism. The progenitors of 'folk Sufism', as well as other 'heterodox' forms of religious beliefs and practices, later came to be known as *ghulāt* or 'extremists'. These were individuals who were nominally Muslim, but who subscribed to doctrines deemed heretical enough to place them outside the pale of Islam. Beliefs such as *tashbīh* (anthropomorphism with respect to God), *tanāsukh* (the transmigration of souls) and *hulūl* (Divine incarnation in man) were prevalent among the early *ghulāt* and later became part and parcel of 'folk Sufism', although doctrines and practices differed greatly from region to region. Today, the *ghulāt* no longer have a discernible profile in the Muslim world, and the term 'folk Sufism' is most often applied to the practices of those largely uneducated Muslims for whom the ritual visiting of important Sufi shrines is an important part of their spiritual life.

SUFISM IN THE MEDIEVAL MUSLIM WORLD

Sufism had existed throughout the Muslim world from the earliest times, and the prevalence and popularity of Sufi adepts in all of the major urban centres is reflected in the histories of the period. The renowned Muslim chronicler al-Maqdisi, describing the Persian city of Shiraz towards the end of the tenth century, tells us that:

Sufis were numerous, commemorating God in their mosques after the Friday prayer and reciting blessings on the Prophet from the pulpit.

Several hundred years later, and especially during the thirteenth and fourteenth centuries, Sufis were still numerous, only now they had become institutionalised into 'Orders' and were spread out across the central lands of the Muslim world. With the proliferation of Sufi Orders came fragmentation, and the growth of a whole host of offshoot groupings and sub-sects, all flourishing openly and commanding the spiritual allegiance of vast numbers of people, educated and uneducated alike. Indeed, to see Sufism as some kind of exotic mysticism confined to a few ecstatic Sufis who found themselves at cross-purposes with the religious 'orthodoxy' is, in fact, to parody what was, for many, their only identifiable link to Islam. It is also to ignore just how commonplace the various manifestations of Sufism were in traditional Muslim society. Very often, tens of thousands of individuals were affiliated in some way or other to an Order in any one of the great cities, and the main Orders were prevalent throughout the whole of the Muslim world.

In the context of the medieval Muslim world at least, while Sufism was a different approach to Islam, and thus to an extent in 'competition' with others, it was by no means peripheral or divorced from 'mainstream' or 'orthodox' religion. Indeed, with the emergence of Sufi Orders in the early medieval period, Sufism was central to Islam and an integral component of the spiritual make-up of many, if not all, Muslim communities and societies, operating in its various forms and guises throughout all levels of society.

SUFI BELIEFS AND PRACTICES

Given the vast range of beliefs and practices included under the definitional 'umbrella' of Sufism, to encapsulate them in a few paragraphs and present them as the definitive outline of Sufi doctrine and ritual is clearly an impossible task. What follows is a tentative overview of those beliefs and practices that are most readily identifiable as Sufi in origin or nature, and which are common to most of the mainstream Orders.

At the heart of Sufi ritual is the practice of *dhikr*, which is the methodical repetition of the names of God. This can be done in virtual silence or aloud, as a chant; it is sometimes done in private, sometimes in public. The word *dhikr* comes from the Arabic verb 'to mention', and it is believed that by 'mentioning' God's 'beautiful Names' in a measured and meaningful way, one is helped in one's attempt to attain constant awareness of the Divine in all of its aspects.

As well as *dhikr*, Sufi ritual also includes the recitation of prayers, invocations, supplications, verses from the Koran and even poems; Sufism, particularly its Persianate variety, has produced a veritable wealth of poetry, including the works of the Iranian national poets, Saadi and Hafez, and arguably the master of all Sufi poetry, the redoubtable Jalal al-Din Rumi, whose *Mathnawi* is known in Iran as 'the Persian Koran'.

In communal gatherings, *dhikr* and other recitations are often accompanied by music, although this depends very much on the particular orientation of the Order involved. Each Order favours its own particular style and format of *dhikr* recitation, reflecting the technique established by the Order's founder. In this, as with all of its devotional exercises, each Order treads its own structurally unique spiritual path. As far as the use of music is concerned, some Orders readily embrace music while others prefer to chant or pray unaccompanied. Similarly, some Orders advocate a type of ritual performance known as *samā*, which involves highly stylised physical movements by its participants – hence the term 'whirling dervishes'.

SUFI BELIEFS

Insofar as Sufism represents an interiorisation of Islam, its beliefs are identical to the core beliefs emanating from the Koran. However, at the heart of the Sufi endeavour is the quest for the purification of the soul. This is articulated in the form of a journey that each individual must undertake, known usually as the 'path'.

THE SUFI DOCTRINE OF THE 'PATH'

By the ninth century, Sufi writers had begun to articulate their core beliefs in short treatises which focused on the spiritual 'path' or *tariqa* which one needed to follow in order to journey towards

God. Most of the early Sufi masters broke the 'path' down into 'stages' (*maqāmāt*), the number of which differed from teacher to teacher but all of which had the same goal: the abnegating of the 'evil-commanding soul' and communion with God. The archetypal Sufi, described as a traveller (*sālik*) on a journey, follows a path of seven stages: repentance; abstinence; renunciation; poverty; patience; trust in God; and complete submission to God's will. At the end of this path, the spiritual traveller attains, with God's grace, a higher level of awareness which enables him to see, through the 'eye of the heart', the fact that knowledge, the knower and the thing known are, in one respect, the same thing. While approaches and methods varied from Sufi to Sufi, the underlying message – namely that man was created in order to know himself and, in knowing himself, to know God – was the same. And, they claimed, it was only through the Sufi path that such knowledge was attainable.

Sufism still exists today, although many would argue that it is but a shadow of its classical self, denuded of its intellectual and emotional vibrancy and fragmented, for the most part, into myriad pseudo-Sufi groupings who pay lip service to the classical ideals yet function mostly as New Age movements with only the most tenuous of links to Islam proper.

However, the principle at the heart of classical Sufism, namely the purification of the self and the desire for communion with God, lives on, even in the teachings of those individuals who claim no formal affiliation to a Sufi *tariqa* or way of life as such. The next step in our search for Islamic spirituality is to meet one of those individuals and consider the ideas at the heart of his discourse – a discourse which has been described as a kind of Sufism for the twenty-first century.

SECRETS OF THE SOUL: THE ENIGMA OF THE HUMAN 'I'

The key to submission, then, lies in the purification of the self. But what is this 'self' that sages and saints in all spiritual traditions talk about so earnestly?

The Turkish scholar Saïd Nursi (1876–1960) is well known throughout the Muslim world for his Risale-i Nur or *Epistle of Light*, a 5,000-page collection of Koranic commentaries which amount to a compendium of the Divine sciences, covering theology, philosophy, the pillars of Islam and much else besides. Nursi's aim in writing the work was to reawaken the faith of a society in which the pull of atheistic materialism was a constant threat.

Among these commentaries was an exposition of the problems caused by man's abuse of his own 'self'. This exposition appears in a short work known as *The 'I' Treatise*. In it, he outlines the nature of that nebulous phenomenon which exists inside all human beings, and which enables us to identify ourselves as unique individuals, distinguishable from all the other unique individuals who make up the human race. To call this phenomenon the 'ego' or the 'self' would be misleading, given the Freudian connotations that such terms have. It is possible that Nursi, a contemporary of Freud, avoided using the word 'ego' for this very reason, knowing perfectly well that the 'ego', 'id' and 'superego' of the Freudian schema are considerably different to the concept of the 'I' in Islamic spirituality. To understand precisely what this 'I' is, and why an understanding of its nature and function is an indispensable prerequisite to the spiritual journey, let us look a little closer at Nursi's exposition.

THE DIVINE 'TRUST'

The ability of each human individual to talk about himself or herself as 'I', Nursi contends, was given to man as part of the Divine 'trust'.

> We did indeed offer the Trust to the Heavens and the Earth and the Mountains; but they refused to undertake it, being afraid thereof: but man undertook it – he was indeed unjust and foolish.
>
> (33:72)

A 'trust' is something that is given to an individual, and over which he has power of disposal: he is expected to use it in the manner prescribed by the giver of the trust, although he also has the power to go against the giver's wishes and dispose of the trust in any way that he likes. In the context of the Creator–creature relationship, what is this 'trust' that man agreed to take upon himself, after cosmic phenomena such as the heavens and the mountains had refused it? Nursi is not alone in defining the 'trust' as man's God-given ability to act as divine 'vicegerent'; in accepting the 'trust', man takes it upon himself to act as God's 'representative' on earth.

To understand exactly what 'representing' God entails, we have to look to those verses in the Koran which refer to the creation of humankind. Several passages discuss the drama of man's first appearance on the cosmic stage, but none is quite so succinct as the account given in verses 30 to 40 of the second *sūra*, *al-Baqara*.

> Behold, thy Lord said to the angels: 'I will create a vicegerent on earth.'

> They said: 'Wilt Thou place therein one who will make mischief therein and shed blood? – whilst we do celebrate Thy praises and glorify Thy holy [name]?' He said: 'I know what ye know not.'

> And He taught Adam the names of all things; then He placed them before the angels, and said: 'Tell me the names of these if ye are right.'

> They said: 'Glory to Thee, of knowledge We have none, save what Thou Hast taught us: In truth it is Thou Who art perfect in knowledge and wisdom.'

> He said: 'O Adam! Tell them their names.' When he had told them, God said: 'Did I not tell you that I know the secrets of heaven and earth, and I know what ye reveal and what ye conceal?'

> And behold, We said to the angels: 'Bow down to Adam.'

> (2:30–34)

The key which unlocks the meaning of this passage lies in the 'names' which God 'taught' to Adam, who as the 'first man' represents the totality of humankind. For Nursi, like other gnostic thinkers in the Muslim tradition, the names taught by God to man are none other than the 'beautiful names' of God Himself. In imparting knowledge of His names, not only does God teach man to recognise all of the divine attributes of perfection, but He also gives him the ability to display those attributes consciously and, in so doing, act as God's 'representative' on earth. In other words, man is able to recognise divine attributes of perfection such as power, wisdom, mercy, beauty and the like simply by virtue of the fact that he is, in one sense, created in God's image.

It is on account of man's potential to act as God's representative that the angels were asked to acknowledge man's creational status by 'bowing down' to him. In the cosmology of the Koran, angels are endowed with limited knowledge of God's names, and while they worship God with perfect sincerity and awareness, they do so because they lack the free will to disobey. Man, on the other hand, is endowed not only with knowledge of all of God's names, but also with free will: if man uses his knowledge of the names wisely and bows down to God of his own volition, he rises above the angels and fulfils his destiny as the jewel in the crown of creation. However, if he abuses his knowledge of the names and fails to fulfil his part of the 'trust', he sinks to a position described by the Koran as the 'lowest of the low'.

The 'trust', then, offers whoever accepts it the ability to know God and to 'experience' Him through His 'beautiful names' and attributes of perfection. But whoever accepts a 'trust' must also undertake the responsibility to dispose of what he is given in accordance with the wishes of the giver: should he discharge his responsibility successfully, he will reap the reward; should he fail, he must face the consequences. In the context of the trust offered by God, the responsibility is a momentous one, for what it actually means in practice is assuming the attributes of God and acting not only in His name, but in complete accordance with His will. It is only when we grasp the significance of the 'trust' and what it means in practice to accept such an undertaking that we can see why cosmic phenomena such as the heavens and the mountains – both symbols of might and grandeur – refused the challenge.

THE FUNCTION OF THE HUMAN 'I'

The 'I', then, is considered by Nursi to be part of the 'trust' given to man by God. The 'I', he goes on to say, is not only the means through which we are able to understand the 'names' of God, but it is also the 'key to the locked talisman of creation'. When we understand the meaning of 'I', Nursi assures us, the locked doors of creation will open and the riddle of cosmic existence will be solved. According to a famous Prophetic Tradition:

Whoever knows himself, knows his Lord.

The ability of the 'I' – the self – to know God stems from the fact that it contains within it what Nursi calls 'indications and samples' which reflect the attributes and functions of God. In this sense, the 'I' is like a unit of measurement which exists solely for the sake of revealing the existence and measure of something else. Like any other unit of measurement, the 'I' does not have a concrete material existence:

> It is not necessary for a unit of measurement to have actual existence. Rather, like hypothetical lines in geometry, a unit of measurement may be formed by hypothesis and supposition. It is not necessary for its actual existence to be established by concrete knowledge and proofs.
> (Bediuzzaman Saïd Nursi, *Man and the Universe*, Istanbul: Sozler Neshriyat, 1987, p. 22)

Whether the 'I' is part of the soul or the spirit, or whether it is a function of the conscience or the psyche, we do not know and possibly cannot tell. What is clear, however, is that the 'I' is an abstract entity whose sole function is to act as a kind of yardstick against which God's names can be 'measured'. Such a yardstick is necessary because, it would seem, in dealing with God we are dealing with a being who is absolute and all-encompassing. The very fact that something is absolute and all-encompassing, without shape or form, means that under normal circumstances it cannot be perceived. If the whole of the cosmos were coloured red, we would be unable to perceive it, simply because there would be nothing against which red might be compared and thus distinguished: if everything were red, we would not be able to perceive it as such. Nursi uses the example of endless light to elucidate his argument:

> For example, an endless light without darkness may not be known or perceived. But if a line of real or imaginary darkness is drawn, it [i.e. the light] then becomes known.
> (Bediuzzaman Saïd Nursi, *Man and the Universe*, Istanbul: Sozler Neshriyat, 1987, p. 22)

Light is discernible only because it exists in degrees. In other words, without the existence of darkness, light would remain imperceptible. Darkness is needed in order to reveal or render perceptible the existence of light. In that sense, it is, like the human 'I', a yardstick. And, like the human 'I', darkness has no concrete material existence. Darkness is simply an absence of light: in and of itself it does not exist.

The yardstick of the human 'I' is needed, then, because the attributes and names of God, such as knowledge, power, mercy, compassion and wisdom, are all-encompassing, limitless and without like. And since they are infinite and absolute, the attributes of perfection cannot be determined, and what they are cannot be perceived. In order to discern them, we have to impose on them an imaginary limit, like the line of darkness that is used to make known the light. This imaginary limit is placed on the Divine attributes of perfection by the human 'I'.

How the 'I' does this is perfectly simple: it imagines that it is the owner of its own self. In other words, it claims ownership over all of the attributes of perfection that it experiences as part of its own existence. The human self looks at the power, beauty, wisdom, compassion and knowledge within its own being and claims to be the owner of them all. As each human being develops, a sense of ownership is developed over the attributes it experiences in its own self. This ownership appears to be very real, but it is illusory, its function being simply to reveal or indicate the true Owner of the attribute. For at the outset, man gauges the attributes of God by comparing them with those he finds in himself:

> For example, with its imagined dominicality over what it owns, the 'I' may understand the dominicality of its Creator over contingent creation. And with its apparent ownership, it may understand the true ownership of its Creator, saying, 'Just as I am the owner of this house, so too is the Creator the owner of this creation.'
>
> (Bediuzzaman Saïd Nursi, *Man and the Universe*, Istanbul: Sozler Neshriyat, 1987, p.23)

Similarly, through his own knowledge, man may understand the knowledge of God; through his own art, man may understand the art of the Creator, and so on. Man uses his own apparent powers of creation as a yardstick by which the powers of the Creator may be gauged. Man looks at his own creative powers and extrapolates from them, concluding that whoever or whatever is responsible for the creation of the universe must possess similar powers, but on a truly cosmic scale. At this embryonic stage of man's spiritual journey, he 'shares' the attributes between himself and God, reasoning that since he has power, God too must have power, but on a scale befitting God; the same applies to all of the divine attributes of perfection.

The 'I', then, is nothing but a mirror-like unit of measurement, or a tool through which man is able to discover the Creator: it has no meaning in itself, and exists only to reveal the existence and meaning of the absolute. However, the 'I' is a double-edged sword, as Nursi points out, for while it is designed to lead man to God, if misunderstood it may lead man in the other direction.

If man uses his 'I' to journey towards God, at some stage – either through his own reasoning or through the grace of revelation – he will realise that only One who is absolute in every sense of the word can be the creator and nurturer of the cosmos. In other words, those attributes of perfection which the 'I' was once content to 'share' conceptually between itself and God now have to be 'surrendered' in their entirety to God alone. For an absolute God must possess absolute attributes of perfection: divine wisdom is absolute, divine power is absolute, divine beauty is absolute, and so on. If God's power is absolute, what status does man's power have? Is it real or is it imaginary?

Nursi argues that man's power is imaginary. Man in fact owns nothing: the ownership he appears to exercise over his attributes is an illusion, there only to reveal the very real and absolute attributes of man's Maker. Realisation of this truth is, according to Nursi, the kernel of real worship and true submission:

> That is to say, the 'I' ... realises that it serves one other than itself. Its essence has only an indicative meaning. That is, it understands that it carries the meaning of another. Its existence is dependent; that is, it believes that its existence is due only to the existence of another, and that the continuance of its existence is due solely to the creativity of that other. Its ownership is illusory; that is, it knows that with the permission of its owner it has an apparent and temporary ownership.

> (Bediuzzaman Saïd Nursi, *Man and the Universe*, Istanbul: Sozler Neshriyat, 1987, p. 29)

THE SUBMISSION OF 'I'

The issue of 'ownership' is key here, for it is the metaphorical 'surrender' of man's temporary and illusory ownership over his own attributes that underpins the notion of *islām* or submission. For it is only by 'giving up' one's claims to ownership of one's attributes that one can begin to comprehend the idea of 'purification of the self', which lies at the heart of Koranic spirituality.

True 'surrender' is only possible if the 'I' is realised for what it is, namely a nebulous, insubstantial mechanism that exists solely to indicate its Creator. Once it has truly accepted this, the 'I' will abandon its imaginary ownership and admit that all attributes belong to God alone. It will realise that whatever it appears to 'own' is there in the form of a loan, to be 'given back' to its rightful Owner. To 'give back' the attributes means to use them in a manner dictated by the One who 'gave' them in the first place. To submit one's (imaginary) knowledge, for example, means to nurture it for God's sake and to use it in accordance with His will alone. It also means to attribute it to Him at all times and under all circumstances, and not to appropriate it for oneself or to imagine that one has any real power of disposal over it. Submission involves the conscious attribution of all of the attributes of perfection to God, thus turning the self quite consciously into a mirror through which God's attributes can be reflected for others to see.

The spiritual journey envisaged by the Koran, and confirmed by Nursi, is one in which man strives to mirror God's attributes consciously. This does not mean that man should aspire to be 'like' God. Rather, it means emptying the self of all claims to ownership and cleansing the mirror of one's being so that God's perfections may be manifested in it. It means abandoning all of our claims to sovereignty and acknowledging the One True Sovereign. For it is only through true submission (*islām*) that peace (*islām*) can be attained.

THE UNREGENERATE 'I'

The alternative, as Nursi points out, is for the 'I' within man to hold onto its illusory ownership and deny that there is a Creator with greater claim to sovereignty. This happens when the 'I' fails or refuses to recognise its true function and sees itself solely in the light of its nominal and apparent meaning. If the 'I' believes that it owns itself, it cannot act consciously and sincerely as the 'vice-gerent' of God, and thus fails the 'trust'.

It is not difficult to understand why an 'I' would choose the path of self-assertion rather than self-submission. If man is created in God's image, with small 'samples' or 'reflections' of the Divine attributes deposited in his innermost being in order to allow him to recognise God, is it not surprising that he should want to claim these attributes as his own? When one is so used to power, wisdom, beauty and the like, to be told that they do not belong to you, and that they must be 'given up', or used only in accordance with the will of another, the immediate response is one of incredulity, often followed by rebellion, and, for many, by rejection and denial. The longer the 'I' claims ownership, the more difficult it will become to submit. Eventually, the 'I' swells, puffed up by its imaginary sovereignty, until it transforms the person into a creature that is propelled purely by considerations of 'self'. Rather than using the 'I' as a yardstick to indicate God, it begins to measure all other things against itself, and becomes the centre of its own universe. And in order to retain the ownership it believes it exercises over its attributes, it begins to 'divide' the absolute sovereignty of God between itself and other beings. Instead of attributing power to God, for example, it attributes it to nature, to causes, and to other beings. As Nursi puts it:

> It is just like a man who steals a brass coin from the public treasury: he can only justify his actions by agreeing to take a silver coin for each of his friends that is present. So the man who says, 'I own myself', must believe and say, 'Everything owns itself.'
>
> (Bediuzzaman Saïd Nursi, *Man and the Universe*, Istanbul: Sozler Neshriyat, 1987, p. 26)

Therein lies the way of *shirk*, or the ascription to God of 'partners' – the cardinal and unforgivable sin which the heavens and the mountains were terrified of committing should they accept the 'trust' and fail.

Readers who are interested in Nursi's spiritual psychology of man will find his short treatise on the human 'I' extremely interesting.

The question it poses, however, is that once man has realised the true nature of his own self, and that he must purify his soul in order to reach his Lord, in purely practical terms, what is he to do? How is he to undertake such a journey?

A WAY FORWARD?

The Sufis of old might have prescribed special ascetic practices, while Christian mystics might have favoured various forms of physical mortification. Yet Nursi would probably be the first to agree that in this day and age, there is no need to impose physical mortification: the incidents of everyday life itself provide enough mortification, without having to resort to sackcloth, ashes and harsh bodily penance. Doing what is prescribed and refraining from what is forbidden, in the Koranic sense of the term, is difficult enough, as is bearing with patience and resignation all that life has to throw at one: poverty, illness, war, the death of loved ones ... the list is, unfortunately, endless. In life itself there is mortification enough, without adding to it artificially.

Yet in order for the purification of the soul to occur, there has to be what the Greeks call *metanoia*, a total and radical 'change of mind'. And not only a change of mind, but a change of heart, and of habit. The Koran, in prescribing belief (*imān*) and submission (*islām*), acknowledges this, and adds:

> Verily never will God change the condition of a people until they change it themselves [with their own souls].
>
> (13:11)

Change, the Koran asserts, *is* possible; however, it must start with man himself. The subject of the final section of this chapter, the practice of *du'ā*, will show us how, for Muslims, such change can be brought about.

CALLING ON GOD: THE PRACTICE OF *DU'Ā*

Finally, we turn to the act of devotion that lies at the very heart of Koranic spirituality, namely the practice of *du'ā*, or 'calling upon' God, particularly through the invocation of His Names and Attributes.

The philosophy of *du'ā* is informed ultimately by the absolute dependence that man, as a created being, is moved to feel when contemplating the Divine. The absolute nature of the Divine Essence and the attributes of perfection that It manifests, together with the concept of continuous creation and the contingency of all created beings, serves to show man that in and of himself, he is nothing, and that all he has, he has on account of Divine munificence and mercy. At every instant, in every breath he takes, man is nurtured and his existence replenished from the treasury of Divine names and attributes. Everything man is, and does, depends continuously on this effulgence of light, as it were, from the very Source of being Itself: were God to withdraw, even for a millisecond, His power from man, man would crumple into the darkness of non-existence.

The purpose of *du'ā*, then, is not only to praise God, but to seek succour and support through the invocation of His names. In doing so, the individual reconfirms his spiritual poverty before God and acknowledges his constant debt of gratitude to God for manifesting His attributes through him, thus allowing him to exist as God's vicegerent on earth. It is the notion of man as God's vicegerent or representative on earth that prevents man from falling into despair on account of his innate nothingness as a creature. For so long as he does not appropriate them as his own, the attributes of perfection that he finds within himself can be his forever, so to speak, so long as they are used *in the name of God*, and for His sake, while man is on this earth.

Misappropriation of the Names occurs when man denies his origins, rejects God and sets himself up as sovereign of his own soul, as we saw previously. The practice of *du'ā* is encouraged in order that man may remind himself constantly who is the true Owner of all creation, and of man himself. Everything man does, he must do as the bearer – but not the owner – of the Names. Thus when we cook food and eat it, we must do so in the name of the Provider, which is why traditionally, all meals eaten by believers are preceded by a softly uttered *bismillah*, or 'in the Name of God'.

The formula *bismillah* is not only used before a meal: Muslim believers everywhere will utter it before they leave the house, before they go on a journey, before they undertake any particularly difficult task, and even – for it is encouraged in the *hadith* – before they make love. The ultimate goal, however, is not that man should spend his whole day repeating the formula verbally, but rather that his whole waking and sleeping life should be lived in a constant state of *bismillah*. As the believer progresses on this spiritual path, constantly invoking God and reminding himself of his utter dependence on Him, he will gain strength, constancy and peace as a result. For he will rely for all things not on his own self – which cannot support even an atom for a single second – but on God, Whose power encompasses all things, and Whose support never fails:

> whoever rejects evil and believes in God hath grasped the most trust-worthy hand-hold, that never breaks.
>
> (2:256)

The *du'ā*, then, is the means by which man can progress on the spiritual road to communion with God, and to the point at which his own soul becomes so effaced in his vision of God, that it is as though God is acting through him at all times. A sacred *hadith* records God's confirmation of this:

> My servant draws not near to Me with anything more loved by Me than the religious duties I have enjoined upon him, and My servant continues to draw near to Me with supererogatory works so that I shall love him. When I love him I am his hearing with which he hears, his seeing with which he sees, his hand with which he strikes and his foot with which he walks. Were he to ask [something] of Me, I would surely give it to him, and were he to ask Me for refuge, I would surely grant him it.

Through supplication and the invoking of God's Names, the soul of the sincere believer can attain the point at which he becomes a mirror for all of the names of God, thus fulfilling his role as vicegerent in the true sense of the word; and by acting as vicegerent, serve as an example to others, as the prophets were an example to him.

FURTHER READING

Works on various aspects of Muslim spirituality abound, with Chittick and Murata's *The Vision of Islam* prominent amongst them. And William Chittick scores yet again with his excellent overview of Sufism in the context of Islam and Muslim history, *Sufism: A Short Introduction* (Oneworld, 2000). A book which delves even deeper into the spiritual psychology of Islam is Hamza Yusuf's *Purification of the Heart: Signs, Symptoms and Cures of the Spiritual Diseases of the Heart* (Starlatch Press, 2004), which is the translation of a fascinating Sufi manual on the diseases of the soul and their prescribed spiritual remedies.

Two examples from the many Shi'ite sources of the formulaic type of *du'ā* that believers are encouraged to recite on various occasions are worth reading. These are 'The supplication of the lame sinner', attributed to Ali b. Abi Talib. He taught it to a young man whose appalling treatment of his own father had culminated in his own spiritual and physical sickness; on his full and sincere repentance, and his continuous use of this supplication, he is said to have been restored to full health. The second is a prayer attributed to the Prophet's great-grandson and fourth Shi'ite Imam, Zayn al-Abidin, in praise of God. While the English translations preserve little of the beauty of the original Arabic, they are still of great interest and worth seeking out.

6

REVIVAL, REFORM AND THE CHALLENGES OF MODERNITY

This chapter, the aim of which is to discuss what basically boils down to 'Islam and politics in the modern world', seems at first glance incongruous with the chapters that precede it, for they were about Islam, while this is about Muslims. The two are often conflated: Islam, it is often believed, is what Muslims are about, and is judged, more often than not, by the behaviours of those who claim to adhere to it. However, this chapter has very little to do with the religion of Islam *per se*, for considerations such as the fundamentals of belief and the articles of orthopraxy – the 'pillars of Islam' – are largely absent from contemporary religio-political discourse.

Yet one would not be able to conclude a book like this without casting some light on the labyrinthine issue of the modern Muslim world, particularly bearing in mind the horror of 9/11 and the subsequent attacks on various parts of the Muslim world by the Anglo-American coalition. Indeed, in the past five years, most of the new books published on Islam would probably never have been written had it not been for the tragedy of the Twin Towers. The case linking Islam to such events appears watertight, at least to most of those who appeared to catapult themselves into print almost before the smoke in Manhattan had cleared.

For many, that case seems as irrefragable now as it was when policy makers, hack journalists and *soi-disant* scholars of Islam and the Middle East presented it back in the autumn of 2001. To the more discerning mind, however, the case is not only unproven, it is totally unfounded – a fabrication from start to finish. To the discerning mind, the link between Islam and what happened on 11 September is as tenuous as the link, say, between Catholicism and the Omagh bombing carried out by the 'Real IRA' in 1998, or the link between Judaism and the bombing of the King David Hotel in 1946, perpetrated by the Jewish underground group, Irgun. And while the link may appear to be strengthened by the fact that the alleged perpetrators of 9/11 carried out their atrocities in the name of Islam, this is nothing more than a case of special pleading: as the old adage goes, simply saying it doesn't make it so.

This chapter will present a concise overview of the political history of certain areas of the world – the Middle East in particular – where Muslims comprise the majority of the population. This time frame is important for the simple reason that it is three hundred years, give or take a decade or two, since the beginning of what, for many, was the slow but inexorable decline of the Muslim world, culturally, economically and politically. For as the three great empires of the medieval Muslim world – the Ottomans in Asia Minor, the Safavids in Iran, and the Moghuls in the Indian subcontinent – entered the eighteenth century, they did so against a backdrop of gradual decay, disillusion and discontent, moving from 'golden age' to old age with depressing inevitability.

The vast range of civilisations which are connected, some more loosely than others, by Islam, and which comprise that vague entity we call the Muslim world, has had more 'golden ages' than one could possibly enumerate here. What constitutes a 'golden age', of course, depends on one's perspective. Arguably the most frequently cited example of a 'golden age' in Muslim civilisation is the age of the Prophet himself, and his establishment of a community-state in the city of Medina. And it is the community-state of Medina which is held up most frequently as the perfect example of the kind of society that man could create if only he were willing to obey God and follow the dictates of the Prophet's *sunna*. Indeed, the phrase 'dreaming of Medina' sums up the nostalgic vision of that highly idealised time in the genesis of Muslim civilisation; a past that is invoked – as is any 'golden age' – to provide psychological compensation for the woes and failures of the present.

The mid-to-late medieval period has also been seen as a 'golden age' in Muslim civilisation, with the Ottomans, Safavids and Moghuls attaining heights of cultural excellence undreamt of by their predecessors and unsurpassed by those who have succeeded them. Towards the end of the seventeenth century, however, all three empires seemed to be waning simultaneously. Decline is difficult to quantify, and depends very much on context and perspective. However, the fact remains that a concatenation of causes – some political, some economic, some cultural – conspired against all three regional powers and precipitated a gradual slide into socio-political decay.

Initially, the decline in the Muslim world was attributed to the fact that Muslims had become deficient in faith and practice. Towards the nineteenth century, however, decline was being discussed in a very different context, namely the increasingly unequal relationship between the Muslim world and Europe, with the latter enjoying the kind of political and cultural prominence to which the former had been habituated for over half a millennium. Eventually, decline would be explained not only in terms of deficient faith, but partly as a result of what seemed like the gradual Western takeover of the Muslim world.

As the nineteenth century gave way to the twentieth, for many in the Muslim world, a return to pristine Islam was seen not only as a means of reversing the moral and social decay in Muslim societies, but also as a way of combating the perceived evils of Western colonialism and cultural imperialism. Others, while decrying the West's political hegemony over areas of the Muslim world, welcomed with open arms the scientific and technological advances available in the West, reiterating the compatibility of Islam and science, and reassuring the more conservative elements of society that Muslims had nothing to fear from modernity apart from subservience to foreign masters, which it must avoid at all costs. A small minority agreed with the rest, but clamoured for a more radical remedy: the introduction, by force if absolutely necessary, of a theocracy akin to the old caliphal system, based squarely on the *shari'a*.

Responses to the new relationship between the Muslim *umma* and the rest of the world were immensely varied, with many different colours and shades of opinion and approach. The common denominator in all of them was the centrality of Islam to the discourse in general, regardless of whether or not the various scholars, thinkers and ideologues who helped to formulate these response were Muslims by conviction or merely by dint of geographical accident.

That responses to the crises of the Muslim world in the nineteenth and twentieth centuries were made often in overtly Islamic terms should come as no surprise. Generally speaking, the contribution of Islam to one's individual sense of identity is, for historical and psychological reasons that need not concern us here, far greater in the Muslim world than the contribution of Christianity is to the identity of those in many parts of the Western world.

A brief digression may help to elucidate. Traditionally, the number of people in Muslim societies willing to self-identify as atheists, for example, has always been lower than in the West. This is not to say that atheists do not exist in Muslim societies; far from it. However, in the more conservative Muslim societies, people prefer to dissemble rather than risk the shame of admitting to unbelief. This problem, which was foreshadowed by the Koran itself, moved one Muslim scholar to remark:

> The problem in the West may be atheism, but our problem is much worse: our problem is one of hypocrisy, of dissembling and pretence. And we all know that the place reserved for hypocrites in hell is much worse than the place reserved for atheists.

This is not the place to examine the faith of Muslims, or to decide whose profession of Islam is sincere and whose is bogus. What the short excursus above attempts to demonstrate is the centrality of Islam to that part of the globe we call the Muslim world, and the inevitability of its inclusion in any discourse on decline, modernity and the need to combat Western hegemony. The very fact that we can talk of a 'Muslim world' shows the extent of the centrality of Islam to the personal identity of most who inhabit that 'world', regardless of whether they are committed believers or not.

Thus the 'Islamic resurgence' which is said to have occurred over the past forty or fifty years should be seen primarily in terms of a *resurgent identity* that has little to do with any surge of interest in, or affiliation to, Islam *per se*. Muslims have not suddenly become better believers or more proficient in their outward expressions of submission, although this may have happened in various individual cases. What has happened in the Muslim world has been an attempt on the part of certain groups to reassert their collective identity in the face of external threats. Some have accentuated their inextricable ties – be they religious, cultural or a mix of the two – to Islam, while others have taken advantage of the centrality of Islam to the socio-political and cultural dynamics of the Muslim world in order to advance their own political and ideological agendas.

Seen in this way, the numerous movements of the past 150 years, characterised almost without exception as 'Islamic movements', have had little if anything to do with the resurgence of religious faith as such. Most of these have actually been political movements, with leaders whose underlying goal has been to solve a specific problem: the problem of the perceived backwardness of the Muslim peoples and their subservience, politically and culturally, to the West. But it is to the origins of these movements at the beginning of the eighteenth century that we now turn.

THE BEGINNINGS OF REVIVALISM

The gradual political decline of the Muslims in the seventeenth and eighteenth centuries provided the backdrop for one of the most important developments in the Muslim world for several hundred years. This was the growth of a revivalist movement, fuelled by the spirit of religious renewal and regeneration, which began in the middle of the eighteenth century and spread to virtually every part of the Muslim world. The movement had as many variations as there were different Muslim communities and traditions: in some areas it was spearheaded by the orthodox *ulama*, in others by the mainstream Sufi brotherhoods. Yet however it manifested itself, the movement had but one central message: the cause of the decline of the Muslim world is the decline of Islam itself. The true practice of Islam, it was argued, had been sullied by centuries of foreign, un-Islamic accretions and innovations, while the continued closure of the 'gate of *ijtihād*' had led to the ossification of jurisprudence, thus robbing Islamic law of its dynamism. As a result, Muslims had fallen away from the true path. To halt this decline, it was asserted, Muslims must therefore return to the first principles – the Koran and the *sunna* – for guidance, and in so doing revive the pure faith of the Prophet and his companions.

THE RISE OF WAHHABISM

The first major manifestation of the Islamic revival in the eighteenth century was the Wahhabi movement, named after its founder, Muhammad ibn Abd al-Wahhab (1703–92). Trained in Hanbali jurisprudence and the teachings of the orthodox jurist and theologian, Ibn Taymiyya (d. 1328), Abd al-Wahhab considered the social conditions of the time to be little better than the 'age of ignorance' – the *jāhiliyya* – of pre-Islamic Arabia. Appalled by the superstitions, innovations and suspect practices of the general population, such as the worship of saints and the veneration of shrines, he called for a complete revival of Islam along the lines of the pristine faith practised by Muhammad in Medina. For Abd al-Wahhab, the community-state founded by the Prophet represented Islam's 'golden age', and was seen as a point of reference and source of inspiration for all future Muslim communities.

Abd al-Wahhab also advocated armed revolt against the Ottomans. To this end, he joined forces with a local tribal leader, Muhammad b. Saud (d.1765), and created a militant revivalist movement that swept like a fire through the Arabian peninsula. In Mecca and Medina, the tombs of the Prophet and his companions were levelled; in the Shi'ite holy city of Karbala, the shrine of Imam Husayn was destroyed and many Shi'ite pilgrims were massacred. By the beginning of the nineteenth century, the Wahhabi movement was in control of most of Arabia, and its influence was felt widely throughout most of the Muslim world.

Today, the staunchly conservative Wahhabi creed enjoys influence disproportionate to its relatively small number of adherents, owing largely to the fact that many mosques, educational establishments and university Islamic societies outside the Muslim world are funded by Saudi money.

SHAH WALI ALLAH

In the Indian subcontinent, Shah Wali Allah of Delhi (1703–62) played a similar role to that of Abd al-Wahhab, albeit with some important differences. Shah Wali Allah espoused a form of Sufism – he was an adherent of the Naqshbandiyya brotherhood – from which foreign accretions and popular superstitions had been removed. This 'purified' Sufism would do in Mogul India, and much of the rest of the Muslim world, what Abd al-Wahhab's 'ultra-orthodoxy' did in Arabia: it would posit a return to the pristine Islam of the Prophet as the only way of solving the problems of the day. Like Abd al-Wahhab, Shah Wali Allah advocated a return to *ijtihad* as outlined by Ibn Taymiyya.

Elsewhere in the Muslim world, the spirit of revivalism grew apace. In Africa a series of revivalist movements culminated in the formation of several Muslim states, such as those of Uthman dan Fodio in Nigeria (1754–1817), the Sanusiyya in Libya (1787–1859), and the Sudanese Mahdi (1848–85). In central and southeastern Asia, too, similar trends were observable, with a whole rash of revivalist movements springing up throughout the eighteenth and nineteenth centuries.

At the end of the eighteenth century, then, one thing was clear: over the course of the past two hundred years, a large number of religious scholars and political thinkers in different parts of the Muslim world had reached more or less the same conclusion: all was not well in the state of Islam, and for the future of the religion and its adherents to be secured, fundamental changes in approach and practice were needed. The causes of discontent differed from region to region, depending on particular social and political circumstances, but there was broad consensus as to the way forward. The solution lay in revival, and a return to the pure Islam as advocated and practised by the Prophet. Again, ideas on how this was to take place differed from one thinker to the next, but take place it must, if Islam were to survive. The greatness once attributed to the three major Muslim powers was in serious decline, and the reason for this, many argued, was the laxity of the people in their adherence to the tenets of the faith. Revive that faith, the argument followed, and the Muslim world would once again be restored to supremacy.

Ultimately, however, the challenge was too great. For not only did Muslims have to grapple with their own internal demons, they also had to face up to an even greater threat from outside: the spectre of European colonialism. It is to the advance of Europe and its encroachment on the Muslim world that we now turn.

EUROPEAN COLONIALISM AND THE MUSLIM RESPONSE

The decline of the Muslim world in the eighteenth century was paralleled by the acceleration of technical and economic development in the West, culminating in the Industrial Revolution and the ascendancy of the European nations in the fields of commerce, trade, industry and technology. The Muslim world lagged behind in all of these areas, and could only watch with envy and consternation as Europe, which had for so long been overshadowed by the brilliance of Muslim civilisation, now began to outpace it on every front. More importantly, the West's maritime might and military prowess were such that at the close of the eighteenth century it was ready not only to outstrip the Muslim world economically but also to dominate it politically. As the nineteenth century dawned, so did the era of European colonialism; by the end of the nineteenth century, much of the Muslim Middle East – and the wider Muslim world beyond – was either directly under the control of the West or in various ways affected irreversibly by Western or Westernising influences.

THE FALL OF THE OTTOMAN EMPIRE

The final stages in the demise of the Ottoman Empire began with Napoleon Bonaparte's occupation of Egypt (1798–1801). This was a watershed in Muslim history because it was the first time since the Crusades that a European power had taken possession of part of the Muslim world. Although the French did not stay in Egypt for long, they were able to have a lasting impact on the elite strata of Egyptian society. The power vacuum left by the departure of Napoleon's forces was filled by the Albanian military officer, Muhammad Ali (1769–1849), whom the Ottomans acknowledged as viceroy of Egypt (1805–48). Muhammad Ali embarked on a French-inspired programme of modernisation that had virtually no precedent in the Muslim world. He confiscated religious endowments (*awqaf*), formed a regular army on European lines, and dispatched a number of educational missions to various parts of Europe. When the Wahhabis invaded Iraq and went on to capture Mecca and Medina, the Ottoman sultan Mahmud II (r. 1808–39) called on Muhammad Ali to crush the rebellion. His victory over the Wahhabis strengthened his position and enabled him to rule Egypt almost independently.

It also made him more ambitious – so much so, in fact, that he later rebelled against his Ottoman overlords and annexed Syria. It is possible that he would have overthrown the sultan himself, had the European powers at Mahmud's behest not stepped in to repulse him. Syria was handed back to the Ottomans in 1840, while the Europeans were rewarded for their intervention with enough mercantile concessions to give them virtual control over almost the whole of the Ottoman Empire.

From the mid-nineteenth century onwards, the disintegration of the empire gained astonishing momentum. Greece gained its independence in 1830, with Serbia following suit a year later. Between 1830 and 1847, Algeria was wrested out of Ottoman hands by the French. Bulgaria became an independent entity in 1878, the same year that Austria seized Bosnia and Herzegovina. Tunisia was made a French protectorate in 1881, while its neighbour Libya was conquered by Italy on the eve of the First World War, by which time most of the Ottoman Empire's remaining European territories had been lost in the Balkan conflicts of 1912–13.

In an effort to remedy the malaise which would, if not checked, cause the Ottoman Empire to fall entirely into the hands of the European powers, Sultan Abdul Mejid (r.1839–61) embarked on a series of Westernising reforms known as the *Tanzimat*, which literally means 'reorganisation'. In the first stage of the *Tanzimat*, begun in 1839, all religious groups were to be regarded as equal before the law. This marked a radical break with Ottoman Muslim tradition, which had always regarded non-Muslims as separate and inferior. In 1856, an imperial decree reaffirmed the equality of Muslims and non-Muslims, and by 1867, Christians, who made up approximately 40 per cent of the sultan's subjects, were being appointed to state councils.

This obvious move towards more equitable integration was followed by radical changes in the legal and educational systems, both of which had been controlled in the past by the religious scholars or *ulamā*. From 1840 onwards, Western-style courts and legal codes were introduced, and the administration was restructured along French lines. The educational system was overhauled, with new secular institutions of learning established to produce elites who would, in turn, continue the process of social and political reform.

Attention was also paid to the country's infrastructure: land was reclaimed and new factories and workshops were built; postal and telegraph systems were set up, and a railway was established.

The Ottoman reformers had realised that in order to survive in a world in which rivalry with non-Muslim powers was inevitable, the empire had to reform – and along overtly European lines if necessary. The *Tanzimat* reforms were the most far-reaching yet attempted in the Muslim world, and easily the most revolutionary. Yet if the purpose behind them was to build the empire up to a point where it might compete on its own terms with its European adversaries, then it may be argued that they were an abject failure. For all the reforms appeared to secure was the triumph of Europe over the Ottoman Empire thanks to the imposition of European institutions and practices, often with the aid of European advisers and experts.

Abdul Mejid was succeeded by his brother, Abdul Aziz (r.1861–76), who continued the Westernising reforms and, in doing so, drove the Ottoman Empire to the brink of bankruptcy. The loans he used to finance his schemes were taken from Western banks, thus giving European governments and their financiers a hitherto unprecedented degree of control over the empire's economy. Under Abdulhamid II (1876–1909), Ottoman fortunes went from bad to worse. While the *Tanzimat* reforms had culminated in the Constitution of 1876, a damaging war with Russia a year later led to the humiliating Treaty of Berlin, which resulted in the loss of most of the empire's European lands. As European powers laid claim to most of the various spheres of influence in the Middle East, Abdulhamid was presented with the pretext he needed to bring an end to liberalisation and proceed with reforms as he personally saw fit – in other words under his own autocratic guidance. By the 1880s, Germany under Kaiser Wilhelm had replaced France and Great Britain as ally and military advisor of the Ottoman Empire, while Abdulhamid was drawn to new ideologies such as Pan-Islamism, a plan – often discussed but obviously never implemented – for the unification of all Muslim lands and peoples.

THE 'YOUNG TURKS'

Abdulhamid's main domestic opponents, known collectively as the Young Turks, favoured a more secular form of Ottoman nationalism, and it was a revolution staged by the Young Turks in 1908–9 that finally brought end to despotism of the Ottoman sultans. Under the Young Turks' Committee of Union and Progress (CUP), constitutional, parliamentary government was established, reflecting the growing trend towards Turkish nationalism. The Balkan Wars which preceded the First World War brought the military element of the Young Turk movement to the fore, culminating in the domination of the political sphere in Istanbul by the so-called 'Young Turk Triumvirate' of Enver, Talat and Jamal Pasha, who led the Ottomans into the First World War on the side of the Germans. The Turkish defeat in the war finally discredited the Young Turks, however, and paved the way for the rise of a new nationalist movement under the leadership of an army officer named Mustafa Kemal, later known as Ataturk or 'Father of the Turks'. Under Ataturk, the nationalist government began to take Turkey in the direction of secularism and Westernisation; to this end, Turkey became an independent republic in 1923, abolishing the caliphate a year later. The 600-year reign of the Ottomans was finally over, and with it the last vestiges of arguably the world's greatest Muslim empire.

EGYPT UNDER BRITISH RULE

Abdul Aziz's mismanagement of the Ottoman economy was paralleled by that of the Khedive Ismail, who ruled Egypt from 1863 to 1879. Ismail's modernising zeal outstripped even that of his grandfather, Muhammad Ali, and was to find ample expression in his construction of the Suez Canal in 1869. The crippling expenditure on this and other projects, such as railways and an opera house, led to the accumulation of an inordinately heavy foreign debt: with bankruptcy looming, Egypt was forced to surrender to Franco-British financial control. A nationalist uprising – the 'Urabi Revolt of 1881' – provoked British intervention; two years later, Britain appointed a Consul-General, Earl Cromer, who was effectively the ruler of Egypt until 1907.

THE ARABS AND THE TRAGEDY OF SYKES–PICOT

British involvement in the area did not end with Egypt, however, for Britain also showed an interest in the Ottoman Empire's other

Arab subjects, of whom there were many millions. Not unsurprisingly, Britain was particularly drawn to those who were disillusioned with Ottoman rule and wished to achieve autonomy. One such example was the Sharif of Mecca. Britain made it clear that as far as the issue of independence was concerned, she was on the side of the Arabs and ready to help them in every way possible. What she did not reveal, however, was the fact that any support that she might give the Arabs in their quest for freedom stemmed not from altruistic considerations but from stark political self-interest: in 1916, unbeknownst to the Arabs, Britain had signed the infamous Sykes–Picot agreement, which was basically a blueprint for the carving up of the post-Ottoman Middle East into British and French spheres of influence. At the end of the First World War, the Sharif of Mecca became King Hussein of the Hejaz, while five new, largely artificial political entities were created out of other parts of the old Ottoman Empire. These new creations were Palestine, Lebanon, Syria, Jordan and Iraq. Hussein's two sons became kings of Jordan and Iraq, albeit under British protection. Palestine was governed directly by British mandate, while Syria and Lebanon were handed over to the French.

THE CASE OF IRAN

The situation to the east of the Ottoman Empire was somewhat different. While Iran was not formally colonised by any European power at this time, she had been the subject of intense Anglo-Russian rivalry throughout the nineteenth century. Weak central government by the self-serving Qajar shahs made it relatively easy for Russia to take control of most of the Caucasus region and Azerbaijan, while Nasiruddin Shah (1848–96) and his infatuation with all things Western opened the way for Britain to gain a foothold in the south of Iran by dint of various commercial monopolies granted by the Persian throne. The commercial stranglehold on Iran enjoyed by both Russia and Britain was completed in 1872, when Baron de Reuters was given vast concessions on banking and mining. Iran may not have been a European colony in the formal sense of the word, but any claims to political or economic independence it may have had prior to 1872 were now looking increasingly hollow.

Opposition to Western influence and interference in Iran was spearheaded mainly by the Shi'ite jurists and scholars, collectively known as the *ulamā*, a word that is sometimes translated misleadingly as clergy. When, in 1890, a British consortium was granted a monopoly on the production and sale of tobacco, the leading Shi'ite cleric of the day issued a famous fatwa, declaring the use of tobacco to be *harām* or forbidden. The edict was obeyed throughout Iran and other Shi'ite communities in the Middle East, and as a result the concession was overturned.

The involvement of the Shi'ite jurists in politics continued into the next century, when they played an important and arguably defining role in the Iranian constitutional revolution of 1905. Thereafter, however, Iran became increasingly secular and Western-oriented, with the British-appointed Reza Khan ascending the throne in 1925. As Reza Shah, the new ruler curbed the power of the *ulamā*, banned the wearing of traditional Muslim attire for both men and women, and, under the guise of modernisation, embarked on a series of Westernising social, educational and political reforms.

THE WIDER MUSLIM WORLD

Beyond the frontiers of the Ottoman Empire and Iran, the rest of the Muslim world was subjected to the depredations of Europe to varying degrees throughout the nineteenth century. In Central Asia, the second half of the century saw Russia extend her territories considerably, swallowing up the ancient khanates of Khiva and Bukhara, the khanate of Khokhand, and the territories we know today as Kazakhstan, Tajikistan and Turkmenistan.

Further south, Britain had achieved control in India by 1820, giving both Muslims and Hindus the freedom to follow their faiths in accordance with the policy of 'divide and rule'. Towards the end of the century, Britain also achieved hegemony over the Malay states, just as the Dutch were completing their colonisation of Indonesia. In Africa, the British established an Anglo-Egyptian condominium over the Sudan and gained control of most of the Sultanate of Sotoko, which was absorbed into the British protectorate of Northern Nigeria. Meanwhile, the colonial endeavours of the French saw much of West Africa come under their control between 1890 and 1912, the year in which Morocco also became a French protectorate.

THE MUSLIM RESPONSE

Just as the internal decline of the three great Muslim empires had provoked strong reactions among Muslim scholars and thinkers during the eighteenth century, leading to the rise of revivalist movements such as Wahhabism, European domination of the Muslim world in the nineteenth struck a similar chord, with differing results. Protest sometimes took the form of uprisings – bracketed under the category of *jihād*, or defensive 'holy war' – against the Europeans: notable examples include the *jihād* of the southeast Asians against the Dutch; that of the Sanussi Brotherhood against Italian rule in Libya; and the Mahdist movement in the Sudan. In other parts of the Muslim world, the *ulamā* took part in constitutional revolutions, such as the one in Iran in 1905.

Underpinning most of these movements was a strong pan-Islamic sentiment that drew on early conceptions of the Muslim *umma* as the basic focus of Muslim solidarity. The most prominent pan-Islamist was the politician, political agitator and journalist, Jamal al-Din al-Afghani (1839–97).

AFGHANI

A mysterious figure about whose life and activities a definitive portrait has yet to be painted, the Iranian-born Afghani travelled the length and breadth of the Muslim world, warning against the blind pursuit of Westernisation and arguing that the blame for the weakness of Muslims stemmed not from any imperfection in Islam but from defects in Muslims themselves. The vast majority of Muslims, he asserted, had lost touch with the spirit of moral, intellectual and scientific excellence that had made possible the great Muslim empires of the past. Furthermore, he claimed that the greatness of Islam could be recaptured with the help of Western technology and learning, but only if Muslims retained their own spiritual and cultural moorings. Without a reconstructed vision of Islam, he argued, Muslims would never be able to regain the vitality they had possessed when they were a dominant force on the world stage, united in a single international community and unaffected by differences of language, culture or outlook.

Afghani influenced Muslim thought in Central Asia, Ottoman Turkey and India, and his teachings inspired not only the 1881 revolt in Egypt but also the whole constitutional movement in Iran.

ABDUH

Afghani's disciple, Muhammad Abduh (1849–1905), argued along the same lines as his master. Rector of the famous al-Azhar university, Abduh believed that the Muslim world had been subjugated to the forces of the West not because of any weakness on the part of Islam, but because most Muslims were actually not very good Muslims. The main cause of Muslim backwardness, claimed Abduh, was the scourge of *taqlid* or 'blind acceptance', be it of legal precepts or fundamentals of faith. What was needed, he said, was a return to the true Islam of the Koran and the *sunna*, to the pristine beliefs and practices of 'the righteous forefathers' (*al-salaf al-sālih*). The reform movement inspired by his teachings came to be known as the Salafiyya, and was influential throughout the Muslim world. Identifying with an ideal time in history – the 'golden age' of the Prophet and the 'righteous caliphs' – the Salafiyya advocated past-oriented change to bring present-day Muslims up to the standards of the earlier ideal, albeit in a way that was reconcilable with the spirit of social and scientific progressiveness demonstrated by the West. This was 'dreaming of Medina' indeed, but a Medina in which the legacy of the Prophet would be located in the context of a modernised society, with all of the advances that science and technology might offer.

DECOLONISATION AND NEO-REVIVALISM

If the nineteenth century was one long litany of woes for Muslims, with most parts of their world coming under direct European domination, the advent of the twentieth century brought new hope.

Signs that Muslim misfortunes were improving came after the First World War. The Ottoman Turks and the Iranians, never colonised formally by the European powers, had begun to solve their internal problems and slowly master their affairs. It now remained for the vast majority of Muslim peoples who had not been able to escape European domination to take their destinies into their own hands. The process of decolonisation which took place throughout the Muslim world in the first half of the twentieth century served precisely that purpose, allowing most Muslims the opportunity of liberation from the direct political control of the Europeans.

Egypt was the first of the former Ottoman territories to achieve independence. When Turkey entered the First World War as an ally of Germany, Britain declared Egypt a protectorate, promising a degree of political change once the war was over. Buoyed by the thought of achieving self-determination, Egyptian nationalists formed the Wafd (literally 'delegation') movement in 1918 to plan for the country's independence. Britain, however, reneged on her promises: the leader of the Wafd was exiled and the Egyptian people rose up in violent revolt. Unrest continued until 1922, when Britain finally declared Egypt an independent monarchy under King Fuad I.

The modern kingdom of Saudi Arabia came into existence several years later. Emerging from exile in Kuwait, the Saud dynasty recaptured their old capital, Riyadh, in 1902; by 1906, Abdul Aziz ibn Saud's forces enjoyed complete control over the Nejd. He took the Hasa region in 1913, Mecca in 1924, Medina in 1925 and Asir in 1926. He then proclaimed himself king of the Hejaz, before going on to reunify the conquered territories and, in 1932, renaming his kingdom Saudi Arabia.

Iraq, Syria, Jordan and Lebanon – largely artificial states that had been created out of former Ottoman territories in the aftermath of the First World War – were next in line. A former British mandate, Iraq joined the League of Nations as a free and independent member state in the autumn of 1932. Syria became a charter member of the United Nations in 1945, after uprisings had led to British military intervention and the subsequent removal of all French forces and administrative personnel. A year later, Britain gave up her mandate over Transjordan, which was duly recognised as a sovereign independent state and renamed Jordan four years later. Also in 1946 Lebanon saw the evacuation of the last French troops from its soil, thus heralding that country's full independence.

Elsewhere in the Muslim world, the move towards independence continued apace after the Second World War. Pakistan came into existence in 1947, followed two years later by Indonesia. Libya became an independent monarchy in 1951. In 1956 Morocco and Tunisia emerged from years of French colonial control and gained independence; Sudan attained its freedom from Britain and Egypt the same year. Malaya became an independent state in 1957, while in 1960 a whole host of African nations with considerable Muslim populations – Mali, Mauritania, Niger, Nigeria, Somalia and Upper Volta (now Burkina Faso) – gained autonomy. Finally, in 1962, Algeria was able to throw off the shackles of French rule, albeit after an eight-year war of independence that had resulted in over a million Algerian casualties, and almost two million refugees.

THE ISSUE OF PALESTINE

One development which ran counter to the general process of decolonisation, and which was to usher in decades of unrest and strife throughout the Muslim world, was the creation of the state of Israel on Palestinian soil in 1948. The British had wrested Palestine from the Ottoman Turks at the end of the First World War, aided by the Arabs, to whom they promised independence once the war was over. However, Britain made two other promises which ran totally at odds with this: in the Sykes-Picot agreement concluded with France and Russia in 1916, she had vowed to carve up the region and rule it along with her allies; in the Balfour Declaration, issued a year later, Britain promised the Jews a 'national home' in Palestine. The latter promise was the one that was upheld when Palestine came under British mandate in 1922. Not surprisingly, the Arab Palestinians rejected the British right to sign their land away to a third party, and a series of anti-Zionist uprisings ensued. Britain denounced Zionist claims to the whole of Palestine, but reconfirmed their support for the Jews and their creation of a new national home. Despite Arab revolts and measures taken by the British to limit the number of Jews entering Palestine, Jewish immigration increased, especially after the Second World War. Unable to find a solution to the problem it had created, Britain finally deemed the mandate impracticable and, in April 1947, called on the United Nations to review the matter.

Despite the fact that the number of native Palestinians was double that of the Jews, the latter had the upper hand in the showdown that followed. Backed by a semi-autonomous government, led by the socialist David Ben-Gurion (1886–1973), and a competent military organisation, the Haganah, the Jews were far better prepared than the Arabs, who had never really recovered from the revolts that had taken place a decade earlier. When, in November 1947, the United Nations proposed the partition of Palestine into Jewish and Arab states, the Arabs rejected the plan while the Jews accepted. In the war that followed, the Arabs suffered an ignominious defeat, and on 14 May 1948 the state of Israel was established.

Conflict between Israel and her Arab neighbours has been a constant feature of Middle Eastern history ever since, with the staunch support offered to the Zionist state by Western nations – the United States in particular – serving as ample proof for many Muslims of the West's determination to maintain a tangible presence, albeit by proxy, in the very heartlands of the Muslim Middle East. The creation of the state of Israel has been a thorn in the side of not only the Arabs of the Middle East, but also of Muslims the world over, many of whom discern, rightly or wrongly, an agenda in the politics of the US–Israeli alliance reminiscent of the Nazi treatment of the Jews in the years preceding the Second World War. Indeed, when world leaders such as George W. Bush describe talk of certain facets of American involvement in the Middle East as a 'crusade', it is not difficult to understand why some Muslims believe that what fuels American foreign policy is hostility to Islam itself.

One of the tragedies of the whole Palestine–Israel issue is the fact that unenlightened people on both sides see the dispute in terms of religion. Israel, however, is a Zionist creation, not a Jewish one. Indeed, many Orthodox Jews are every bit as opposed to the existence of the state of Israel as Palestinians are, and are just as vocal in their denunciation of the human rights abuses perpetrated by the Zionist regime against those living under occupation. Unfortunately, however, many Muslims are unaware of this, and cite the occupation of Palestine as anti-Islamic, thus adding fuel to the fire of religious unrest in the region. With Arafat now gone, and a Bush–Blair coalition determined – or so they allege – to bring peace to the region, it remains to be seen what twists and turns lie in store for the beleaguered people of the Holy Land.

DECOLONISATION AND DISILLUSION

Although most of the Muslim world had thrown off the colonial yoke of Europe by the mid-twentieth century, for many Muslims the whole process of decolonisation appeared to be little more than a shambolic façade: a cosmetic exercise designed to lull the Muslim masses into a false sense of security. While independent Muslim states emerged one after the other with welcome rapidity, the underlying and increasingly unpalatable truth was lost on no-one: in the vast majority of cases, the individuals, groups and parties that had shaken off the shackles of European domination and led their lands to freedom were, more often than not, members of the Western-educated – and, more than likely, Western-oriented – elite. Although their rise to power did indeed signal the formal end of European control over the Muslim Middle East, the fact that the new masters were largely the product of the West meant that it was relatively easy for Europe – and, increasingly, the USA – to continue to dominate the region by proxy. Economic aid and the proliferation of industrial, agricultural and educational projects were but a few of the mechanisms employed by Western powers to retain a degree of control over their former colonies – and, indeed, over countries never before colonised in the literal sense of the word, such as Iran. Gradually it became clear to many Muslims in the Middle East that they had not thrown off the yoke of Western colonialism at all.

THE NEO-REVIVALISTS

The development of a nominally independent Muslim Middle East was paralleled by the rise of a marked neo-revivalist trend, fuelled partly by the growing realisation that the Muslim world was, despite its apparent independence, still subject to implicit Western hegemony. The aim of the neo-revivalists was nothing less than a complete transformation of society along what they saw as Islamic lines: to this end, they blended the moral and legal precepts of the Koran with overt – and at times radical – social activism. For the neo-revivalists, Islam is a 'complete way of life': an all-embracing ideology, even, which is capable of lifting the Muslim world from the mire of ignorance, factionalism and superstition into which it was deemed to have sunk. However, unlike the modernist reformers a century earlier, they did not reinterpret Islam to accommodate Western ideas. Whereas those reformers had looked to the West, and in so doing attempted to provide a Koranic rationale for the appropriation of the most beneficial aspects of Western learning and culture, the neo-revivalists emphasised the perfection of Islam and the comprehensiveness of Koranic teaching. While not opposed to progress, technology and other fruits of modernity, the neo-revivalists wished to move forward on Islamic terms, rather than on terms dictated by the West.

DREAMING OF MEDINA: AL-BANNA AND MAWDUDI

Neo-revivalism is epitomised by two movements whose influences have lasted until the present day: the Muslim Brotherhood (*Ikhwān al-Muslimin*) and the Islamic Society (*Jamā'at-i Islāmi*).

The Muslim Brotherhood was founded in 1928 by an Egyptian schoolteacher, Hasan al-Banna (1906–49). Begun initially as a youth group, from the outset its emphasis was on moral regeneration. However, with the growth of Zionist activity in Palestine, it began to espouse more overtly political ideals, and in 1939 it was transformed into a political party. Its aims were simple: to liberate the Muslim world from foreign domination and to create a truly Islamic government. In 1948 the Brotherhood was outlawed, ostensibly because it had blamed the Egyptian government for the Israeli victory over the Arabs. This provoked one of the Brotherhood members to assassinate the Egyptian prime minister; in retaliation, al-Banna was murdered by government agents, even though he had personally condemned the assassination. A year later the ban on the Brotherhood was lifted, and for several years there was an uneasy truce between the movement and the government, which, in 1952, had overthrown King Farouk. The involvement of the Brotherhood in the attempted assassination of Colonel Nasser in 1954 culminated in the execution of four of its members and the incarceration of several thousand others. As government opposition to the movement intensified, popular support for the

Brotherhood increased accordingly, with branches appearing all over the Muslim world.

Parallel to the growth of the Muslim Brotherhood in Egypt was that of the Islamic Society in the Indian subcontinent. The Society was founded in 1941 by Mawlana Mawdudi (1903–79), initially as a vehicle for his opposition to the Muslim League's demands for the creation of Pakistan, which he regarded as un-Islamic and liable to encourage Hindu nationalism. Following the Partition in 1947, Mawdudi was forced to move to Pakistan, where the Society became a persistent thorn in the side of the government.

There are many similarities between the ideological beliefs and political ideals held by al-Banna and Mawdudi, and it is to their teachings that we are able to locate the first unambiguous call in the modern Muslim world for the creation of an 'Islamic state' on theocratic lines. For both of these ideologues advocated nothing less than the full implementation of the *shari'a*, partly for what they believed was its intrinsic value as God's intended plan for human-kind, and partly as a means of eradicating Western imperialism from the heartlands of Islam. According to Mawdudi, the 'Islamic state' would be ruled by one man – a throwback to the caliphate – so long as that man adhered to state ideology, which was the ideology of Islam. And in this he would be assisted by those who are able to interpret the *shari'a*, namely the *ulamā*.

Mawdudi's programme for an Islamic state was ignored for decades, and it was only after the loss of East Pakistan – Bangladesh – in 1971 that many began to think of Islam as a possible way forward for the state. Mawdudi remains a popular figure among Muslims some twenty-five years after his death, and his influence on modern Muslim political thought cannot be overestimated.

THE MUSLIM WORLD TODAY

Today, halfway through the first decade of the third Christian millennium, nominal adherence to Islam is a truly global phenom-enon. It is possible to travel from the Atlantic in the West along a wide belt of land that stretches across northern Africa and through the Middle East into Central Asia, before heading southwards to the Pacific across the northern regions of the Indian subcontinent, the Malay peninsula and the Indonesian archipelago, without ever

leaving the world of the Muslims. Today, the community of individuals who claim affiliation to Islam is a billion strong: Muslims
constitute a majority of the population in over forty nation-states
and a sizeable minority in many others, including much of Western
Europe and North America. And some 1,400 years after the death
of Muhammad, the Islamic faith continues to expand, arguably
with greater rapidity than any other major world religion.

'TRANSPLANTED' ISLAM

The migration of huge numbers of Muslims to various parts of
Europe – Turkish 'guest workers' to Germany; Algerians, Mor-
occans and Tunisians to France; and vast numbers from the Indian
subcontinent to the United Kingdom – has, along with events such
as the increase in oil prices in the mid-1970s and the concomitant
rise of the Arab nations as major players on the global political
stage, ensured a high profile in the West for Islam and the Muslim
world. The vocabulary of Islam, too, is everywhere, from the *ayatollah* and his *fatwa* in the evening news, to the neighbourhood
imām and his campaign to introduce *halal* meat into the local primary school. Islam has made itself felt in numerous ways
throughout the global village, with Muslims enjoying a visibility
unprecedented in their collective history.

THE IMAGE OF ISLAM IN THE WEST

Unfortunately, however, one of the ways in which the world of
Islam has impacted on the West has little to do with the way Europeans or Americans as private individuals see their Muslim next-
door neighbours, or engage on a mundane level with their Muslim
friends or colleagues in the workplace. It is an unpalatable fact that
for the past twenty-five years in general, and the past five years in
particular, Muslims in general have become the focus of an irre-
fragably negative, and at times downright hostile, press: this was
true even before the events of 9/11, which we will discuss at the
end of this chapter.

The Western image of Islam as a harsh, uncompromising religion that demands strict and unquestioning obedience from its followers, who, if pushed, will not hesitate to spread their faith with

violence and terror, is one not confined to the rhetoric of twelfth-century Crusaders: fear of Islam and Muslims, or 'Islamophobia' as it is currently known, is sadly as visible today as it was then. Just as pictorial depictions of Muslims as child-eating demons abounded in the days of Richard the Lionheart, so too some 800 years later do we come across ostensibly serious works on Islam whose front covers carry photographs of gun-toting mullahs, or balaclava-clad terrorists, often against the backdrop of blown-up embassies or hijacked airliners. While the responsibility for the creation of this negative image lies largely with the sensationalist tabloid press, which is always ready to prey on its readers' fear of the unknown, much damage has been inflicted by writers and academics who, one assumes, should know better. The Muslim world, it would now seem, is the new bogey man to be feared and held at bay as we approach, in the words of one academic, the 'end of history'.

Yet the notion of Islam as a religion that is not averse to using violence in order to realise its goals is not a construct of Western interests alone. Over the past twenty-five years there has been a proliferation of avowedly militant and militaristic groups through-out the Muslim world that have proposed – and sometimes used – violent means to achieve their aims, be it in internal power struggles such as those in Algeria and Afghanistan, or in struggles against perceived enemies from outside, such as the continuing troubles in occupied Palestine and the surrounding territories. Other groups, while not overtly violent, are deemed to be so when they appear to coerce whole populations into adhering to their beliefs: various so-called 'Islamic fundamentalist' movements, such as those which have come to power in Iran, Sudan and Afghanistan over the past quarter-century, are among them.

All of these groups have two main features in common. First, like all revivalists before them, they profess the desire to return their societies to the pristine rule of Islam, and in so doing to ameliorate the myriad problems which have come about as a result of over-hurried modernisation, slavish imitation of alien cultures, and the hegemony of the West; second, by dint of the high profile they naturally enjoy on the global political stage, the are portrayed consistently as representatives and purveyors Islam.

ISLAMISM AND ITS ROOTS

What these groups represent, however, is not Islam but Islamism: Islam made political and transformed into ideology. One must add, in order to prevent accusations of inaccuracy on the grounds that Islam is inherently political anyway, the rider that such groups represent only one face of the 'Islamist' outlook. For Islamism, or 'Muslim political activism', comes in a variety of guises and is not the monolithic whole that it has often been portrayed. Although it invariably involves and encompasses the politics of power, Islamism is characterised by a substantial diversity. While the goals of the various Islamist groups are similar – and are balanced on the fulcrum that is the restoration of 'Islamic government' – the strategies they adopt in order to implement their goals differ considerably. Indeed, there are as many kinds of Islamism as there are of Islam itself.

Islamism is, to a large extent, a by-product of the general reassertion of Muslim identity that has taken place over the past half-century. This revivification of the collective Muslim spirit – the so-called 'Islamic resurgence' – has emerged as a response to a whole host of factors, both internal and external. The problems of rapid modernisation; the inability of local rulers to eradicate poverty; rural-to-urban migration; globalisation and the contact with the wider, non-Muslim world; and the inability to accommodate new developments and cultures – all these have contributed to the emergence of problems which, given the failure of secular remedies such as socialism and nationalism, have prompted many Muslims to look to their identity as followers of Islam in order to find a solution to their ills.

Between the 1950s and the 1990s, certain events on the wider world stage also acted as catalysts in the reassertion of Muslim identity. The burning of the al-Aqsa mosque in Jerusalem in 1969, for example, led to the formation of a whole new political movement, culminating in the creation of the Organisation of the Islamic Conference (OIC), in which foreign ministers from throughout the Muslim world, together with the Islamic Development Bank and other institutions dealing with economic, educational, and scientific issues, voiced their concerns about the unity of the umma. Following on from this, universities, religious institutions and professional groups throughout the Muslim world began to pay renewed attention to Islam and its role as a viable socio-political alternative to the failed ideologies of the past.

The 1967 Arab–Israeli war, while constituting a political setback, was also important ideologically since it marked a shift from Arab nationalism to a search for some kind of stable Muslim identity that might provide a steadier basis for unity and cooperation among the Muslim peoples of the world. And the 'Islamic Revolution' of Iran in 1979 was a watershed of inestimable importance. Whatever one thinks of the direction in which Ayatollah Khumayni's revolution has moved since his death in 1989, one cannot deny that his anti-Shah movement, and the subsequent creation of the first democratically elected Muslim theocracy in history, provided a huge boost to both Muslim and Islamist morale in all parts of the *umma*, giving many the feeling that Islam is able to respond successfully to the problems of the contemporary Muslim world. For many, it seemed, the 'Islamic Revolution' in Iran proved that 'dreams of Medina' do come true if you work hard enough to realise them.

Yet while Islamism attracts all the headlines, there are other social and intellectual currents at play within the Muslim world that are equally worthy of attention. In Iran, for example, where the Islamist experiment is taken by outsiders as paradigmatic, the revolutionary zeal of the first decade of the Revolution has, in recent years, given way to a more pragmatic and conciliatory approach to domestic and international issues – a *realpolitik* anchored in the growing awareness that international neighbours have to be lived with, socio-political and economic realities accepted, and ideological adversaries often accommodated if the affairs of an avowedly Islamic government are to run smoothly.

'LIBERAL ISLAM'

The gradual rehabilitation of Iran – its apparent nuclear standoff with the US notwithstanding – is partly a result of the natural recognition of limits that all revolutionary movements reach eventually. It is also partly a result of the growth – both inside Iran but also throughout the rest of the Muslim world – of a new reformist trend among Muslim thinkers and academics which seems to draw strength from Islam's innate capacity for self-renewal and the same spirit of self-critical analysis that fuelled both the revivalist movement at the end of the eighteenth century and the modernist movement at the end of the nineteenth. This largely intellectual movement has come to be known as 'liberal Islam'.

'Liberal Islam' has grown out of the thoughts and writings of certain Muslim academics and thinkers who are committed to Islam, but who consider Islamism to be misrepresentative of the Koranic ideal. This, they argue, not only connotes a liberal under-standing of the Islamic revelation, but also actively commands man to follow liberal positions in all matters Islamic. Thus it is that the supporters of 'liberal Islam' champion issues such as the freedom of speech, the freedom to choose one's religion and not be coerced into following Islamic law if one is not a committed believer, and the freedom to practise *ijtihād* – all of which, they claim, are rights guaranteed by the Koran itself. Other concerns they discuss include: the question of democracy; the separation of 'church' and state; the real meaning and role of secularism; the issue of gender and the rights of women; the position of religious minorities; and environmentalism and the notion of human progress.

'Liberal Islam' is a thriving concern, aided by rising education throughout the Muslim world, by the growing trend of democrati-sation, and by the disenchantment that many educated Muslims feel with direction taken by political Islam. Naturally, 'liberal Islam' has its detractors. Some see the nebulous group of ideolo-gues around whose writings and teachings the movement is based as apologists, whose main goal is not to create an 'Islamic state' but to adapt Islam to modernity – in order, it is often claimed, to pro-mote political trends that can find a home among the globally dominant values advocated by the West such as liberal democracy and secularism. Many conservative Muslims denounce 'liberal Islam' as un-Islamic, while policy makers in the West, who gen-erally applaud its ideals, often assert that it is not liberal enough.

Such criticisms echo the response given to the modernist reform movement of the early twentieth century, when Muslim reformers were denounced by their more traditional peers as 'dupes of Satan'. Yet if the peoples of the Muslim world are to survive and flourish in today's rapidly shrinking global village – and flourish from a position of strength and dignity – then it is clear that reform of some sort is desirable. Whether 'liberal Islam' will play a significant role in the future of the Muslim world remains to be seen. Suffice to say that there are some Muslims who are uncomfortable with Islamism and see a safe haven for their ideals in the embrace of 'liberal Islam'. And there are some who see both 'Islamism' and 'liberal Islam' as complementary parts of the same discourse of power, vying with each other to see whose version of the truth proves more authentic, and whose interpretation of the Koran prevails. And there are some – a silent majority, perhaps – who look on bemusedly, remaining aloof from politics – that 'parentless child', to paraphrase the Persian – and endeavouring to live as best they can the truth that others contest with such alacrity.

AN EPILOGUE: ISLAM AND TERRORISM

Although it is strictly speaking beyond the scope of this book, a word should be said on the vexing subject of 'Islamic terror' – this strange beast that seems to have reared its head in the past twenty-five years or so. It is a beast, it appears, that belongs in the annals of crypto-zoology rather than a normal natural history tome, for the more one tries to pin it down, the more phantom-like it becomes. Even noted Western analysts concede that an entity such as al-Qaida – the 'mother of all terrorist groups' – has no actual existence in the way that, say, the IRA or the Basque Separatists exist. The same analysts also pour cold water on claims that hundreds of 'Islamic terrorists' are poised, ready to inflict untold suffering on innocent and unsuspecting Western civilians.

The term 'Islamic terrorism' is oxymoronic. Even allowing for the most hawkish interpretations of those Koranic verses which talk of 'slaying the unbelievers wherever you find them', one is confronted with the unpalatable fact that the Koran sanctions fighting, and in terms which, if interpreted a certain way, may even be seen as a green light for offensive rather than defensive war. Let us say, for the sake of argument, that the Koran goes so far as to support the kind of pre-emptive strike against its enemies that, say, the Americans used against Iraq in order to topple Saddam Hussein. Let us say that the Koran defends the use of the sword against those who oppose it. However much a travesty of the actual message of the Koran it may be, let us allow for all of that. But 'Islamic terror'? Where in the Koran does God give the believers carte blanche to terrorise their enemies? To strike terror into the heart of one's foes is one thing, but to terrorise them in the way that terrorism is understood today is another thing entirely. Taking the alleged atrocities of the Bin Ladens and the Zarqawis of this world as our yardstick, where in the Koran do we find sanction for this kind of behaviour?

Again, the main problem here is one of definition. After all, one man's terrorist is another man's freedom fighter, and we must make allowances for fundamental differences in interpretation. Here we are not concerned with the kind of anti-state 'terror' that can be construed as legitimate, carried out by individuals who wish to free their nation from the yoke of foreign oppression. Was the late Arafat a terrorist or a freedom fighter? The answer, of course, depends on which side of the conflict you happen to be sitting. By Israeli standards, no doubt, Arafat was a terrorist. However, how different were the acts of violence that he endorsed from those carried out by the likes of Menahim Begin, for example, who helped to blow up over ninety innocent people at the King David Hotel in 1946, yet went on to win the Nobel Prize for Peace, as indeed did Arafat himself.

Separating the freedom fighters from the terrorists does not mean, however, that Islam sanctions the use of violence for the sake of causes that are nationalistic in origin. Whether or not those freedom fighters who campaign under the umbrella of Islam are actually justified in doing so is not our concern here. The point that needs to be made here is that 'terrorism' is a contested term, and we need to be sure what we mean by it before we can discuss it with any coherence.

Assuming, then, that our frames of reference with regard to terrorism are clear, and we agree that the Bin Ladens and Zarqawis of this world are, by universal consensus, terrorists in the true sense of the term, we can also agree that to describe such individuals as 'Islamic terrorists' is grossly misleading, and in some cases intentionally so. For there are some who would attribute to Islam the kinds of inhumane behaviour that simply have no place there, neither in the practices of Muhammad nor in the precepts of the Koran. The fact that some self-professed Muslims commit acts of terror is neither here nor there: their terrorism does not become

'Islamic' simply by dint of the fact that they are Muslims. Let us revisit a tired old analogy: Adolf Hitler was a self-professed believer in Jesus, but this hardly makes his persecution of the Jews an act of Christian genocide. Similarly, does anyone use the term 'Christian terrorism' to describe the atrocities carried out by the IRA? Even the excesses of Torquemada and his fellow inquisitors went under the term 'Spanish' rather than 'Christian' Inquisition, doubtlessly to spare the Christian faithful the ignominy of attributing such foul atrocities to the teachings of Christ, who preached nothing but love, compassion and tolerance.

In fact, 'Islamic terror' is a chimera, a Western construction dreamt up by the neoconservative strata of American political thinkers who, bereft of the old bogeyman of communism, have created a new monster to unleash on an unsuspecting public: the spectre of Muslim fundamentalism in its most brutal and threatening incarnation: not the sword-wielding Saracen this time, but the suicide bomb-bearing Islamist with *jihād* and the promise of heavenly virgins as his impetus.

That the media in the West – and particularly in North America – should see 'Islamic fundamentalism' as the implacable enemy of all things Western is doubly ironic when one considers the symbiotic relationship that has existed in the past between American foreign policy and Wahhabism. US military intervention in Afghanistan during the 1980s was supported by armed Wahhabi missionaries from Saudi Arabia, who trained the Taliban in US-sponsored religious seminaries in Pakistan and Afghanistan. The CIA itself is on record as having provided guerrilla training for these groups in Pakistan, where preparation for the military campaign against the Russians went hand-in-hand with classes on Islamic law and theology. The thousands of religious teaching establishments which mushroomed under General Zia and his successors, and in which the germ of the future Taliban was nurtured, flourished thanks to the support of the United States. The American-backed 'jihād' planned in these seminaries was designed to destabilise the secular, Soviet-backed regime in control of Afghanistan at that time. The *mujāhidin* or 'holy warriors' who were to wage this war were recruited largely by Saudi Arabia – the cradle of Wahhabi 'fundamentalism' – with overt American backing. Recruitment was facilitated by the publication of a series of authoritative juristic edicts, issued by the ultra-conservative Wahhabi clerics in the Saudi kingdom, which appealed to the religious sensibilities of the younger Muslim generation. These edicts 'urged Saudi and non-Saudi youths to go to Afghanistan in order to carry out jihād there, praising those who sacrificed their lives for the sake of the Islamic nation's causes'.

> What is the difference between jihad in Afghanistan and jihad in Iraq? What is the difference between the Soviet occupation of Afghanistan and US occupation of Iraq? What is the difference between the jihadic groups in Afghanistan and their counterparts in Al-Fallujah, Samarra, and Al-Ramadi? We ask these questions and know their answers in advance. The difference is clear. Jihad in Afghanistan was supported by the Americans under a US plan to revenge against the Soviets and make up for the defeat in Vietnam. Therefore, this jihad was legitimate from the viewpoint of the ulema and officials in Saudi Arabia. However, jihad in Iraq is illegitimate because the occupying forces are American and America is a strategic ally of the ruling family in Saudi Arabia.
>
> (*Al Quds al-'Arabi*, Editorial, 14 November 2004)

That the genie unleashed largely thanks to the Americans should not only refuse to go back into the bottle, but should turn around and bite the hand that fed it, would, had the consequences not been so tragic, smacked of a most delicious irony. 9/11, however, provided nothing to gloat over for anyone. Regardless of who actually carried out that atrocity – and there are many who are simply unwilling to believe the official line – it is clear that the one thing it did provide was a pretext. That pretext was a 'war on terror' that began with the pulverisation of Afghanistan and the destruction of Iraq, and which also threatens to engulf Syria, Iran and possibly as many other 'rogue states' as necessary. The 'war on terror', characterised in its first stage by the virtual annihilation of Baghdad and the political subjugation of Iraq, would appear to be a long-term strategy, with nothing less than the gradual assimilation of vast regions of the Muslim world into the New American Empire. How Muslims will respond, and what the perceived role of Islam will be in this very uncertain future, time alone will tell.

FURTHER READING

While there are literally hundreds of books to choose from here, the reader is not really spoilt for choice since the key word with most of them is mediocrity. For a sober overview of religion and politics in the modern Muslim world, one would be hard pressed to beat Esposito's *Islam: The Straight Path*. Also packing a punch is Edward Mortimer's excellent *Faith and Power: The Politics of Islam* (Vintage Books, 1988), despite being almost two decades old.

OTHER TOPICS

Majid Fakhry's *Islamic Philosophy, Theology and Mysticism: A Short Introduction* provides a well-written and concise overview of his subject matter in an enlightening and challenging way. On the development of jurisprudence, law and the *shari'a*, readers are well served by N. J. Coulson's *A History of Islamic Law* (Edinburgh University Press, 1989), while A. Rahman Doi's *Shar'iah: The Islamic Law* gives us a Muslim perspective on more or less the same issues. Finally, Heinz Halm's *Shiism* (Edinburgh University Press, 1991) is a packed but accessible look at Shi'ite history and doctrine, while Moojan Momen covers the same ground, but with much greater depth, in his excellent *An Introduction to Shi'i Islam: The History and Doctrines of Twelver Shi'ism* (Yale University Press, 1985).

APPENDIX A
THE SUCCESSION CRISIS AND THE BIRTH OF SHI'ISM

Since we are trying to keep to the original remit by covering only the 'basics' of Islam, a detailed discussion of the meteoric rise of Muslim civilisation following the death of Muhammad is sadly beyond the scope of this work. This is unfortunate, because the history of the expansion of Islam beyond the confines of the Arabian peninsula is a fascinating one, and interested readers are referred to some of the best books on the subject in the Further Reading section of the book's Introduction and at the end of each chapter.

However, this book would not be complete without a brief overview of the birth and evolution of an approach to Islam that is known as Shi'ism. Approximately 10 per cent of all Muslims adhere to Shi'ite teachings, and Shi'ism has been the 'state religion' of Iran since the beginning of the sixteenth century. More than 50 per cent of Iraqi Muslims are Shi'ites, and there are also large Shi'ite minorities in Pakistan and the Gulf states.

The word actually derives from the Arabic *shi'a*, which means 'faction' or 'party'. The 'party' in question was composed of all those who supported the candidacy of the Prophet's cousin, Ali, for the position of Caliph or leader of the community after Muhammad had died. The 'succession crisis' which occurred after the death of Muhammad has left its mark on all areas of Muslim life and thought down to the present day, colouring perspectives on law, theology, exegesis and, more importantly, political theory. Let us delve a little more deeply.

THE SUCCESSION CRISIS

When Muhammad died, his prophethood died with him: he was proclaimed the 'seal of the apostles' and the last in the long line of messengers tasked by God to bring the message of Divine Unity to mankind. However, the need for a temporal leader, one who might guide the community politically as well as spiritually, continued.

Muhammad's death plunged the nascent Muslim community of Medina into crisis, simply because most people believed that Muhammad had failed to nominate a successor.

Some, however, were of the opinion that the Prophet had indeed chosen the man who would carry on his role as leader and guide of the young community-state. This man was his cousin and son-in-law, Ali, one of the first to have converted to Islam when Muhammad began to receive the revelations a quarter of a century earlier. Those who believed that Ali was Muhammad's rightful successor cited numerous verses in the Koran to support their belief that the 'family of the Prophet' – and particularly the male line issuing from Ali through his marriage to Muhammad's daughter, Fatima – had a greater right to rule the Muslim community than anyone else.

However, the Meccans and the Medinese who gathered after the death of the Prophet chose Abu Bakr as the new leader of the *umma*, and he was duly declared Caliph. Ali's partisans continued to grow in number, but he was passed over for the caliphate three times in all: when Abu Bakr died, he was succeeded by Umar, and when Umar died, Uthman took his place. Following the assassination of Uthman in 556, Ali became the fourth of the *rāshidūn* or 'rightly-guided' caliphs.

The birth of Shi'ism is traced by many to the troubled caliphate of Ali, and particularly to his assassination in 661. Following Ali's death, the caliphate went to Ali's bitter rival, Mu'awiya, who founded the Umayyad dynasty (661–750). With Ali's demise, authority in the Muslim world became divided. The Umayyads continued as caliphs, ruling from Damascus, but in the east, and in Iraq in particular, there existed a separate community that did not recognise the authority of the Umayyad caliphs. Instead, they claimed that only the blood successors of Ali were the true leaders of the Muslim *umma*. These successors were given the title of Imam, which means both spiritual and religious leader, in contradistinction to the title of Caliph or Sultan, which has more temporal or secular connotations.

In the year 680, one of Ali's sons, Husayn, who had risen up against the corrupt Umayyad regime, was martyred at Karbala, in Iraq. The merciless slaughter of the Prophet's grandson and his family shook the Muslim world, and its reverberations can still be felt today: in Iran, which is predominantly Shi'ite, the martyrdom of Husayn is commemorated annually as an emblem of defiance in the face of oppression. And the concept of martyrdom – the readiness for self-sacrifice in order to combat tyranny – was a recurring motif in the social struggles which preceded the Iranian revolution of 1979.

THE TWELVE IMAMS

Of the several sub-groups within Shi'ism, the largest is that of the Twelver Shi'ites, who believe that Muhammad vouchsafed the succession to twelve imams or leaders, beginning with Ali and continuing down his blood line to the Imam known as Mahdi, who allegedly disappeared as a young child and will, it is believed, return towards the end of time to spread peace and goodness through a troubled world. The messianic role of the Mahdi has great importance for Shi'ites, who find comfort and fortitude in the belief that one day, tyranny and oppression will be removed from the face of the earth.

Shi'ites have in the past been quietist in their approach to politics, generally accepting the status quo and remaining aloof from political involvement. Shi'ism's reputation for radical action in the face of political oppression is a recent phenomenon, forged largely by a new generation of Shi'ite thinkers and leaders who have reinterpreted motifs such as martyrdom and Mahdism and imbued them with the kind of revolutionary spirit which enabled the Ayatollah Khumayni to overthrow the regime of Muhammad Reza Shah and establish arguably the world's first 'Islamic republic'.

Approximately 10 per cent of the world's Muslims self-identify as Shi'ites, most of whom live in Iran and Iraq. For more on Shi'ite law, see Appendix D.

APPENDIX B
THE CHAPTERS OF THE KORAN

No.	Arabic name	English name
1	al-Fātiha	The Opening
2	al-Baqara	The Cow
3	Āl-i 'Imrān	The Family of Imran
4	al-Nisā	The Women
5	al-Mā'ida	The Feast Table
6	al-An'ām	The Cattle
7	al-A'rāf	The Heights
8	al-Anfāl	The Spoils of War
9	al-Tawba	Repentance
10	Yūnus	Jonah
11	Hūd	The Prophet Hud
12	Yūsuf	Joseph
13	al-Ra'd	The Thunder
14	Ibrāhĭm	Abraham
15	al-Hijr	The Rocky Tract
16	al-Nahl	The Bee
17	al-Isrā	The Night Journey
18	al-Kahf	The Cave
19	Maryam	Mary
20	Tā Hā	Tā Hā

(continued on next page)

No.	Arabic name	English name
21	al-Anbiyā	The Prophets
22	al-Hajj	The Hajj
23	al-Mu'minūn	The Believers
24	al-Nūr	The Light
25	al-Furqān	The Criterion
26	al-Shu'arā	The Poets
27	al-Naml	The Ants
28	al-Qasas	The Stories
29	al-'Ankabūt	The Spider
30	al-Rūm	Rome
31	Luqmān	Luqman
32	al-Sajda	Prostration
33	al-Ahzāb	The Confederates
34	Sabā'	Sheba
35	Fātir	The Originator
36	Yā Sīn	Yā Sīn
37	al-Sāffāt	Those in Ranks
38	Sād	(The letter) Sād
39	al-Zumar	The Crowds
40	Ghāfir	The Forgiver
41	Hā Mīm	(The letters) Hā Mīm
42	al-Shūrā	Consultation
43	al-Zukhruf	Glittering Trinkets
44	al-Dukhān	The Smoke
45	al-Jāthiya	The Kneeling
46	al-Ahqāf	The Sandy Tracts
47	Muhammad	Muhammad
48	al-Fath	The Victory
49	al-Hujurāt	The Chambers
50	Qāf	Qāf
51	al-Dhāriyāt	The Scattering Winds
52	al-Tūr	The Mountain
53	al-Najm	The Star
54	al-Qamar	The Moon
55	al-Rahmān	The Compassionate
56	al-Wāqi'a	The Inevitable Event
57	al-Hadīd	Iron
58	al-Mujādila	The Woman Pleading

(continued on next page)

No.	Arabic name	English name
59	al-Hashr	The Gathering
60	al-Mumtahina	That Which Examines
61	al-Saff	The Battle Line
62	al-Jumu'a	Friday
63	al-Munāfiqūn	The Hypocrites
64	al-Taghābun	Loss and Gain
65	al-Talāq	Divorce
66	al-Tahrīm	Prohibition
67	al-Mulk	The Dominion
68	al-Qalam	The Pen
69	al-Hāqqa	The Inevitable Reality
70	al-Ma'ārij	The Ways of Ascent
71	Nūh	Noah
72	al-Jinn	The Jinn
73	al-Muzammil	The Enfolded One
74	al-Mudaththir	The One Wrapped Up
75	al-Qiyāma	The Resurrection
76	al-Insān	Man
77	al-Mursalāt	Those Sent Forth
78	al-Nabā	The Great News
79	al-Nāzi'āt	Those Who Tear Out
80	'Abasa	'He frowned ... '
81	al-Takwīr	The Folding Up
82	al-Infitār	The Cleaving Apart
83	al-Mutaffifīn	The Fraudsters
84	al-Inshiqāq	The Rending Asunder
85	al-Burūj	The Constellations
86	al-Tāriq	The Shooting Star
87	al-A'la	The One Most High
88	al-Ghāshiya	The Overwhelming
89	al-Fajr	The Dawn
90	al-Balad	The City
91	al-Shams	The Sun
92	al-Layl	The Night
93	al-Duhā	Morning Light
94	al-Sharh	The Expansion
95	al-Tīn	The Fig
96	al-'Alaq	That Which Clings

(continued on next page)

No.	Arabic name	English name
97	al-Qadr	The Night of Power
98	al-Bayyina	The Clear Proof
99	al-Zalzala	The Earthquake
100	al-'Ādiyāt	Those That Gallop
101	al-Qāri'a	The Great Cataclysm
102	al-Takāthur	The Piling Up
103	al-'Asr	Time
104	al-Humaza	The Scandalmonger
105	al-Fīl	The Elephant
106	Quraysh	The Tribe of Quraysh
107	al-Mā'ūn	Neighbourly Charity
108	al-Kawthar	The Pool of Kawthar
109	al-Kāfirūn	The Unbelievers
110	al-Nasr	The Succour
111	al-Lahab	The Flame
112	al-Ikhlās	Sincerity
113	al-Falaq	Daybreak
114	al-Nās	Mankind

APPENDIX C
MUSLIM THEOLOGY

In the Muslim world, learned discussion and debate concerning the fundamentals of belief have traditionally been the preserve of the discipline known as *kalām* (lit. 'discourse'), which is usually translated as 'scholastic theology'. Discussion on the nature of Divine Unity, the necessity for prophethood, and logical proofs for the existence of a hereafter occupied the mind of Muslim thinkers from comparatively early on.

The origins of Muslim theology remain obscure, but the first recorded theological discussions came about in the middle of the seventh century as a result of distinctly political concerns. When the fourth Caliph, Ali, was challenged by Mu'awiya, a rival claimant to the caliphate, hostilities broke out and a civil war ensued. Ali had the upper hand in battle, and might have secured victory had the enemy not resorted to shock tactics. Holding aloft pages of the Koran on their spears, they called on Ali to let the Holy Book act as arbitrator in their dispute. This came to nothing, and Ali was denigrated by a number of his followers, who said that he should have ignored the plea for arbitration and settled the issue there on the battlefield, as they believed God intended. Eventually, these followers broke away from Ali and formed their own grouping, known as the Khārijiyya (from the Arabic term meaning 'those who break away').

The Khārijiyya began as a political faction, but developed theological ideas of their own. Prominent among them was the notion that sin casts an indelible stain on faith, and that those who sin – as Ali was held to have done – fall outside the pale of Islam and become unbelievers. The question of who is a believer and who is not, and the degree to which sins – trivial or cardinal – damage or destroy faith, was possibly the first to come under scrutiny. Another group involved in discussions on the nature of belief and faith were the Murjiites, a century later. They concluded that belief and practice were separate things, and that sin was not enough to disqualify anyone from membership of the brotherhood of Islam.

Later still, two important groups emerged that would dominate theological discussion in the early medieval period of Muslim history. These were the Mutazilites and the Asharites. More is known about these two groups than about any other theological faction, and their debates still have resonance for Muslims today. Known misleadingly as the 'free thinkers' or 'rationalists' of Muslim theology, the Mutazilites championed the idea of God's unity and justice. With regard to Divine Unity, they were keen to stress that while God has many attributes of perfection, these attributes are not separate from Him; rather they are part of, and virtually synonymous with, His essence. Thus while God describes Himself as all-powerful, all-knowing and all-merciful, for example, He does not possess power, knowledge and mercy as separate attributes: this would imply their co-eternity with Him, thus adulterating His absolute unity with plurality. With regard to justice, the Mutazilites argued that acts are good or bad inherently, and not because God says they are so. Out of their perspective of God's absolute justice came the belief that man was equipped with free will and the ability to choose between right and wrong. While some groups believed that all of man's acts were predetermined by God, thus allowing little if any room for freedom of choice, the Mutazilites argued that God does not force man to do anything: God is just, they asserted, and would not punish a man for sins he did not choose freely to commit.

A third issue debated by the Mutazilites was the 'createdness' of the Koran. The assumption had always been that the Koran, as the word of God, was eternal. However, the Mutazilites argued that this would make the Koran co-eternal with God – a clear infringement of Divine Unity. Similarly, they dismissed the idea that what the Koran describes as the 'hands' or the 'face' of God should be understood literally: rather, such terms can only ever be metaphors: God's 'hands', for instance, signify His all-encompassing power, while His 'face' denotes His attributes as made manifest in the created world.

Underpinning all of the Mutazilite positions was their staunch belief in human reason, which they held to be the supreme criterion by which not only all theological issues should be judged, but also by which revelation itself must be appraised.

The main rivals of the Mutazilites were the Asharites, who came to the forefront in the tenth century, and whose teachings still hold sway in many Muslim theological circles today. Asharite theology began largely as a response to what certain scholars saw as the rather unorthodox views of the Mutazilites, who were seen as disturbingly over-reliant on human reason.

The Asharites matched the Mutazilites argument for argument. On the issue of Divine Unity, they claimed that God's essence and attributes were necessarily separate: were they not so, they said, we might just as well declare 'knowledge' or 'power' our god rather than God. They conceded, however, that the kind of knowledge that we predicate of God is different to the knowledge that we experience as humans, and that by way of compromise we should conclude that while God's knowledge is not identical with His essence, it is not separate either – at least not in the sense that human knowledge is separate from the human essence.

On the issue of justice, the Asharites agree that God is absolutely just. However, they claim that good and evil are determined not by the nature of things or actions themselves, but by God: it is God who creates good and allows evil, in order to test mankind. An act which has been declared evil is evil only because God has declared it such, and not because it is inherently devoid of good. For if, they argued, God outlaws an act because the act is bad, this implies that His will is secondary to the evil of the act in question, and that His prohibition is in a sense contingent upon it. Evil, for the later Asharites at least, is a wholly relative category, and should be seen merely as the 'lack of good'. In short, evil is a relative rather than an absolute concept. An earthquake on the moon, for example, would most likely not be seen as evil, simply because there are no casualties. An earthquake in Japan, however, is likely to be seen by many as evil, particularly if there is huge loss of life. As a 'lack' – a lack of good, or a lack of mercy – evil has a reality, but it has no external existence.

On the issue of free will, the Asharites argued that man has the choice only to act. As soon as he chooses, everything he does is created by God. While God creates man's acts, He does not coerce man into performing them: the choice is man's; the creation of the outcome of that choice is God's. In short, 'Man proposes, God disposes'. God even creates those acts which are deemed sinful, but man has to accept responsibility for them on account of having chosen them in the first place. One scholar likened this to one man sitting on the shoulders of another: when the first man says, 'Take me forward,' the second man goes forward; when the first says, 'Sit me down,' the second sits down. If the first man were to say, 'Throw me onto the ground,' would he have the right to complain when he was thrown?

On the question of the 'created Koran', the Asharites argued that while the paper and ink with which the Koran is created, the word of God which is enshrined in them is eternal. To substantiate this, they cited the famous Koranic verse in which God says:

> For to anything which We have willed, We but say the word, 'Be', and it is.
>
> (16:40)

This verse implies the eternity of God's speech, and thus if the Koran is indeed His speech, it must be eternal and uncreated.

Many other issues were debated in theological circles across the Muslim world throughout the medieval period. However, Muslim theology has never achieved the kind of profile enjoyed by Muslim jurisprudence, and after the Asharites there were few theological groupings to rival them in popularity and influence. Today, most of the Sunni majority adhere to the teachings of the Asharites, demonstrating how little theology has advanced in the Muslim world in the past thousand years.

APPENDIX D
THE NOTION OF 'ISLAMIC LAW'

For the majority of contemporary Muslims, 'Islamic law' is that corpus of rites, rules and recommendations that are given by God so that man may order all of his actions and behaviours – be they personal or societal – in accordance with the 'Divine will'. As such, the reach of 'Islamic law' is considered to be all-inclusive: there is no facet of man's personal behaviour that is not catered for or covered by some divine ordinance or other, and no area of man's social or political life that is untouched by the 'law' or 'laws' of God. Popular belief has it that there is no aspect of human existence that is not regulated or legislated for by this all-encompassing code, hence the perennial mantra, 'Islam is not just a religion, it is a *whole way of life.'*

However, as we have already seen in the previous sections, there is no such thing as a practice or action that is inherently sacred, religious or 'Islamic': an action is only as good, bad, sacred or pro-fane as the intention which engenders it and the attitude which underpins it. The same applies, but for slightly different reasons, to that codified body of rules and regulations known as 'Islamic law', most of which is a purely human construct, and much of which has little or nothing to do with the precepts enshrined in the Koran. A whole host of practices – from those staples of Western tabloid interest such as the ritual stoning of adulterous females to the more trivial practices such as veiling, or circumcision – are passed off as 'Islamic' but in fact receive no mention at all in the Islamic revelation.

The fact that most of the laws by which Muslims have endeavoured to regulate their lives are in fact human concoctions may come as a bracing surprise to most readers, and a shock to many, particularly if they are Muslims with traditionalist views. However, that 'Islamic law' is mostly 'human law' is not particularly earth-shattering. What is shocking is the fact that it has masqueraded as a sacred code for so long, its spurious provenance allowing it to avoid criticism and to act as a virtually impregnable barrier to legal, social and political reform.

That which passes in most Muslim societies as 'Islamic law' is in fact a hybrid of Koranic precepts; moral and social codes abstracted from the personal practice or *sunna* of the Prophet; and the rulings of jurists, which are based largely on their personal interpretation of the so-called 'sources of law', the most important of which are the Koran and the *sunna* of Muhammad. While the 'Muhammadan code' or *sunna* enshrines the sayings and behaviour of a mere mortal, it is held to be divinely inspired. However, the *sunna* is suspect as a source of law on account of the problematic nature of the Traditions that comprise it, many of which may be later fabrications. This leaves the rulings of jurists, which, as we shall see shortly, are human and fallible through and through. Of the whole melange, only the Koran can claim to be divine, and even then, in comparison with the other two components, its direct contribution to the body of Islamic law is minimal. The term 'Islamic law' is at best misleading, and at worst a travesty; to call it 'law abstracted by Muslims from a mixture of divine and human sources' would be cumbersome and unfeasible, but much closer to the truth.

SEEING 'ISLAMIC LAW' AS MUSLIMS SEE IT

Before we go back in time to the era of the Prophet and the earliest Muslim communities to trace the gradual development of Islamic law, let us first clear up a few 'definitional' grey areas and look at Islamic law – on the surface at least – as Muslims see and understand it.

The laws that God is said to have devised so that man may order and regulate his life are described in their totality as the *shari'a*.

Over the past thirty years the profile of Islamic law internationally has become such that the word 'Sharia' has found its way into most of the well known English dictionaries.[1] Readers may have heard of or read about endeavours and campaigns by Muslims in various parts of the world to 'bring back the *shari'a*' or to 'reinstate *shari'a* law'. Sometimes, such efforts are undertaken to revive Islamic law with respect to a certain area of socio-political life: to bring back Islamic criminal codes, for example, or Islamic laws of inheritance – rules and regulations that were in force when the nation or society in question operated according to the *shari'a*, but which have long since been superseded by secular codes. Other endeavours to reinstate the *shari'a* have harboured the objective of applying the 'sacred code' in its totality, thus turning the nation or society into an 'Islamic state', run solely on legal principles said to be derived directly from the Koran through the medium of Islamic law. The most famous example of this, of course, is Iran, which refashioned itself as an 'Islamic republic' after the revolution of 1979.

Let us now turn to the history of early Islamic legal doctrine so that we may throw a little light on the development of the complex phenomenon we have been trying to deconstruct in the previous paragraphs.

THE *SHARI'A*: THE EVOLUTION OF MUSLIM JURISPRUDENCE AND 'ISLAMIC LAW'

The Arabic word *shari'a* means 'a path or an approach to a watering place', but in the technical sense it is understood as the laws prescribed, directly or indirectly, by God. It is the aim of *fiqh* – or jurisprudence – to understand how practical laws are to be derived from the main 'sources of law', namely the Koran and the Prophetic *sunna*. For complex reasons, *fiqh* has always been the most popular and important discipline in the Muslim world of learning.

Fiqh has two principal components: *furū al-fiqh* (the 'branches of understanding') and *usul-al-fiqh* (the 'roots of understanding'). The 'branches' comprise the various laws, which are classified under two headings: *ibādāt*, or acts of worship (namely: ritual purity, prayer, almsgiving, fasting, pilgrimage, and so on); and *mu'āmalāt*, or transactions, which include family law, commercial law, civil law and criminal law. The roots are more extensive, covering the various categories or values of law (the obligatory, the recommended, the permitted, the discouraged and the forbidden); the sources of law (which vary according to different 'schools of law', but which always include the Koran, the *sunna* and scholarly consensus or *ijmā*); the rules for extrapolating norms from the sources; and the principle of *ijtihād*, which is the right to exercise independent judgement.

THE PRINCIPAL SCHOOLS OF JURISPRUDENCE

Although there is a certain amount of legislative material in the Koran, it is not a book of law and thus one will not find written in it any systematic code of law. While the Koran does tell those who adopt Islam as their chosen creed what they are supposed to do to express their submission in practical terms (e.g. through praying, fasting and the like), it does so only in a very general manner. Muslim orthopraxy is firmly rooted in the Koran, but the Koran itself gives believers only very vague and general guidance on how their obligations are to be fulfilled. In the case of prayer, for example, there are verses in the Koran which stress the importance of prayer, and which mention the times when people should pray, but nowhere can we read precisely when and how the prayers are to be performed; for that one has to refer to the *sunna* – the practice of the Prophet. Another example is the issue of the punishment of theft. The Koran does indeed state that the thief's hand should be cut off, but it leaves many questions unanswered. For example, does the law apply to minors as well as adults? Should the punishment be carried out if the thief is old, pregnant or insane? Are there mitigating circumstances such as poverty? Must the object taken be of value? What evidence is required to convict a person of theft? And so on.

While the Prophet was still alive, the Koran's silence on these issues was unproblematic. Sometimes he would receive additional revelations which would throw light on difficult issues, but more frequently he gave his own judgement, or relied instead on the customary law of Medina. After his death, however, the situation changed dramatically. There were no further revelations, and no-one else like Muhammad who could act as lawgiver in his own right. The first four caliphs administered justice on the basis of the

Koran and the decisions of the Prophet. Like him, they too gave *ad hoc* rulings of their own and relied on the customary law of Medina. However, these last two elements proved increasingly difficult to justify. In matters of administration, for example, the third caliph, Uthman, was criticised severely for reversing many of the policies of his predecessors. More importantly, as the Arab conquests took Islam halfway around the world, it became increasingly less practical to rely on the customary law of Medina.

A watershed development took place during the Umayyad period (661–750), when the provincial governors in various parts of the Arab Muslim empire appointed *qādis* (judges) to whom they delegated their judicial authority. The governors reserved the right to judge any case themselves if they so desired, and they could of course dismiss the judges if they saw fit. Nevertheless, the judges were in charge of the day-to-day administration of justice. The historical sources portray them mostly as devout Muslims who were concerned to proceed in accordance with the Koran and Islamic tradition, but they also drew on local custom and frequently had to use their own discretion. Many of the decisions which they took were incorporated into law. The appointment of judges who were legal experts led, in turn, during the early Abbasid period (750–900), to the emergence of distinct 'schools of jurisprudence' (*madhhab*) in different parts of the empire. Four schools of law still exist in the Sunni world: the Hanafi, Maliki, Shafi'i and Hanbali; the Shi'ites have their own 'school of jurisprudence', the Ja'fari school, named in honour of its founder, Ja'far al-Sadiq, a direct descendant of the Prophet.

THE HANAFI SCHOOL

The Hanafi school is named after Abu Hanifa (d. 767), a native of Kufa in Iraq. He was an academic lawyer and never served as a judge. The Hanafi school is seen as the most liberal and flexible of the four Sunni schools.

In establishing points of law, Abu Hanifa relied in the first instance on the Koran, then on 'analogical reasoning' (*qiyās*). He actually regarded the latter as more important than Prophetic Tradition although of course he took *hadiths* into account. A jurist's use of analogical reasoning to extend a Quranic ruling to a new case depends on his ability to identify the underlying cause or reason (*illa*) for the original ruling. For example, according to the Koran, after the *adhān* has been sounded for the Friday congregational prayers, it is forbidden to buy or sell goods until the prayers are over. The underlying reason for this is that buying and selling tend to distract people from praying. Therefore, by analogy, all other transactions are likewise forbidden at this time because they too are a distraction.

Abu Hanifa invoked the principle of 'juristic discretion' (*istihsān*, which literally means to approve or deem something preferable) in order to justify departing from the letter of the law in circum-stances where the rigid application of it would lead to unfairness. For example, the Koran requires men and women to dress modestly when in the presence of members of the opposite sex to whom they are not married or closely related. However, Hanafi jurists argue that this rule may be set aside in the case of a person who is ser-iously ill and needs a medical examination. A similar principle, *istislāh*, gives the jurist the authority to overrule a law which is not in the public interest, even if that law is religiously binding in the sense of being *fard*. These principles, which give jurists tremendous scope for 'creative legislature', came under attack by the more conservative juristic majority and were discontinued, much to the chagrin of modern Muslim reformers.

As well as allowing ample room for the use of reason, Abu Hanifa also relied on scholarly consensus (*ijmā*) to establish points of law. He held that only the consensus of the qualified legal authorities of a given generation was absolutely infallible, but in practice, jurists of the Hanafi school have often accepted a local consensus, sometimes involving only a handful of scholarly opinions.

The Hanafi school was the dominant school during the Abbasid period and subsequently became the official school of the Ottoman Empire. Largely because of this it has continued to be the most widespread school. It is adhered to by the majority of Muslims in Syria, Jordan, Turkey, North India, Pakistan, China and Central Asia. Approximately a third of all Muslims are Hanafis.

THE MALIKI SCHOOL

The Maliki school was founded by Malik b. Anas (d. 796), who was born and died in Medina. This school of law represents a reaction against the earlier, more speculative approaches to law. Malik's magnum opus is *al-Muwatta* (lit. The Trodden Path), which is essentially a law book based on Prophetic Tradition. In dealing with each topic, he cites the precedent set by the Prophet, followed by reports about the opinions and acts of the Companions and other eminent Medinese Muslims. Then he discusses them and accepts or rejects them in the light of the legal tradition of Medina and his own reasoning. In the last analysis, what counted for Malik was the legal tradition of Medina. In his view, it was this that enshrined the will of the Prophet as understood by the Companions. Thus, where Abu Hanifa had understood *ijma'* as the consensus of the qualified legal authorities of a given generation, Malik understood it as the consensus of the people of Medina.

Malik is also credited with having supported the principle of *istislāh*, or taking into account the public interest. He held that new laws could be introduced which had no textual basis in the Koran or *sunna*, provided that they are created to bring about benefit or prevent harm, and are consonant with the aims of the *shari'a*. The principle of *istislāh* was often called on by rulers who wished to impose taxes or introduce other social or political measures which might have appeared to be Islamically suspect. The Maliki school dominates in Egypt and North Africa, but finds no favour in Medina, its birthplace, where a far more conservative jurisprudence holds sway.

THE SHAFI'I SCHOOL

This was founded by Muhammad b. Idris al-Shafi'i (d. 820), who studied in Mecca, Medina, Iraq and Syria. He was thoroughly acquainted with the various schools of law which existed in his time, but refused to identify with any one in particular. Instead, his life's endeavour was to unify them by providing a sound theory of the sources from which laws are derived. For Shafi'i, the 'sources of law' were hierarchical. First and foremost came the Koran. Then he relied on evidence from the Koran to show that Muslims were duty-bound to follow the Prophet because his legal decisions were divinely inspired. Thus the *sunna* as enshrined in the *hadiths* became the second most important authority. In many people's views, however, the *hadiths* were often contradictory. Shafi'i therefore tried to show that apparent contradictions could be explained in terms of a later *hadith* abrogating an earlier one, or one *hadith* representing an exception to the rule laid down in another.

Next in Shafi'i's hierarchy of authorities came *ijma* (consensus). Both Hanafis and Malikis accepted this as a source of law, although they disagreed over its scope and application. Shafi'i's solution was to redefine it to signify the agreement of the entire Muslim community, including both jurists and laymen. In effect, this meant that its value was acknowledged in theory, but that its importance in practice was reduced. Shafi'i's final source of law was analogical reasoning (*qiyās*). Owing to his emphasis on the *sunna*, he accorded *qiyās* much less importance than Abu Hanifa, and rejected both *istihsān* and *istislāh* as legitimate principles of jurisprudence. Today, adherents of the Shafi'i school are to be found scattered throughout the Muslim world, and predominate in the Indian subcontinent and Southeast Asia.

THE HANBALI SCHOOL

The Hanbali school, seen by many as the most conservative of the four, is named after Ahmad b. Hanbal (d. 855). He was a native of Baghdad, but travelled extensively in search of *hadiths*, many of which he gathered into an enormous collection known as the *Musnad*. Ibn Hanbal never actually wrote anything on jurisprudential theory: he was more of a collector of *hadith* than a jurist, travelling far and wide to collect Prophetic traditions, many of which formed the basis of the *Musnad*. He was a pupil and admirer of Shafi'i and had an even higher opinion of the value of the *sunna* than the latter. He insisted that the Koran and the *sunna* were the primary sources of law, and that both were to be understood literally. Later Hanbalites recognised four further sources of law, ranking them in the following order: the legal rulings of the Companions of the Prophet, provided that they do not contradict the Koran or *sunna*; the sayings of individual Companions so long as they are consonant with the truths enshrined in the Koran and *sunna*; Prophetic Traditions with weak chains of transmission; and, finally, analogical reasoning, but only when absolutely necessary. The most famous Hanbali scholar was probably Ibn Taymiyya

(d. 1327), whose writings greatly influenced the eighteenth-century reformers, the Wahhabis. The success of the Wahhabis led ultimately to the recognition of Hanbalism as the official law school in Saudi Arabia and Qatar. It also has adherents in Iraq and Syria.

THE CLOSURE OF THE 'GATE OF *IJTIHĀD*'

The process of using independent judgement to derive new laws, known as *ijtihād*, was criticised by some scholars because they believed it encouraged over-confidence in the role of human reason. Also, by the end of the tenth century, the proliferation of schools of law – at one point there were at least nineteen – was such that some scholars thought Muslim jurisprudence might become over-fragmented, leading to splits and schisms in the fabric of Muslim society. The idea began to emerge in certain quarters that the 'gate of *ijtihād*' must be closed, and instead of using independent reasoning in the future, scholars should confine themselves to studying and reinterpreting the laws that were already in existence. From this point onwards, principles such as *qiyās*, *istihsān* and *istislāh*, all vital components of independent reasoning, were to be abandoned, and scholars of jurisprudence were to emulate (*taqlid*) their illustrious jurist predecessors rather than foster legal innovation in their own right.

Today, many Muslim thinkers believe that the 'gate of *ijtihād*' has never really been closed, and that Muslim jurists continued down the ages to practise independent reasoning in order to derive laws for new, unprecedented situations. The alleged closure of the 'gate of *ijtihād*' has been cited by many as the reason why Muslim law appeared to ossify after the twelfth century.

SHI'ITE LAW

Shi'ite law developed along markedly different lines, and was based on Traditions handed down not only from the Prophet but also the Imams who were deemed to have succeeded him. Shi'ite jurisprudence came into existence largely thanks to the efforts of Ja'far al-Sadiq, the sixth Shi'ite Imam, who had actually been the teacher of many important Sunni jurists, including Abu Hanifa. The Shi'ites differ slightly from the Sunnis on the sources of law, and for the Shi'ites the 'gate of *ijtihād*' was never considered closed.

When the line of successors to Muhammad – the Twelve Imams – came to an end, the last in that line, the Imam Mahdi, was deemed to have gone into 'occultation', to return at the end of time. During his absence, jurisprudential authority was devolved upon the most learned Shi'ite jurists, who acted as representatives of the Hidden Imam. The development of Shi'ite legal theory culminated, in the nineteenth century, in the notion that the most learned Shi'ite jurists of the age are in fact representatives of the Imam in all his functions, both temporal and spiritual, leading in turn to the principle known as *wilāyat al-faqih*, the simplified meaning of which means the right of the jurist to rule. This theory was elaborated by Ayatollah Khumayni, who made it a cornerstone of the Islamic Republic of Iran.

THE DIFFERENCES BETWEEN SUNNISM AND SHI'ISM

From a practical point of view, there is little to separate Shi'ite from Sunni in terms of everyday law and jurisprudence. Sunnism, strictly speaking, means adhering to the *sunna* of the Prophet, which is something that all Shi'ites would claim to do anyway. Sunnis, however, depend on the *sunna* alone, while Shi'ites also include the Twelve Imams as sources of spiritual inspiration and socio-political guidance. However, the difference between the two are few and relatively minor. And while there are some theological differences between the two approaches, on the three 'fundamentals of faith' – Divine Unity, Prophethood and the Last Day – they are in complete agreement. In fact, there are arguably more differences – jurisprudentially, at least – between different Sunni groups than there are between Sunnis and Shi'ites.

NOTE

1   Chambers, for example, spells it 'Sheria' and defines it as 'the body of Islamic religious law'.

CHRONOLOGY

THE ERA OF MUHAMMAD

625   The Battle of Uhud
627   The Battle of the Ditch
628   The Treaty of Hudaybiya is concluded between the Muslims
      and the Meccans
630   The conquest of Mecca
632   The death of Muhammad; election of Abu Bakr as first
      caliph; Arab expansion begins

THE POST-PROPHETIC MUSLIM WORLD:
A SOCIO-POLITICAL CHRONOLOGY

633   Wars of apostasy
634   Death of the first caliph, Abu Bakr
635   Conquest of Damascus
637   Battle of Qadisiyya between Arab Muslim forces and Persian
      army
638   Arab Muslim forces capture Jerusalem
641   Arab Muslim conquest of the Persian Empire
644   Death of the second caliph, Umar, who is succeeded by
      Uthman
645   Fall of Alexandria; first wave of Arab Muslim conquests ends
653   Fall of Khurasan marks complete conquest of Persia
656   Uthman murdered; the Prophet's cousin Ali becomes fourth
      caliph; war breaks out between Ali and the Prophet's widow,
      Aisha
657   Battle of Siffin between Ali and Muawiya
658   Battle of Nahrawan between Ali and the Kharijites
660   Muawiya proclaims himself caliph in Damascus
661   Ali is assassinated; Muawiya becomes the first Umayyad
      caliph
667   Arabs in North Africa construct the garrison town of
      Qairawan, in modern-day Tunisia
680   Martyrdom of the Prophet's grandson, Husayn, at Karbala
      on the orders of the caliphate
684   The Marwanid branch of the Umayyad clan assumes control
      of the caliphate
692   Defeat of the rebel Ibn Zubayr in Mecca; completion of the
      Dome of the Rock in Jerusalem, the first great achievement
      of Muslim architecture

705	Second wave of Arab expansion begins under the caliph Walid
711	Arabs cross from North Africa to Gibraltar, which is named in honour of an Arab commander
718	Arab siege of Constantinople broken
732	Muslim forces advance through Europe as far as Tours in northwest France
750	The Abbasid revolt against Umayyad rule takes place; the Abbasid dynasty is established
756	The Umayyad Abd al-Rahman establishes himself as sole ruler of Andalusia
760	Arabs adopt Indian numerals and develop algebra and trigonometry
762	Baghdad is built by the caliph Mansur
765	Death of the sixth Shi'ite Imam, Ja'far al-Sadiq, founder of the (Shi'ite) Ja'fari school of jurisprudence
767	Death of Abu Hanifa, founder of the Hanafi school of jurisprudence
786	Harun al-Rashid becomes caliph; Abbasid dynasty at its zenith
795	Death of Malik b. Anas, founder of the Malikiyya school of jurisprudence
800	The Aghlabid dynasty begins its hundred-year rule of Tunisia
809	Death of Harun al-Rashid
819	The Samanid dynasty takes control of eastern Iran (819–1005); death of al-Shafi'i, founder of the Shafi'ite school of jurisprudence
855	Death of Ibn Hanbal, founder of the Hanbali school of jurisprudence
864	The Shi'ite Zaydi dynasty takes control of the Caspian littoral (864–928)
868	The Tulunids establish independent rule in Cairo (868–906)
909	The Fatimids establish an independent caliphate in North Africa, lasting over sixty years
921	Abd al-Rahman III breaks away from the caliphate in Baghdad and declares himself Caliph of Andalusia
945	The Shi'ite Buyids take control of Baghdad, reducing the Abbasid caliphs to puppet rulers

969	The Fatimids conquer Egypt and found Cairo
1020	Death of the poet Ferdowsi, reviver of the Persian language and author of the Iranian national epic, the *Shahnameh* or 'Book of Kings'
1037	Death of the Persian philosopher Ibn Sina, known to the West as Avicenna
1055	Baghdad is captured by the Turkish Seljuk dynasty
1056	The Almoravids conquer North Africa and southern Spain
1066	The first Muslim university or *nizāmiyya* is established
1071	The Seljuks defeat the Byzantines at the Battle of Manzikert
1091	Imam Ghazali, the classical Muslim world's most illustrious thinker, becomes head of the Baghdad *nizāmiyya*
1095	First Crusade begins: the Franks invade Anatolia and Syria, establishing Crusader states there
1099	Crusaders recapture Jerusalem
1100	Persian poet Omar Khayyam composes the *Rubaiyyat*
1111	Death of Imam Ghazali
1135	The Almohads become dominant in northwestern Africa and Muslim Spain
1144	The Second Crusade begins
1171	Salah al-Din (Saladin) defeats the Fatimids and conquers Egypt
1188	Saladin destroys the Frankish Crusader kingdoms
1189	The Third Crusade begins
1202	The Fourth Crusade begins
1220	Mongol forces capture Samarkand and Bukhara
1258	Baghdad is sacked by the Mongols, who put an end to the 500-year-old Abbasid caliphate
1299	The Ottoman Turks begin to expand in Anatolia
1326	Ottoman forces capture Bursa
1366	Edirne is established by the Ottomans as their European capital
1392	Taymur-i Lang (Tamburlaine) begins his conquest of Persia; death of Hafiz, Persian lyric poet
1453	Ottomans capture Constantinople, which they rename Istanbul
1501	Ismail I proclaims himself Shah of Iran at Tabriz and declares Shi'ism the state religion

1520 Sulayman the Magnificent becomes ruler of the Ottoman Empire

1530 Establishment of Moghul rule in India

1533 The Ottomans capture Baghdad

1555 Treaty of Amasya marks the end of Ottoman–Safavid hostilities

1556 Akbar the Great comes to power in Moghul India

1566 Death of Sulayman the Magnificent

1587 Abbas I ascends the Safavid throne

1598 Isfahan becomes the Safavid capital

1600 Formation of the British East India Company

1605 Death of Akbar the Great

1629 Death of Shah Abbas

1699 Treaty of Karlowitz: Ottomans forced to surrender territory in the Balkans

1718 Treaty of Passarowitz: Ottomans forced to surrender Serbia

1722 Isfahan falls to Sunni Afghan forces

1736 Nadir Shah becomes ruler of Iran

1739 Nadir Shah captures Delhi

1744 Revivalist leader Abd al-Wahhab joins forces with Muhammad Ibn Saud

1764 The British become rulers of Bengal; Moghul power begins to wane

1794 The Qajar dynasty is established in Iran

1798 Napoleon occupies Egypt

1839 The Ottomans begin widespread reforms known as the *Tanzimat*, the first attempt at modernisation in the Muslim world

1884 Britain becomes the de facto ruler of Egypt

1905 Iran undergoes a 'constitutional Revolution'

1917 The Balfour Declaration promises Jews a national home in Palestine

1922 Egypt is declared an independent monarchy under Fuad I; Palestine comes under British mandate

1923 The Ottoman Empire comes to an end

1928 The Muslim Brotherhood is founded by Hasan al-Banna

1932 Saudi Arabia comes into existence under Abdul Aziz ibn Saud; Iraq becomes an independent state

1941 The 'Islamic Society' is founded in Pakistan by Mawdudi

1945   Syria becomes charter member of the UN
1946   Jordan and Lebanon gain independence
1947   Partition of India and creation of the state of Pakistan
1948   The state of Israel is created on Palestinian soil; the first
       Arab–Israeli war; Egypt outlaws the Muslim Brotherhood
1949   Indonesia becomes independent
1951   Libya becomes an independent monarchy
1952   King Farouk of Egypt is overthrown by Gamal Abdul Nasser
1956   Tunisia, Morocco and Sudan become independent; second
       Arab–Israeli war; the Suez Crisis and the Anglo-French
       invasion of the canal zone
1957   Malaya gains independence
1960   Mali, Mauritania, Niger, Nigeria, Somalia and Upper Volta
       (Burkina Faso) gain independence
1962   Algeria gains independence from France
1963   Anti-government unrest in Iran leads to the exile of its
       leading Shi'ite cleric, Ayatollah Khumayni
1967   Third Arab–Israeli war
1971   Indo-Pakistan war leads to breakaway of East Pakistan
       (Bangladesh)
1973   Fourth Arab–Israeli war
1977   Egypt-Israel peace talks culminate in Camp David Peace
       Treaty
1979   Khumayni returns to Iran to lead 'Islamic revolution';
       Russia invades Afghanistan
1981   President Sadat of Egypt is assassinated by Muslim
       'fundamentalist' extremists
1982   Israel invades Lebanon
1989   Khumayni dies
1990   Saddam Hussein attacks Kuwait
1991   'Operation Desert Storm' launched by US-led forces against
       Iraq; Kuwait retaken
1992   Military government installed in Algeria in order to prevent
       first round election winners, the Muslim FIS, from coming
       to power
1993   The Oslo Accord between Palestine and Israel
1996   The Taliban come to power in Afghanistan
1997   Muhammad Khatami becomes president of Iran and
       promises wide-reaching reforms

2001   Terrorist attacks on World Trade Center and the Pentagon, 11 September; Khatami re-elected as President of Iran; US-led attack on Afghanistan culminates in the apparent fall of the Taliban

2003   US begins bombardment of Baghdad in order to effect 'regime change'; Baghdad falls and Saddam Hussein is captured

GLOSSARY OF ARABIC TERMS

adab	etiquette
adhān	call to prayer
ahadiyya	God's oneness
al-Fātiha	the opening chapter of the Koran
ansār	(lit. 'helpers') the residents of Medina who gave refuge to Muhammad and his followers, thus paving the way for the *hijra*
asbāb al-nuzūl	the circumstances attending the revelation of certain Koranic verses
āyā	verse (of the Koran); sign (of God)
āyāt	verses; signs
barzakh	the 'intermediary world'; purgatory
bayt al-māl	the public treasury
bismillah	'in the Name of God'
dhikr	the methodical repetition of the names of God, a devotional practice
du'ā	supplication; invoking God
Eid al-Adhā	the festival which follows the pilgrimage to Mecca
Eid al-Fitr	the festival which follows Ramadan
fard	obligatory, in the jurisprudential sense
fitriya	an amount of money payable as alms at the end of Ramadan

ghulāt	(lit. 'extremists'); folk Sufis with unorthodox and sometimes un-Islamic beliefs
ghusl	full ablution (of the whole body)
hadith	Prophetic Tradition
hajar al-aswad	the black stone in the *ka'ba*, kissed by pilgrims and said to be a meteor
hajj	pilgrimage to Mecca
hanif	pre-Islamic monotheism of the Arab hermits
haram	the sacred precinct (of shrines, particularly in Mecca)
harām	forbidden by Muslim law
hijra	the migration from Mecca to Medina in 622
hijri	pertaining to the Muslim lunar calendar, which began with the *hijra*
hulūl	the concept of Divine incarnation in man, rejected by Islam
i'jāz	inimitability (of the Koran)
ibādāt	acts of worship
ihrām	the ritual garb of the *hajj* pilgrims
imām	leader; prayer leader; Shi'ite imam
imān	belief; faith
infāq	charitable giving; generosity
Injil	the Gospels
islām	submission; Islam
'isma	infallibility
isrā	Muhammad's 'night journey' or ascension
jabr	compulsion; the concept of predestination or predetermination
jāhiliyya	the 'age of ignorance' prior to the advent of Muhammad
jihād	(lit. 'struggle') defensive war
ka'ba	the cuboid structure in Mecca towards which all Muslims turn in prayer
khutba	Friday prayers sermon
kiswa	the drapes covering the *ka'ba*
kufr	unbelief
ma'ād	the resurrection after death
madhhab	rite of jurisprudence; school of Muslim law
makrūh	discouraged, in the jurisprudential sense

malā'ika	angels
masjid	mosque
masjid al-harām	the central shrine area in Mecca
mi'rāj	Muhammad's 'night journey'; the ascension
mu'āmalāt	the category of transactions in jurisprudence
mu'jiza	miracle
mubāh	allowed, in the jurisprudential sense
muezzin	one who proclaims the call to prayer
muhājirūn	those who migrated from Mecca to Medina in 622
munāfiqūn	hypocrites
murid	follower of a Sufi *shaykh*
muslim	one who submits; a Muslim
mustahabb	recommended, in the jurisprudential sense
nabi	apostle; prophet
nabuwwa	prophethood
nāfila	supererogatory *salāt*
qibla	the direction of Mecca, towards which Muslims turn in prayer
qur'ān	the Koran
rak'a	a unit (of canonical prayer)
rasūl	messenger; prophet
rukū	bowing (in prayer)
sadaqāt	alms; charitable donations
sahari	the food eaten before daybreak during Ramadan
Sahih	authoritive collection
saj	semi-verse (in the Koran)
salām	peace
salāt	canonical prayer
salāt al-asr	late afternoon prayer
salāt al-ishā	evening prayer
salāt al-jamā'a	congregational prayer
salāt al-maghrib	early evening prayer
salāt al-subh	morning prayer
salāt al-zuhr	midday prayer
sālik	a 'traveller' on the Sufi 'path'
samā	ritual music and movement performed by some Sufi groups

sawm	fasting
shahāda	professing Islam; bearing witness that there is no god but God, and that Muhammad is His messenger
shari'a	Muslim law
shaykh	elder; spiritual guide in Sufism
shirk	associationism; attributing 'partners' to God
shurā	consultation
silsila	chain
sira	biography of the Prophet
suhūf	pre-Islamic scriptures
sujūd	prostration (in prayer)
sunna	the Prophetic practice
sūra	chapter (of the Koran)
tahāra	ritual purity
tanāsukh	concept of transmigration of souls, rejected by Islam
taqlid	emulation; imitation; blind acceptance
tarāwih	supererogatory prayers offered during the nights of Ramadan
tariqa	Sufi path or brotherhood
tashahhud	'bearing witness' at the end of the canonical prayer
tashbih	anthropomorphism, with respect to God
tawāf	circumambulation of the *ka'ba* during the *hajj*
tawhid	Divine unity
tayammum	ritual ablution with clean dry sand or stones in the absence of water
ulamā	(lit. 'those who know') scholars; jurists; the 'clergy'
umma	the Muslim community
umra	non-obligatory pilgrimage to Mecca
wāhidiyya	unity or unicity of God
wājib	obligatory, in the jurisprudential sense
wudū	lesser ablution, taken before prayers
Zabūr	the Psalms of David
zakāh or zakāt	a form of charitable giving, incumbent on those who can afford it

INDEX

Religion: The Basics

Malroy Nye

How does religion fit in with life in the modern world? Do you have to 'believe' to be a part of one?

From televangelism in the American South to the wearing of the hijab in Britain and Egypt; from the rise of paganism to the aftermath of 9/11, this accessible guide looks at the ways in which religion interacts with the everyday world in which we live. It is a comprehensive introduction to the world of religion, and covers aspects including:

- Religion and culture
- How power operates in religion
- Gender issues
- The role of belief, rituals and religious texts
- Religion in the contemporary world

Religion: The Basics offers an invaluable and up-to-date overview for anyone wanting to find out more about this fascinating subject.

"Finally, a book written for the general reader that communicates clearly and authoritatively the many advances that have taken place in the academic study of religion over the past generation."

Russell T McCutcheon
University of Alabama

0-415-26379-4

Available at all good bookshops
For ordering and further information please visit
www.routledge.com

Roman Catholicism: The Basics

Michael Welsh

From Africa to South America, Asia to Europe, Catholicism plays a fundamental role in the lives of over 1.07 billion Catholics worldwide. Its history is significant, its beliefs and values intricate; and its hierarchical structure complex. *Roman Catholicism: The Basics* offers readers with a plain-speaking introduction to roman Catholicism. It covers:

- Roman Catholic Beliefs and traditions;
- Practices and devotional life—rituals, prayer, mass;
- The Church structures and authorities—from Vatican to parish church;
- The Church hierarchies and people—from bishops to the laity;
- The role of the Church in society.

With glossary, further reading sections and an appendix on the history of the Papacy, this is the perfect guide for anyone wanting to understand more about Roman Catholicism.

0-415-26381-6

Fifty Eastern Thinkers

Diané Collinson, Kathryn Plant
& Robert Wilkinson

Close exposition and analysis of fifty major thinkers in eastern philosophy and religion form the core of this introduction to a fascinating area of study. The authors have drawn on the major eastern traditions, examining founder figures such as:

- Zoroaster
- Confucius
- Muhammad

Through to modern thinkers such as

- Mao Zedong
- Nishitani
- Gandhi

General introductions to the major traditions and a glossary of philosophical terms, as well as bibliographies and recommended further reading for each thinker, make this a comprehensive and accessible work of reference.

0-415-20284-1